Cases in European Business

DR D. NOBLE
45 HUMBERSTONE ROAD
CAMBRIDGE
CB4 1JD

Phone/Fax: 01223 312094

Cases in European Business

Edited by Jill Preston

Anglia Polytechnic

Pitman

Pitman Publishing
128 Long Acre, London WC2E 9AN

A Division of Longman Group UK Limited

First published in 1992

British Library Cataloguing in Publication Data
A catalogue record for this book can be obtained from the British
Library.

ISBN 0 273 03740 4

Printed in Great Britain by The Bath Press, Avon

Contents

List of figures   *vii*
List of tables   *viii*
Contributors   *ix*
Preface   *x*
Acknowledgements   *xi*
List of abbreviations   *xii*

Introduction   1

Part 1   The European business environment

Chapter 1   The European Community   *Jill Preston*   13

Chapter 2   The Single European Market and the wider
            Europe   *Jill Preston*   23

Chapter 3   The impact of Single Market legislation on
            business   *Jill Preston*   40

Part 2   The case studies

Case 1   Arthur Andersen & Co. SC – A UK practice in an
         international context   *Jill Preston*   61

Case 2   The Olympic Insurance Company, Greece – A study
         in European collaboration   *Theo Kiriziadis*   77

Case 3   Labsworth World Wide PLC – European brand pricing
         issues   *James W. Dudley*   90

Case 4   The National Bank of Greece (NBG) – A case of a
         State-controlled bank preparing for the Single
         Market   *Theo Kiriziadis*   110

Case 5   Gate Hydraulics Ltd – Total Quality Management
         and the Single Market   *John Pike*   123

Case 6   Greater Peterborough Training and Enterprise Council
          (GPtec) – A study of a training response to the Single
          Market   *Jill Preston*   150

Case 7   Pan-European motoring assistance – A suitable case for
          National Breakdown?   *Alan Marchant* and *Ian Cox*   174

Case 8   Essex Water PLC – A case study in market extension
          Tony Bennett   218

Case 9   Airbus Industrie – A study in European collaboration
          Ron Allison and *Ian Barnes*   228

Case 10   Competition and change in the British and German
          brewing industries   *Ron Allison, David Kinnear* and
          Henry Schietzold   247

Index   289

Figures

1.1.1	Distribution of Community expenditure	14
1.1.2	The EC policy-making process summarized	21
1.2.1	External debt per head 1989	36
1.2.2	Joint ventures with Eastern European countries (at the beginning of 1991)	39
1.3.1	Major common transport policy initiatives in road transport	51
2.1.1	Arthur Andersen's fee income in comparison to other international accounting firms	63
2.1.2	Fee income of Arthur Andersen 1980–90	64
2.1.3	The five phases of the IAR process	69
2.1.4	Arthur Andersen's pan-European advertising campaign	73
2.3.1	European self-medication sales 1987–95, advertised brands RSP	98
2.3.2	Cold remedies 1989 – four key markets	100
2.3.3	Competitive advantage	100
2.3.4	Price differences in the EC markets (using Portugal as an index)	102
2.3.5	Pricing analysis	103
2.3.6	Price comparisons of Nasalvine in Europe (1989)	104
2.5.1	Organization chart – quality management	145
2.6.1	Comparison of 16–18-year olds in education and training (1986)	151
2.6.2	GPtec area	158
2.6.3	The functional and organizational chart of GPtec as of August 1991	166
2.8.1	Essex Water Company PLC organization and structure	222

Tables

1.2.1	Economic assistance to Eastern European countries	38
2.2.1	Expenditure on insurance ($) EC ranking	81
2.2.2	Per capita expenditure on insurance ($) EC ranking	82
2.3.1	Company sales and profits 1980–89 in $ millions	91
2.3.2	Markets and activities	91
2.3.3	Turnover and profits by activity	91
2.3.4	Top 10 European self-medication companies' sales in Europe 1990	94
2.3.5	Basic data	106
2.3.6	Nasalvine sales consumer OTC *v* Doctor's prescription	107
2.3.7	Nasalvine gross profit	107
2.3.8	Nasalvine advertising	107
2.3.9	Nasalvine sales Europe	107
2.3.10	German profit and loss account	109
2.6.1	GPtec's budgets (£)	167
2.7.1	Enrolled membership of National Breakdown	178
2.7.2	RAC membership (UK)	190
2.7.3	UK membership of motoring organizations via new car warranties	191
2.7.4	AA membership	193
2.7.5	Financial performance of Britannia Rescue/recovery in £000s	196
2.7.6	Estimated UK membership of motoring organizations (000s)	204
2.7.7	UK membership of major organizations (000s)	205
2.7.8	Cross Channel ferry traffic by user type – Port of Dover	207
2.7.9	Foreign tourism by mode of transport 1989	208
2.9.1	Airbus product range	240
2.9.2	The order book at 31.10.89	241
2.10.1	UK beer production by company 1967–85	249
2.10.2	Number of brewing companies and breweries in the UK	250
2.10.3	UK beer consumption 1960–89	251
2.10.4	UK beer market by type and packaging measured in terms of percentage of sales volume	251
2.10.5	Some comparative aspects of the EC beer market in 1988	254
2.10.6	Advertising and marketing expenditure by brewers in the UK in 1985 (£m)	257

Contributors

Dr Jill Preston is Head of the European Business R&D Centre, Anglia Business School, Anglia Polytechnic, Cambridge.

Ron Allison is Director of International Business Programmes, Anglia Business School, Anglia Polytechnic, Cambridge.

Ian Barnes is Associate Dean, Humberside Business School, Humberside Polytechnic, Hull.

Tony Bennett is Principal Consultant in Marketing at Anglia Business School, Anglia Polytechnic, Danbury.

Ian Cox is a Business Planner in the Commercial Development Section of Yorkshire Water PLC.

James W. Dudley is Head of the consulting firm James Dudley Management.

David Kinnear is Head of the Business Studies Department, Anglia Business School, Anglia Polytechnic, Cambridge.

Dr Theo Kiriziadis is a Research Assistant in the European Business R&D Centre, Anglia Business School, Anglia Polytechnic, Cambridge.

Alan Marchant is a Senior Lecturer in Strategic Management and Economics at Humberside Business School, Humberside Polytechnic, Hull.

Professor John Pike is Head of the Total Quality Management R&D Centre, Anglia Business School, Anglia Polytechnic, Cambridge.

Henry Schietzold is Production Manager, Schultheiss Brewery, Berlin.

Preface

The completion of the European Single Market, planned for the end of 1992, plus the developments in the wider Europe are already having a major impact on business across Europe and beyond. By using a case-study approach, this book aims to show how a variety of companies are responding strategically to these events.

The authors of the individual studies have not attempted to be prescriptive but the reader is encouraged to use his/her knowledge and expertise to evaluate the strategic choices made. To assist in this process, each study is followed by a series of questions/discussion topics.

To give coherence to the studies there are a number of themes running through the book. The underlying point being that competitive intensity has increased and is likely to increase further in most business sectors. In answer to this developing situation, companies are responding in a variety of ways.

The European business environment is changing rapidly, therefore this book attempts to identify broad issues within this environment. Business needs to keep abreast of this change, for each new development within the EC and/or Eastern Europe can bring with it fresh challenges. For students of business and management the need to be aware of these changes and their possible implications is crucial.

Jill Preston
Anglia Business School
September 1991

Publisher's note

Whilst this book has been written as a stand-alone casebook, it is an ideal companion volume to *European Business* by Richard Welford and Kate Prescott (Pitman, 1992). It is for this reason that, where appropriate, reference has been made to particular sections of the latter volume.

It is hoped that the simultaneous publication of this textbook and casebook will help students to find their way through the complex issues raised in European Business teaching at undergraduate and postgraduate levels.

Acknowledgements

I should like to put on record my thanks to each of the authors of the case studies: Ron Allison, Ian Barnes, Tony Bennett, Ian Cox, James W. Dudley, David Kinnear, Theo Kiriziadis, Alan Marchant, John Pike and Henry Schietzold.

I should also like to express my gratitude for the help and support given in the development of this book from the organizations studied:

David Oliver, Conor Boden and Marguerite Deliege-Sequaris of Arthur Andersen & Co SC;
Ron Scouse of Gates Hydraulics Ltd;
Lynda Purser of Greater Peterborough Training and Enterprise Council;
Mr I. Angelides of the National Bank of Greece;
Ron Stevenson of the BBC;
David Parr and David Knight of Essex Water PLC;
Bob Slicer formerly of National Breakdown;
George Bateman of Bateman's Brewery;
John Smith of Ridley's Brewery;
Herr Koller of Landshuter Brewery;
Hans-Joachim Timme of Felsenkeller Brewery.

Many people from a wide range of organizations have been involved in this project and my thanks go to them all, but special mention must be made of Professor John Davies and my colleagues at the Anglia Business School for their support and encouragement in this venture. I should also like to put on record my debt to June Cheetham, Secretary at the European Business Centre, for her endeavours and enthusiasm.

Abbreviations

BGTS	Business growth through training scheme
BRITE-EURAM	Basic research in industrial technology for Europe and European research in advanced materials
BSI	British Standards Institute
BWTE	Brewers without tied estate
CAP	Common Agricultural Policy
CET	Common External Tariff
CMEA	Council for Mutual Economic Assistance (COMECON)
COMDOC	Commission documents
COMETT	Community action programme in education and training for technology
COREPER	Committee of Permanent Representatives
CTP	Common Transport Policy
DDR	Former East Germany
DG	Directorate-General of the EC
DTI	Department of Trade and Industry
EAEC	European Atomic Energy Community (Euratom)
EAGGF	European agricultural guidance and guarantee fund (CAP)
EAS	Enterprise allowance scheme
EBRD	European Bank for Reconstruction and Development
EC	European Community
ECJ	European Court of Justice
ECSC	European Coal and Steel Community
ECU	European Currency Unit
EEA	European Economic Area
EEC	European Economic Community
EFTA	European Free Trade Association
EIB	European Investment Bank
EMF	European Monetary Fund
EMS	European Monetary System
EMU	European Monetary Union

EP	European Parliament
EPC	European Political Co-operation
ERM	Exchange Rate Mechanism
ESC	Economic and social committee
ESPRIT	European strategic programme for research and development in information technologies
ET	Enterprise training
FDR	Federal German Republic
FORCE	Action programme for the development of continuing education in the EC
G24	Group of the 24 leading industrialized countries
GATT	General Agreement on Tariffs and Trade
GDP	Gross domestic product
HORIZON	Programme to promote equal opportunities for people with a handicap
IMF	International Monetary Fund
LEC	Local Enterprise Company
LINGUA	EC's languages initiative
MEP	Member of the European Parliament
MES	Minimum efficient scale
MMC	Monopolies and Mergers Commission
NCVQ	National Council for Vocational Qualifications (Britain)
OJ	Official Journal of the European Community
PETRA	Community action programme for the vocational training of young people and their preparation for adult and working life
PHARE	Poland and Hungary Assistance Economic Restructuring
SAD	Single Administrative Document
SEA	Single European Act
SEM	Single European Market
TA	Training Agency
TEC	Training and Enterprise Council
TEED	Training Enterprise and Education Division (of the Employment Department)
TQM	Total Quality Management
UKREP	UK permanent representative
VAT	Value added tax
YT	Youth training

Introduction

A guide to using the book

This book provides the reader with a series of case studies which illustrate how a variety of companies, most of which located in Western Europe, are responding strategically to the completion of the Single European Market and other activities in Central and Eastern Europe. The reader is given the opportunity to apply his/her knowledge and skills in the area of business strategy to the issues facing organizations as we approach the planned completion of the market in December 1992.

In the choice of cases the aim has been to provide the reader with a wide variety of companies, but we have not attempted to be representative either in terms of types of responses, or indeed in terms of commercial/industrial sectors. The cases are not intended to serve as a basis for illustration of either good or bad management practice.

Each of the cases has been written in co-operation with, and has the approval of, the senior management of the organization concerned. A number of themes run through the case studies representing ways in which organizations could respond to the challenges of the Single Market and other developments in Europe. Each case is followed by a series of questions that can be used as a basis for group activity or individual work.

Themes

The underlying theme running through each of the cases is that competitive intensity is likely to increase in most industrial and commercial sectors and that organizations are responding to this fact in a number of different ways. For example, public procurement accounts for about 15 per cent of the Community's GDP; by opening up public procurement to greater competition many companies are likely to lose these protected markets.

The themes identified represent various ways in which companies could respond to the needs of the Single Market; this response could, of course, include doing little or nothing. It is implicit that most organizations ought at least to consider a wide range of these issues.

A major aim of this book is to assist the reader in applying his/her skills to analyse how a range of business organizations are responding to the challenges of the Single Market and to guide them to come to some conclusions about the effectiveness of individual responses. As in all case studies, the student is not provided with total information and will find that in some of the cases the themes to be explored are explicitly identified for the reader, while in other studies they are implied.

Issues to address

Whilst studying the cases the reader should keep the following points in mind.

(a) **Internal organizational response and intelligence gathering**

- Has the company established some type of Single Market structure?
- Has an intelligence gathering system been established, e.g. to monitor EC legislation?
- Has the organization reconsidered its recruitment policies as a result of European developments?
- Has the firm responded to the needs of training, including management development, that have resulted from the Single Market?
- Is the information system capable of meeting a growth in demand?
- Is the firm developing a Single Market strategy?

(b) **New market identification**
Is the organization asking the following questions:

- Has the market changed for our business?
- Should we become a European business, looking upon Europe as our primary market?
- Are there markets which are likely to become more accessible?
- Have we identified additional potential customers?

- Have we identified competitors and assessed their strengths, weaknesses, products, prices, design, package and services?
- Have we obtained intelligence about how the competitors sell and their structure of distribution into the market?
- Do we know our existing customers' buying plans?
- Will our market research be carried out in house or shall we commission external consultants?

(c) **Purchasing**

Has the company addressed such issues as, are we properly equipped to purchase in a wider market?

(d) **Production**

To compete in the Single Market, production costs will have to be kept down but quality improved. This simple fact raises a number of issues, for example, will the company's production performance be competitive in the Single Market or will it have to change its production processes?

(e) **Product development**

The completion of the Single Market and other developments in Europe raise a number of issues for product development, for example, to what extent is the company adapting existing products and services plus developing new ones to exploit new opportunities and defend existing markets?

(f) **Sales**

If a company is looking at the possibility of exporting goods or developing its exporting capability, a range of issues arise. For example, how will the company reach its customers, what sales methods have been examined, what sales literature and advertising have been considered?

(g) **Distribution**

To what extent has the company addressed the following issues?

- What changes are needed in our distribution requirements?
- What distribution requirements will best achieve the customer service we are seeking?

- What transport services should we be using?

If in the service sector:

- Should we be providing services direct from the UK or do we need a presence in local markets?

(h) **Marketing**
The Single Market will result in more potential customers but it will also see the development of increased competition in most sectors. Has the organization addressed the following issues?

- What new customers can we reach?
- Is the wider market attractive?
- How do we get the right market information?
- Are our product/services suitable?
- What new competition are we likely to face in our existing market?

(i) **Pricing policies**
Have Single Market issues affected the organization's pricing strategies?

(j) **New ways of doing business**
As part of its Single Market strategy is the company considering new ways of doing business, for example, joint developments for R&D purposes, franchising, licensing or agency agreements? Has it considered the possibility of mergers or acquisitions?

Using case studies

A case study is normally a written description of an organization, but cases can be written about groups, institutions, or nations. A case study details events and circumstances, including the organization's history, external environment and internal environment, for example, its organizational structure. A case normally provides a description of a particular situation facing the organization. Cases may be long or short, fact or fiction. Organizations often require their identities to be disguised for fear of revealing information which may be useful to competitors. By its nature a case is a partial and incomplete picture, this is a simulation of the real situa- tion, as business decisions have to be taken with incomplete information.

Analysis of each case should be based on the information given, although some tutors may require some library research. Part 1 of the book provides a European business context for the studies and should be read before individual cases are tackled. The purpose of a case analysis is to present, justify and defend recommended courses of action. This type of work enables people to practise problem solving and decision making in a simulated situation.

The cases in this book can be used for class discussion and/or written submission; each study is followed by a number of questions. The questions can be used for individual work, although many more benefits are obtained if some group work is involved. For example, a situation where a student has to defend a decision before peers is very similar to the situation facing managers.

Case study work uses and develops a wide range of skills but it also imparts knowledge about the organizations concerned. It is assumed that readers will have some knowledge of writers on business strategy such as M.E. Porter and H. Igor Ansoff.

Skills used and developed in a case method include:

- *analytical skills*: classifying, organizing and evaluating material; recognizing when vital information is missing;
- *application skills*: judging which techniques are appropriate and applying these techniques;
- *communication skills*: oral and written skills are usually required, group work normally encourages the development of presentational skills;
- *social skills*: group work involves listening, supporting, arguing;
- *creative skills*: cases require creative ideas as well as analytical skills.

The student should read the case through quickly to get a general overview of the study. Then he/she should read the case through more slowly to look at the nature of the information given and how it may be used. In general terms, a 'SWOT'[1] analysis may be useful to identify strengths and weaknesses.

1 SWOT analysis involves identifying Strengths, Weaknesses, Opportunities and Threats facing an organization.

Structure of the book

Part 1   The European business environment

Business organizations do not exist in a vacuum, therefore an appreciation of the European business environment is a crucial factor in understanding business activities. The movement towards the completion of the Single Market and the developments in the wider Europe are critical elements in this environment.

Chapter 1 provides a brief description of the European Community (EC); it focuses on the general aims of this organization as well as its policy-making processes. Chapter 2 provides a brief overview of the Single Market and associated issues. This chapter also looks at the developments in the wider European framework and identifies some of the implications for business. It concentrates on developments in EFTA countries as well as countries of Central and Eastern Europe. Chapter 3 looks at the likely impact of Single Market legislation on business. It covers a number of areas, for example, technical standards, public procurement and employment legislation, to illustrate the point that for many business sectors the impact of this legislation is likely to be substantial.

Part 2   The case studies

The case study section of the book contains examples from a range of organizations. A major focus of each study is to show how the organization in question is responding to the challenges of the Single Market and the activities in the wider Europe. Each case is followed by a number of questions. A brief synopsis of each organization studied follows.

1. Arthur Andersen – a UK practice in an international context

Arthur Andersen provides audit, business advisory and tax services as well as management consultancy services. It also provides a range of products related to the completion of the Single Market and it is taking advantage of the opportunities presented by developments in Central and Eastern Europe. Arthur Andersen prides itself in its international approach to service provision and the training that it gives to its personnel. The study describes these activities.

2.   The Olympic Insurance Company, Greece – A study in European collaboration

The Olympic Insurance Company is a relatively small organization in one of the less developed areas of the Community. The company was faced with trying to respond to the threats resulting from the completion of the European financial market. Olympic is fully aware that with deregulation, large transnational insurance companies will enter the Greek market. In this case study Theo Kiriziadis describes Olympic's response to this situation.

3.   Labsworth World Wide PLC – European brand pricing issues

In this study, James W. Dudley identifies some of the issues involved when Labsworth World Wide PLC, a medium-sized international pharmaceutical company headquartered in the UK, considers the regionalizing of its pricing policy in response to the needs of the Single Market.

4.   The National Bank of Greece (NGB) – A case of a State-controlled bank preparing for the Single European Market

In his study of the NGB, Theo Kiriziadis describes how the bank is attempting to respond to the challenges of the Single Market. He shows how this organization is being seriously constrained in these attempts by the State controls still operating in Greece.

5.   Gates Hydraulics Ltd – Total Quality Management and the Single Market

Survival and growth in the highly competitive Single Market will depend, to a large extent, on how companies perceive opportunities and threats, and how they respond strategically to these. In his study of Gates Hydraulics Ltd, John Pike shows how one company has adopted a Total Quality Management strategy as a response to these challenges.

6.   Greater Peterborough Training and Enterprise Council (GPtec) – A study of a training response to the Single European Market

Vocational training is a major factor in the successful completion of the Single Market. It is generally accepted that the UK is lagging behind many countries in the Community in terms of both the education standards being achieved and the training provided for people in work. Training and Enterprise Councils (TECs) are the latest attempt by the UK Government to reform the training system. This study describes how, in the general context of UK training policy, GPtec is developing a response to the training needs of the 1990s, including training for the Single Market.

7. Pan-European Motoring Assistance – A suitable case for National Breakdown

In their study of National Breakdown, Alan Marchant and Ian Cox describe the development of the company in what has proved to be a very favourable business environment. The issue now facing both National Breakdown and its rivals, is whether this environment will remain favourable as the key players attempt to succeed and to operate increasingly in the pan-European market.

8. Essex Water Company – A study in market extension

In this study of Essex Water PLC, Tony Bennett examines the partnership that has developed between that company and the French organization, Lyonnaise des Eaux. The general theme of the study is that this partnership provides an example of international co-operation that has resulted not from aggression, but genuine collaboration.

9. Airbus Industrie – A study in European collaboration

The Airbus project predates the Single Market initiative by a number of years but it illustrates one of its most important themes, the need for European industry to develop an appropriate response to a global market, characterized by a need for large-scale production. In their study, Ron Allison and Ian Barnes describe the development of this project and identify some of the political and financial factors involved in the process of collaboration. They make the point that the increasing use of collaboration as a method of operating within the European market has revealed a number of significant problems.

10. Competition and change in the British and German brewing industries

Ron Allison, David Kinnear, and Henry Schietzold outline some of the developments that have taken place in the British and German brewing industries. The study is also concerned with some of the issues arising from the movement from a command economy to that of a market economy as found in the brewing industry of the former East Germany. To illustrate some of the general issues explored, two local British breweries are examined: Bateman's and Ridley's, and three German breweries: the

Landshuter Brauerei, the Berliner Kindl Brauerei and the Felsenkeller Brauerei.

Bibliography

Ansoff, H.I., *Corporate Planning* (Penguin, 1975).

Boseman, G. and Phatak, A., *Cases in Strategic Management* (New York, Wiley, 1989).

Easton, G., *Learning from Case Studies* (Hemel Hempstead, Prentice Hall International, 1982).

Johnson, G. and Scholes, K., *Exploring Corporate Strategy* (Hemel Hempstead, Prentice Hall International, 1989).

Porter, M.E., *Competitive Strategy* (New York, Free Press, 1980).

Porter, M.E., *Competitive Advantage* (New York, Free Press, 1985).

Part 1
The European business environment

Chapter 1
The European Community (EC)

Historical background

The origins of the EC go back to 1950 when Robert Schuman, the French Foreign Minister, put forward a plan for France and Germany to pool their coal and steel production. This plan became a reality with the signing of the Treaty of Paris on 18 April 1951, establishing the European Coal and Steel Community (ECSC). Further important developments occurred with the signing of the Treaty of Rome on 25 March 1957, which created the European Economic Community (EEC) and the European Atomic Energy Community (EAEC) better known as Euratom. Important amendments to these treaties were achieved in 1986 with the signing of the Single European Act.

The founding States of the three Communities were Belgium, West Germany, France, Italy, Luxemburg, and the Netherlands. Successive accessions brought the number of Member States to twelve. Denmark, Ireland and the UK became members on 1 January 1973, Greece on 1 January 1981, and Spain and Portugal on 1 January 1986. The former Republic of East Germany automatically became a member upon German re-unification in November 1990. On 16 February 1976 the European Parliament resolved that the three Communities should become one, and designated the 'European Community'(EC).

Aims

In effect the treaties that established the EC provided a blueprint for action with specific targets in a number of policy sectors, ranging from agriculture, employment creation, transport, the environment and the quality of life, to free and fair trade, relations with the Third World, and scientific and technological co-operation.

A general overview of the functions of the EC is provided in Fig. 1.1.1 which gives details of the distribution of EC expenditure.

The European Community has a number of general aims, these include:

- upholding peace in Europe by integrating national economies;
- increasing prosperity by developing a common market;
- pooling the energies of Member States for technological and industrial development;
- easing the inequalities between people and regions;
- assisting people of the Third World;
- developing an effective means of resolving political disputes.

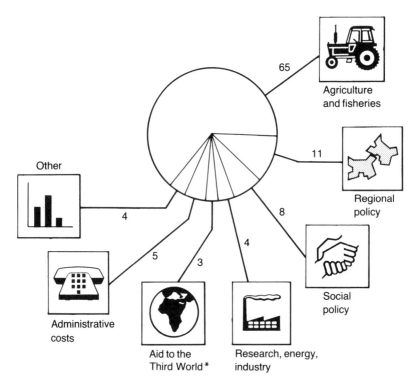

* excluding similar expenditure financed outside the budget by the European Development Fund.

Fig. 1.1.1   Distribution of Community expenditure (as %, 1989 commitments)
Source: EC Commission

The responsibility for achieving these aims rests with four institutions: the Commission, the Council of Ministers, the European Parliament (EP) and the Court of Justice (CJ); and three auxiliary bodies, the Economic and

Social Committee (ESC), the European Investment Bank and the European Court of Auditors.

The Commission

The Commission consists of 17 members; France, Germany, Italy, Spain and the UK designate two members each, the other Member States of the EC only one. The members of the Commission and its President are appointed by 'common accord' of the Member States' Governments. Each Commissioner is responsible for an area of Community policy. The Commission is currently divided into 23 Directorates-General (DGs) plus a number of specialized services.

Each Commissioner has a 'cabinet' of six or more permanent administrators plus secretarial support. The cabinets have an important part to play in the decision-making process. However, the main bulk of the Commission's personnel are grouped in the 23 DGs – this group is often referred to as 'the services'. The DGs are responsible for the technical preparation of legislation and its implementation. The services are usually staffed by career officials.

Directorates-General of the Commission

The 23 DGs of the Commission are:

DGI	External relations
DGII	Economic and financial affairs
DGIII	Internal market and industrial affairs
DGIV	Competition
DGV	Employment, industrial relations and social affairs
DGVI	Agriculture
DGVII	Transport
DGVIII	Development
DGIX	Personnel and administration
DGX	Information, communication and culture
DGXI	Environment, nuclear safety and civil protection
DGXII	Science, research and development
DGXIII	Telecommunications, information and innovation industries
DGXIV	Fisheries
DGXV	Financial institutions and company law
DGXVI	Regional policy
DGXVII	Energy

DGXVIII	Credit and investments
DGXIX	Budgets
DGXX	Financial control
DGXXI	Customs union and indirect taxation
DGXXII	Co-ordination of structural instruments
DGXXIII	Enterprise policy and trade, tourism and 'economic sociale'

The work of the Commission

The Commission acts in the general interest of the Community and is completely independent of each Member State in the performance of these duties. The treaties assigned to the Commission a range of functions, these include:

(a) **Initiating legislation.** The Commission is the starting point for every Community action; it tables proposals to the Council of Ministers after wide-ranging discussions with national experts and other organizations.

(b) **The Commission is the 'guardian of the treaties'.** It has to ensure that the provisions of the treaties and the Community legislation are properly implemented. Whenever these are infringed, the Commission can intervene, either on its own initiative or on the basis of complaints from Governments, companies or private individuals.

(c) **The Commission is an executive body and it has responsibilities for implementing policy decisions.** This task has given the Commission increased power, although this is often ignored by commentators because the set piece political conflicts are over. In many areas, policy is actually administered by Member States with the Commission supervising programmes.

The Commission is collectively responsible to the European Parliament and can be removed by a vote of censure carried by a two-thirds majority. There is no procedure for removing individual Commissioners.

The Council of Ministers

The Council consists of representatives of the Governments of the Member States. Over the course of time, 'specialist' councils have evolved dealing with particular areas of policy, for example, education, research, foreign affairs, agriculture, budget, finance, industry, and the internal market. Councils are attended by the relevant ministers from each of the Member

States and by the President of the Commission, who is present as of right and participates in discussion as an equal partner. It is in the Council that the individual interests of the Member States and the EC are balanced and reconciled.

The Council is the final decision-making body of the EC. The votes of its Members are weighed as follows:

Germany, France, Italy, UK	10 votes each
Spain	8 votes
Belgium, Greece, Netherlands, Portugal	5 votes each
Denmark, Ireland	3 votes each
Luxemburg	2 votes

When a Council decision requires a 'qualified majority' it must achieve at least 54 votes (out of 76) in favour. Most of the Single Market programme requires a qualified majority, but this depends on the provision of the Treaty of Rome under which individual items are made. For very important issues, such as enlargement and amendments to the treaties, unanimity is required.

When the Heads of State or Government meet, the Council is referred to as the European Council. In addition to the Heads of State and Government, the European Council consists of the Foreign Affairs Ministers and the President of the Commission. The European Council meets at least twice a year in 'summit' conferences. It determines long-term policy objectives for the Community. Member States assume the President of the Council can exercise considerable influence within the Council.

The term 'Council' embraces not only the ministerial meetings but also working groups of officials from the Member States and the Committee of Permanent Representatives of the Member States in Brussels (COREPER). COREPER is composed of national officials of ambassadorial rank, they have the task of discussing all proposals coming from the Commission and going to the Council and identifying areas of agreement and conflict. The UK is represented on COREPER by members of the UK representatives in Brussels. The UK representatives are mainly members of the Foreign Office, but increasingly people from other departments, for example, the Department of Trade and Industry (DTI), and the Ministry of Agriculture, Fisheries and Food (MAFF) are being seconded to this unit.

A wide range of specialist committees composed of national Civil Servants report to COREPER; their main function is to discuss the details of policy proposals. In addition to their formal role, the UK representatives play a crucial part in the policy-making and implementation processes via informal discussions with Commission officials and civil servants from other Member States. The Council is accountable to the European Parliament.

The European Parliament

The European Parliament (EP) is a directly elected body of 518 members, 81 of which come from the UK. The EP is not a Parliament in the normal Western European sense in that it cannot initiate legislation, and in most areas it does not have the final say in passing laws. Under the EC treaties its formal opinion is required on most proposals before they can be adopted by the Council. Members are elected for a period of five years, the next election year being 1994. The Secretariat of the Parliament is in Luxemburg, although the Parliament's plenary sessions are held in Strasbourg and its committees meet in Brussels.

The EP's powers are mainly budgetary; it has the final word on all 'non-compulsory expenditure', that is expenditure that is not the inevitable consequence of EC legislation (roughly 25 per cent of the Community budget). Funding for both vocational education and research and develop-ment is viewed as 'non-compulsory expenditure'. The EP can reject the budget in total, and it did this in 1979 and 1984, whereas in both 1985 and 1986 it held up the budgetary timetable.

With the passing of the Single European Act, the EP has become directly involved in decisions affecting the Single Market, for example, the Council can reject the Parliament's views only by a unanimous vote.

Most of the detailed work of the EP is done in specialist committees, divided by subject area; one of the functions of these committees is to examine Commission proposals before they are put to the EP as a whole. For each policy proposal a committee appoints a 'rapporteur' who is an MEP charged with preparing a report. After discussions, the draft opinion is put to the EP as a whole, it is then adopted, sometimes with amendments, as the Parliament's opinion.

The European Court of Justice (ECJ)

The European Court of Justice (ECJ) is an important part of the Community policy-making process as it rules on the interpretation and application of EC rules, and its decisions apply directly in the Member

States. The Court has 13 judges, at least one from each Member State. In 1989 a Court of First Instance was established to relieve the backlog of cases which had steadily built up in the Court of Justice. This Court is able to determine certain types of cases at first instance, subject to a right of appeal to the Court of Justice on a point of law.

In addition to the main policy-making institutions at the EC level, there are three auxiliary bodies.

The Economic and Social Committee (ESC)

The ESC is a consultative body made up of 189 members, 24 of whom come from the UK. The ESC consists of representatives of employers, trade unions, and 'special interests' such as consumer groups. The Committee must be formally consulted by the Commission on proposals relating to economic and social issues. In most instances the Committee's influence in the policy-making process is limited.

The European Investment Bank (EIB)

Based in Luxemburg, the EIB is a financing agency whose main aim is to assist in the 'balanced and smooth development' of the Community, by providing loans and guarantees to promote the economic and technological developments of less developed regions, to modernize or convert undertakings, create new jobs and assist projects of common interest to Member States.

The European Court of Auditors

The European Court of Auditors has twelve members; they examine the accounts of Community institutions to ensure sound financial management. The Court can also examine the accounts of any organization in receipt of EC funding.

The EC policy-making process

In simple terms, it is the Commission that initiates a policy proposal. This proposal then goes to two consultative bodies, the European Parliament and the Economic and Social Committee. During the consultation process, proposals are also sent to national legislatures for discussion. After the consultation stage, the proposal goes to the Council of Ministers for a final decision. Much of the preparatory work for the Council is carried out by the Committee of Permanent Representatives (COREPER).

The Commission is responsible for implementing policy. In some policy sectors it is concerned directly with implementation, but in others it is responsible for ensuring that Member States are implementing EC decisions. The Court of Justice may become involved in this process if there is an area of judicial dispute. Figure 1.1.2 illustrates a simplified version of the Community policy-making process.

Community policy-making styles

The EC is a unique supranational organization and its main policy objective is to persuade Member States to co-ordinate policies and, where legislation is required, to obtain agreement by consensus.

Different types of policy initiatives tend to affect Member States in different ways; it is useful to divide these types into five categories:

(a) The policies which regulate internal and external trade between Member States.
(b) Certain policy areas such as agriculture, where national policies have, to a major extent, been replaced by EC policies.
(c) In many areas – for example, vocational training and R&D – EC policies are supplementing existing national policies.
(d) In some areas – for example, the European Monetary System (EMS) – Members have some choice with regard to their level of participation.
(e) There are areas which develop as a common concern, for example, Third World issues.

Features of EC policy-making styles

(a) The policy-making process is about encouraging the twelve Member States to co-ordinate and, if necessary, change their laws. Inevitably, policy making is slow and each decision involves compromise; at times, the final decision is considerably different from that originally proposed.
(b) The treaties provide a blueprint for action, and decision making can only be based on the treaties or a formal amendment of them.
(c) The Commission proposes new policies but the Council of Ministers is the final decision-making body and the EP is mainly a consultative

assembly, thus individual national governments are firmly in control of EC policy making.

(d) The Commission is highly compartmentalized and co-ordination between the different departments is something of a problem.

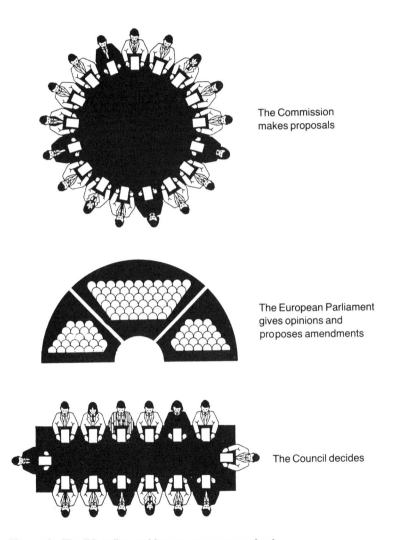

The Commission makes proposals

The European Parliament gives opinions and proposes amendments

The Council decides

Fig. 1.1.2 The EC policy-making process summarized
Source: DTI *The Single Market – 'Brussels can you hear me?'*

Types of EC law

Under the treaties, the Council and the Commission may make regulations, issue directives, take decisions, make recommendations or deliver opinions:

- regulations have general application and are directly applicable in all Member States;
- directives are binding on Member States as to the results to be achieved within a stated period, but leave the method of implementation to national governments;
- decisions are specific to particular parties and are binding in their entirety on those to whom they are addressed, whether Member States, companies or individuals.
- recommendations and opinions have no binding force but merely state the views of the institution that issues them.

Bibliography

Budd, S. A. and Jones, A., *The European Community: A Guide to the Maze*, 3rd edition (London, Kogan Page, 1989).

DTI, *The Single Market* – *'Brussels can you hear me?'* 'Latest edition, London.

Chapter 2
The Single European Market and the wider Europe

Background to the Single European Market

In June 1985 the Heads of State and of Government of the twelve Member States of the European Community committed themselves to establish a true Single European Market, a 'Europe without frontiers'. They did so by endorsing the Commission's White Paper, *Completing the Internal Market.* This Paper contains a 300-point plan and a detailed timetable of measures which need to be adopted by the Council of Ministers in order to achieve a market free of practically all restraints to competition by the end of 1992. The White Paper identifies three types of barriers to trade:

- physical barriers
- technical barriers
- fiscal barriers.

It is generally accepted that these barriers, which result in a fragmented Community, are costly to business and expensive for consumers. A number of studies conducted by the Commission and the European Parliament in the 1980s suggested that frontier formalities alone were causing a loss throughout the Community of over 12 billion ECU (£8 billion) per year. It was estimated that differences in national standards and technical regulations relating to a variety of products cost firms at least 50 billion ECU a year.

The ideas behind the completion of the Single European Market are that the removal of physical, technical and fiscal barriers to trade will enable European business to develop more effectively, leading to greater economic growth and the ability to compete more successfully with US and Japanese companies, especially in high-technology industries.

The idea of creating a single market is not new; this was the aim of the Treaty of Rome when it was signed in 1957. One difficulty in achieving

European integration has been the situation that, for many legislative measures, the Council of Ministers was obliged to act unanimously. Any one Member State could successfully block a measure which, for nationalistic reasons, it disagreed with. However, in 1986 the Council of Ministers signed the Single European Act (SEA), which amended the Treaty of Rome and provided for majority voting in the Council of Ministers for most measures covering the Single Market programme.

Almost all the White Paper proposals take the form of directives, which are binding on the Member States but leave them some discretion as to how they will be implemented by internal legislation. Each directive and proposed directive contain a time limit within which the Member States are required to adopt the necessary legislation.

The comprehensive programme contained in the White Paper affects EC policies in a wide range of areas, for example, agriculture, competition, employment, the environment and transport. Many of these policies are well developed and will facilitate the implementation of the Single Market programme.

Physical barriers

Physical barriers, in the form of customs posts and immigration controls, are perhaps the most visible signs of the national boundaries that fragment the EC. They restrict the movement of goods and people, cause delays and increase costs. The Commission aims to abolish these controls. The liberalization of internal frontier controls on goods and people will be accompanied by tightening up the controls at the Community's external borders, and by the development of a common approach to problems affecting national security, such as crime, drugs and terrorism.

To facilitate the free movement of goods, the Commission has developed a two-stage programme. The first stage was achieved in 1988 by the adoption of the Single Administrative Document (SAD). The adoption of SAD has simplified the paperwork involved in transporting goods. Previously there were as many as 70 different administrative forms which had to be completed for the transport of goods between Member States, this has now been replaced with just one document. Stage two of this process will consist of the co-ordination of policies and the adoption of common legislation so that internal frontiers and controls are completely abolished by the end of 1992.

A significant barrier to trade exists because of the separate national requirements for hauliers and the safety of the vehicles which they use.

Virtually all intra-Community transport has been subject to quotas by which countries have limited the number of journeys that foreign hauliers may undertake. The Commission aims to abolish all such quotas by January 1993, thus adopting a common transport policy which will allow haulage companies to operate freely throughout the Community.

Technical barriers

Technical barriers result from different product regulations and standards in the different Member States. These differences are particularly important in fields such as financial services, foodstuffs, pharmaceuticals and telecommunications. In some instances the costs involved in modifying the product for individual markets or gaining product certification are simply too high. Until the early 1980s the Community tried to eliminate these barriers by detailed harmonization of national regulations to conform to European standards. However, this process was very complicated and slow, and little progress was being made.

The procedure of eliminating technical barriers was facilitated by the Cassis de Dijon case in 1979. In this case the European Court ruled that in principle, goods legally manufactured and marketed in one Member State should be able to be sold in another. Restrictions on free movement should only be applied in certain limited circumstances where real public interest issues were at stake. This is the principle of mutual recognition. The White Paper distinguishes between those areas in which technical details must be harmonized and those in which they need not. Where harmonization is not considered necessary from an environmental, health or safety point of view, then the principle of mutual recognition will apply and Member States must allow goods to circulate freely if they have been lawfully produced and marketed in another Member State. In areas where harmonization is thought to be necessary, the proposed legislation will be confined to setting out essential minimum health and safety standards.

The Commission has developed the principle of mutual recognition in a wide range of educational, technical and professional qualifications awarded in one country by all others. This means that people with qualifications will be freer to move from one Member State to another. In particular, it will also mean that companies offering professional services will have greater freedom to operate throughout the Community. The White Paper treats goods and services equally and the Commission's aim is to open up the market for services on the basis of mutual recognition of qualifications.

Liberalization will affect all service industries but, particularly, financial services, new technologies, broadcasting, transport and insurance.

Fiscal barriers

Fiscal barriers arise from varying approaches to indirect taxation, for example, different levels of excise duties and VAT. The rates and the structure of the rate bands vary so widely as to represent a significant impediment to free trade in the Community. When goods cross internal frontiers, the correct revenue accrues to the right Member State. Under the present system, tax is payable in the country in which the goods are ultimately consumed. Exporters receive a tax rebate when they export their product, whilst importers must pay the tax on import. The whole system depends on checks at internal frontiers. In order to avoid the distortions of trade caused by different rates of indirect taxes, the Commission has proposed a harmonization of the tax levels in different Member States. The proposal is that the levels of VAT in Member States will be replaced by two bands applicable in all Member States. VAT at a rate of between 4 and 9 per cent would be levied on basic goods and services. All other goods and services would attract a new rate of between 14 and 20 per cent. The argument being that the harmonization of the levels of VAT would reduce the incentive to smuggle goods and therefore the need for frontier controls. It should be noted that this part of the White Paper is particularly controversial.

The Single Market – some associated issues

Economic and Monetary Union (EMU)

An issue closely associated with the Single Market programme is the establishment of economic and monetary union, the development of which is already having a major impact on business. The development of a central Community bank and a common currency are important issues if the EC is to take full advantage of the Single Market. Under EMU a European central bank would set interest rates and regulate exchange rates for all EC Member States. If the Twelve agree on full monetary union, the pound could become a thing of the past. Most Member States are committed to the idea of a shared European currency within ten years. The British Government is opposed to the idea of a single currency. Economic union will mean some kind of common European budget and common economic and industrial policies.

The idea of EMU is not new. As long ago as 1970, the Werner Report set out a three-stage process for greater economic and monetary integration, but the process never really got off the ground. This was in part due to the lack of convergence between the economies of the Member States. This failure brought with it a degree of disillusionment with the whole idea of EMU. However, the establishment of the European Monetary System (EMS) in the late 1970s put the issue back on the agenda.

The EMS was launched in 1979 to create a zone of monetary stability in Europe by attempting to move towards more stable exchange rates within the EC. It was hoped that there would be greater co-ordination of national economic policies. Finally, there was the hope that the EMS might become part of a step-by-step approach to complete monetary union within the EC.

The exchange rate is the price of one currency in terms of another; this is important because it determines the price at which goods and services are traded internationally. The EMS operates through a mutually linked web of currency exchange rates: all participating currencies have values expressed against all other currencies and against the European Currency Unit (ECU). The ECU is used mainly for accounting purposes, it is a basket currency and the share of a particular Member State is determined by its Gross Domestic Product.

The Exchange Rate Mechanism (ERM) keeps most EC currencies, including sterling, tied to each other within fixed rates. The currencies move as a block against other world currencies such as the US dollar. EC member governments must set their interest rates at a level that will keep their currency at its ERM rate. If a currency is falling on the money markets, a government must make it more attractive by raising interest rates. If it is rising, interest rates are cut to make money traders less keen to hold that currency.

The time-scale for EMU

In 1989 a Committee chaired by Jacques Delors, President of the Commission, considered how the Community could best progress towards full economic and monetary union. The Delors Report suggested that the move towards EMU could be split into three stages, no deadlines were given. Only Stage One could be accomplished within the existing treaties. Stage One was to consist of:

- the completion of the Single Market;
- the co-ordination of national budgetary policies;
- the establishment of the Committee of Central Bank Governors as an autonomous body.

Stage Two is viewed as a period of transition:

- monetary policy would be the responsibility of the EC central bank (Eurofed) which, in turn, would report to the European Parliament;
- fluctuating margins within the ERM would be narrowed.

Stage Three is to consist of:

- fixed and locked exchange rates;
- Eurofed taking on the full responsibility for monetary policy;
- a single currency being established.

The UK Government is against the idea of a single currency and a European central bank, and has proposed the idea of a hard ECU which in effect would be a thirteenth currency running alongside the existing twelve currencies.

At the time of writing, the Community is working on a draft EMU treaty which should be signed by the end of 1991. The draft treaty proposes that Stage Two should start in 1994; the Committee of Central Bank Governors would call itself a council and try to co-ordinate national monetary policies. The new central bank would be established in 1996. The Commission and the bank would report to the EC Finance Ministers on progress towards economic convergence. An EC summit would then decide if the Community was ready to set a date for the final stage. If all went well, it is envisaged that ECU could replace national currencies by the end of 1998.

All the EC Finance Ministers agree that EMU would be easier if economic convergence really happened. According to the draft treaty, the Community would have major powers over national budgets. For example, if the Finance Ministers decided by majority vote that a country's deficit was 'excessive', it could recommend policy changes. All Member States, including Britain, expect a compromise to be reached, so that Britain will not stop other members moving towards EMU, and they will not force Britain to move faster than it wants to.

On the central bank idea, the draft treaty states that the bank's President will report annually to the EP and the EC Finance Ministers. The Finance Ministers will set an exchange rate policy for it to follow.

EMU – the implications for business

Currency volatility would be removed, leaving companies to make overseas investment decisions without the need to worry about currency risk. The second major advantage is the costs saved in transactions; for example, exchanging sterling into another EC currency involves costs which would not apply with a single currency.

There are two arguments against the establishment of EMU. Firstly, that it will only be possible to create a single currency at great cost to some of the poorer regions of the EC. Secondly, the loss of monetary sovereignty would mean that nationally elected parliaments would no longer have control over their national currency. Yet, in reality, with the dominance of the Bundesbank, much monetary sovereignty has already been lost, for example, the interest rates of all Community countries are greatly influenced by the decisions of the Bundesbank.

Political union

Most Member States agree that national loss of sovereignty resulting from EMU necessitates Community institutions being subject to greater democratic control. Political union involves closer co-operation on law making, foreign policy and perhaps defence between the Member States. There is much dispute among Member States as to what should be included in the draft treaty on political union and the document in final form is unlikely to be ready before the end of 1991. The work on the treaty for political union is running in parallel with the draft document on EMU. However, any change to the Treaty of Rome, which would result, requires unanimity within the European Council as well as endorsement by national legislatures.

The draft treaty on political union, as drawn up in April 1991, proposes the creation of a common EC foreign and security policy; an increase in the powers of the EP by giving it right of 'co-decision' with the Council of Ministers on certain legislation; a right for EC citizens to vote elsewhere in the Community; and the reduction of the Commission to one representative for each Member State. The document also endorses, for the first time, inter-governmental co-operation among the Twelve on police and immigration issues. Jacques Delors is concerned that the draft treaty might lead to the weakening of some of the Commission's existing powers. For example, the Commission would lose its power to accept or reject the EP's amendments to a law before it went to the Council of Ministers.

The SEA has the effect of clarifying the EC competence in a range of areas which are likely to have an increasing impact on business. For example, until 1986 the Community's legal competence to develop policy in the area of research and development was in question. The establishment of a European Research and Technology Community was a major aim of the SEA, 'to strengthen the scientific and technical basis of European industry and to encourage it to become more competitive at the international level'. By developing a range of R&D initiatives, the EC sees itself as a catalyst in the process of encouraging a wider range of joint ventures in R&D at the European level.

Social Europe

The Single Market programme is mainly concerned with removing barriers to competition and enabling companies to obtain maximum economic advantage. But the Community also has both a regional and a social dimension which may in time have a major impact on European business, particularly in the area of employment legislation, personnel practice and industrial relations.

EC regional policy aims to reduce regional disparities within the Community. The Charter of Fundamental Social Rights aims at the upward harmonization of working and living conditions and includes:

- the improvement of living and working conditions;
- the right to freedom of movement;
- the right to employment and remuneration;
- the right to social protection;
- the right to freedom of association;
- the right to vocational training;
- the right of men and women to equal treatment;
- the right to worker participation;
- the right to health protection and safety in the work place.

From these general principles the Commission has developed an action programme, elements of which have attracted much criticism, especially within the UK. The main point of criticism is that the proposed programme which is to be implemented by 1993 will result in much higher costs for industry.

Environmental policy

The EC's legal competence in the field of environmental policy, including pollution controls, was clarified in the SEA. A major element behind EC environmental policy is 'the polluter pays' principle. In addition, the Community's environmental impact assessment directive, which came into force in July 1988, should ensure that environmental considerations are taken into account when formulating other national and Community policies. The Commission is also developing a draft environmental auditing directive which will require most significant industrial operations to carry out audits on environmental acceptability. This directive will be binding on Member States, but it will take the form of a 'framework directive', allowing individual Member States to determine how they will implement the directive in the context of their own legislation. The finalization of the full text is expected in 1992; it is likely to contain the following:

- information availability on emissions to air, land and water;
- company policy on hazards and operations nuisance;
- site waste management analysis;
- clean technologies promotion;
- energy conservation measures.

A verification of the audit would be carried out by independent registered environmental auditors.

For certain industrial sectors, such as chemicals, EC environmental policy is likely to become an increasingly important issue.

Fortress Europe?

When the Single Market programme is implemented, the EC will become the single largest industrial market in the world, but many external trading partners are concerned that a new 'Fortress Europe' will emerge. One of the main problems in this area is that the White Paper makes little reference to the external implications of the programme. Under Article 115 of the

Treaty of Rome, Member States may impose quantitative restrictions against each other on goods originating from third countries. The White Paper states that 'temporary measures' will replace national importing policies.

GATT and the EC

The General Agreement on Tariffs and Trade (GATT) Uruguay round is running in parallel to the Single Market programme. Originally negotiated in 1947, GATT was designed to encourage trade liberalism, and it established an international code for the conduct of world trade. In 1986 a new round of trade liberalization negotiations was launched, called the 'Uruguay round'. This aims to roll back some of the trade restrictions that have developed over the last few years. But a crucial stumbling block has been the failure of the EC to make concessions on farm reform that would facilitate a compromise with the USA. The USA argues that the large subsidies, enjoyed by EC farmers, distort free trade in agricultural products. The question of subsidies and their effect on trade is an issue addressed in the Airbus case study in Part 2 of this book. At the time of writing, GATT members had stated that they hoped to reach some agreement by the end of 1991.

The GATT negotiations include a wide range of trade issues, such as:

- intellectual property – the EC is seeking to develop common standards of protection but these may be in conflict with the ambitions of the USA, for example, on the length of patent protection;
- trade investment rules – the EC has now acknowledged that local content rules are an inadmissible barrier to foreign investment;
- reciprocal access and the extent to which non-EC firms will be allowed access to the Single Market.

In 1988, Commissioner Wily de Clerc outlined the principle of 'reciprocity'. This means that the benefits of internal liberalization will not extend unilaterally to third countries. For example, US banks already resident in one Member State cannot expand into another Member State, unless EC banks are granted the same privilege in return.

It is intended that the wide variety of import arrangements within the Community will be eliminated, but for a transitionary period 'appropriate measures' will be implemented. For example, until 1992 these measures will involve Community-wide quotas for imported cars. An issue still to be decided is whether or not Japanese and other third country models built at manufacturing plants within the Community should be included in these quotas.

In July 1991 the EC and Japan signed a joint declaration pledging 'heightened international co-operation' but a deal between Japan and the EC on the sale of Japanese cars in the EC was being held up by the refusal of Toyko to accept any curb on production inside the EC.

The wider Europe – extending the EC

The European Free Trade Association (EFTA)

Before the publication of the White Paper in 1985, talks began on the possibility of closer links between EC countries and members of EFTA (Switzerland, Austria, Norway, Sweden, Iceland and Finland). For example, Jacques Delors's offer to EFTA was that its members could share, at a price, some of the benefits of the Community's post-1992 Single Market, by the possible creation of a 'European economic space', composed of all Community and EFTA members. The Community only offered EFTA members consultation on early drafts of laws. It has been suggested that Delors made this offer in an attempt to keep these countries out of the EC for as long as possible and that he was more concerned with 'deepening' the Community, rather than with 'widening' it.

The EC and EFTA have entered into co-operation on a range of issues. For example, on the harmonization of technical standards, the use of the Single Administrative Document, and the opening up of public procurement. A number of EFTA countries have implemented some EC directives into their own laws to enable harmonization to extend beyond the boundaries of the Community. However, in the summer of 1991 the negotiations for a 19-nation common European economic area reached stalemate.

EFTA countries will not be full participants in the Single Market programme but there is a general wish within these countries to have more extensive links with EC countries. This, in turn, not only provides opportunities for companies within the EC, but also those in EFTA countries are developing strategies in response to the completion of the Single Market. Austria and Sweden have already applied for EC membership and others could follow in their footsteps, although the EC decided that none of the EFTA countries can be members of the EC before 1995.

The re-unification of Germany

The re-unification of Germany in October 1990 is likely to cause much upheaval as the former East Germany attempts to catch up with the Single Market measures already in force in the Western part of the country. The former West German Government has given assurances that it will shoulder the financial and economic burden involved in this process but, inevitably, the Community will have to take ultimate responsibility. The legacy of the regime in the former East Germany – outdated industry and infrastructure, inefficient agriculture and massive pollution problems – will take time to overcome. A number of these problems are explored in the German part of Case 10 on the British and German brewing industries. The needs of the former East Germany may provide business opportunities for Western firms, although the early indications would suggest that German-based firms are taking up most of these opportunities.

Central and Eastern Europe

In 1989 revolution swept across Bulgaria, Czechoslovakia, Hungary, Poland, Rumania, the USSR and Yugoslavia. After 40 years of Leninism, these countries needed help to build up democratic structures and market economies. These needs are pressing and the task is enormous. The common feature of these economies is one of centralized resource allocation, monopolistic production structures, autarkic trade policies, non-convertible currencies and the widespread use of subsidies. The result has been a distortion of the price of goods, services, labour and capital.

Economic problems

A major problem facing all these economies is that of price distortion: the price of goods and factors of production do not reflect the true cost of the resources used. The debt problem facing these countries represents a major impediment to economic liberalization. It contributes to the balance of payments problems and deters these countries from opening up their economies to the world markets. It also leads to a limited credit worthiness which prevents foreign investors from injecting urgently needed finance and investment capital.

The basic requirements to develop a market economy include:

• an open pricing system: that is, a system where prices are set by willing buyers and willing sellers;

- privatization of state-owned enterprises and the right to own and transfer property;
- an active competition policy: a government policy committed to low rates of protection against imports would provide an important shield against anti-competitive behaviour;
- the provision of vocational education, training and business advice to assist in the creation of an entrepreneurial base;
- a central banking/monetary policy which gives confidence in the currency;
- the provision of banking services;
- a convertible currency.

Rapid privatization is essential in order to maintain the momentum of the reform programme. However, privatization has proceeded more slowly than many observers expected, the private sector's contribution to output is small. For example, in 1990 only 3 per cent of industrial output in Hungary came from the private sector. In all these economies, private savings are not sufficient to support rapid privatization. There are considerable opportunities for acquisition by Western companies.

Political problems

On the political front, the stability of the new regimes is by no means secure. Issues include:

- the lack of a recent democratic tradition;
- possible political unrest arising from what, in the short term at least, may well be declining living standards;
- ethnic and nationalistic unrest.

Eastern European countries and the EC

Developments in countries of Central and Eastern Europe have raised important questions as to how these countries are to participate, or be affected by, the completion of the Single Market. In June 1988, the EC and the Council for Mutual Economic Assistance (CMEA) signed a joint declaration of mutual recognition. This not only established diplomatic relations between the two organizations but it also opened the way to the establishment of diplomatic relations between the EC and individual Eastern European countries. The declaration also provided a stimulus to negotiations on trade and other forms of agreement. Hence, relations between the EC and countries of Central and Eastern Europe were already improving before the revolution that occurred in the second half of 1989.

It seems certain that these fragile democracies with backward economies will require underpinning by close involvement with the Twelve. Equally, the Member States of the Community are aware that the security of Europe is in part dependent on the stability of these new regimes. The changing balance of power between a fragmenting Soviet Union and a unified Germany threatens all manner of instabilities and problems associated with them. The EC is the only organization likely to be able to deal with some of these problems. What is uncertain is whether or not the Community will be able to cope with the burdens which are being placed on it. For example, Eastern European countries are saddled with large foreign debts, owed largely to European governments and commercial banks. Figure 1.2.1 shows the external debt per head of population in 1989.

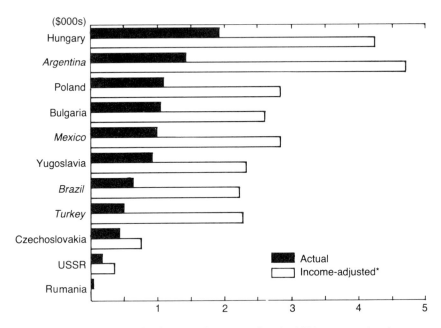

* Population weighted by ratio of average income per head to US income per head

Fig. 1.2.1   External debt per head 1989
Source: European Economy Special Edition No. 2 1991, p.301

The new authorities which have taken office in Central and Eastern European countries have expressed their wish that the EC should play a major role in re-inforcing the process of political reform and economic liberalization. The EC is likely to establish 'Association Agreements' with Czechoslovakia, Hungary and Poland, although, at the time of writing, these negotiations were being threatened by the reluctance of some EC governments to open their markets to the farm, textile and steel exports vital for Eastern Europe's economic recovery.

The G24 group of the 24 leading industrialized countries charged the EC Commission with co-ordinating the PHARE Programme (Poland and Hungary Assistance for Economic Restructuring) in 1990. Originally, the programme applied to Hungary and Poland alone but it has now been expanded to include other Eastern European countries. The priority areas of this programme are:

- agriculture and rural development;
- access to markets, i.e. removing restrictions on imports from Eastern Europe into the markets of the G24 group;
- finance, i.e. loans from the European Investment Bank designed to assist in restructuring;
- vocational training;
- the environment.

In May 1990 the European Bank for Reconstruction and Development (EBRD) was established, its main aim being to promote private sector investment in East European countries. Table 1.2.1 shows the level of economic assistance given to Eastern European countries from 1989 to 1991 by the G24 group.

The assistance provided by the G24 group is small in comparison to the persistent problems facing these countries. For the countries of Eastern and Central Europe, future trade policy will be the acid test of repeated Western declarations of support, as it is essential for these countries to have free access to Western markets.

The range of agreements does offer certain long-term opportunities to companies in Western Europe, especially within the services sector. In the course of economic reforms there has been much interest in direct investment. Joint ventures between foreign and domestic partners are the main form of Western direct investment in Central and Eastern Europe.

Table 1.2.1   Economic assistance to Eastern European countries. (Commitments mid-1989 to January 30, 1991)

Recipients	Members of G24	Donors Multilateral organizations ECU bn[1]	Total
Poland	5.9	1.8	7.7
Yugoslavia	0.2	1.2	1.4
Romania	0.3	0.1	0.4
Czechoslovakia	0.8	0.3	1.1
Hungary	4.0	1.1	5.1
Bulgaria	0.2	0.2	0.4
Unallocated	11.5[2]	–	11.5
Eastern Europe	22.9	4.7	27.6
Of which: loans	9.1	4.7	13.7
grants	13.8[2]	–	13.8

1   1 ECU = approx. $ 1.35 as of early March 1991
2   Including ECU 8.2 bn in share capital from the European Bank for Reconstruction and Development
Source: Commission of the EC, Progress Report on G24 Assistance to Central and Eastern Europe, Brussels, January 30, 1991

The domestic partner provides the infrastructure and links with national authorities, while the Western companies provide technological, marketing and management skills. Figure 1.2.2 shows the number of joint ventures existing with Eastern European countries at the beginning of 1991. This diagram illustrates the point that countries such as Hungary and Poland, which are well ahead in the reform process, attract more joint ventures.

The case studies illustrate how a number of organizations from a range of industrial/commercial sectors are evaluating the opportunities provided by Central and Eastern European countries – for example, Arthur Andersen, Gates Hydraulics Ltd, and National Breakdown. However, any form of direct investment in these countries is difficult. The present imperfections in the price system, the lack of a convertible currency, the bureaucratic regulations, the inefficiency of the public authorities and the political instability are restricting further investment. The flow of Western venture capital has been relatively modest. The EC Commission estimated it at a total of about £1.5 billion as of mid-1990. It seems necessary for these countries to develop efficient legal and administrative frameworks to accept private property and profit if Western investment is going to gain momentum.

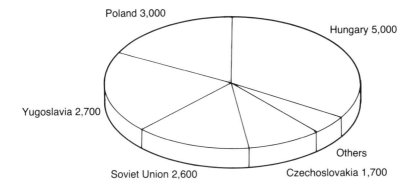

Fig. 1.2.2   Joint ventures with Eastern European countries (at the beginning of 1991)
Source: Austrian Economics Ministry

Bibliography

Budd, S.A. and Jones, A., *The European Community: A Guide to the Maze*, 3rd
    Edition (London, Kogan Page, 1989).

El Agraa, A.M., *The economics of the EC*, 3rd Edition (London, Philip Allen,
    1990).

Cecchini,P., *The European challenge - the benefits of the single market*
    (Wildwood House, 1988).

Lodge, J., *The European Community and the Challenge of the Future* (London,
    Pinter, 1989).

Pelkmans, J. and Winters, A., *Europe's Domestic Market* (London RII/RKP,
    1989).

The Times Guide to Eastern Europe (London, Times Books, 1990).

The Times Guide to 1992 (London, Times Books, 1989).

Chapter 3
The impact of Single Market legislation on business

There is little doubt that the impact of Single Market legislation will be substantial. And although the importance of the impact will vary from sector to sector, there are a number of developments that will be common to a wide range of them. All companies should find that trading within the Community is eased, although the impact is likely to be greatest on small companies and those who are currently discouraged from expanding because of the mass of regulations. There will, of course, be new patterns of trading, as domestic markets are open to organizations from other Member States. For example, there will be an increased number of joint ventures, as well as acquisitions of smaller companies, to benefit from economies of scale. In addition, these changes will affect suppliers, customers, competitors and those with a financial interest, whether they be lenders, investment analysts or potential predators.

A wide range of surveys show that many UK companies, especially the smaller ones, erroneously view the Single Market as being simply about exporting, and hence as having very little impact on their domestic markets. As many smaller companies do not export, they misguidedly ignore the warnings.

In Chapter 2 some of the general implications for business of removing barriers were identified as well as the possible impacts resulting from EMU, Community environmental policy, and developments in EFTA countries and Central and Eastern Europe. A major theme of the impact of the completion of the Single Market is that the vast majority of companies will face increased competition at home and there will be a need to increase efficiency through price and quality control. The study of Labsworth World Wide PLC examines the issue of a pricing strategy. Whilst the Gates Hydraulics Ltd case study illustrates how one organization is responding to this challenge by adopting a Total Quality Management strategy.

Most of the Single Market programme is concerned with liberalizing trade within the Community, both for manufacturing and service industries. The rules of the EC are intended to ensure that competition is not distorted. This aim is not only to facilitate the goal of market integration, but also to preserve effective competition as a spur to innovation and economic efficiency for the benefit of the EC as a whole. EC competition law can affect the type of alliances that businesses can forge. Therefore, a brief overview of some of the areas covered by the Single Market programme must be viewed within the broad context of EC competition policy. Then a number of Single Market issues will briefly be examined to illustrate the likely impact of the Single Market and associated legislation on business.

Competition policy

The main competition rules of the EC are contained in Articles 85 and 86 of the Treaty of Rome. In general terms, Article 85 prohibits anti-competitive agreements between businesses and Article 86 prohibits abuses of monopoly power. The Commission has been given considerable powers to investigate and enforce the provisions of these Articles.

Article 85 prohibits collusive agreements between businesses where such agreements prevent, restrict or distort competition within the EC and affect trade between Member States. For example, price fixing and marketing or customer sharing is normally prohibited, and in some instances, exclusive purchase or distribution agreements, as well as some franchising agreements, can be illegal. This Article prohibits not only formal written agreements but all kinds of informal arrangements, whether or not they are intended to be legally enforceable.

Article 85 applies only if an agreement has an appreciable effect both on inter-State trade and on competition within the EC. The Commission considers that an agreement will not normally infringe Article 85 if it is between undertakings belonging to groups which have a combined turnover of less than £130 million. Companies are expected to notify the Commission of any agreements which might infringe Article 85. Many organizations have notified the Commission in order to be considered for an exemption.

The Commission has identified a number of types of agreements which do not normally infringe Article 85. For example, agreements between a principal and his agent; co-operation agreements on a range of technical matters; and most sub-contracting agreements where the sub-contractor uses the contractor's technology to produce goods exclusively for the contractor.

The Commission is empowered to grant exemptions in certain cases, for example, if an agreement produces economic benefits in which consumers share and it does not eliminate competition. The Commission may grant exemptions either by an individual decision relating to a specific agreement or by use of a 'block exemption'. In the case of a specific agreement, individual exemptions can only be granted for limited periods of time. Block exemptions are contained in regulations issued by the Commission and provide automatic exemption for certain categories of agreement. For example, there are block exemptions for 'tied house' arrangements for the supply of beer, an issue which is illustrated in Case 10 on the British and German brewing industries. Joint research and development agreements are covered by block exemption, an issue which has implications for the Airbus Project examined in Case 9.

Infringement of Article 85 can involve fines which, in theory, can amount to 10 per cent of the worldwide turnover, termination of the agreement and damages to third parties who have suffered.

Article 86 prohibits an organization which enjoys a dominant position within the EC from abusing that position, if it may affect trade between Member States. Abusive conduct includes: predatory pricing where prices are artificially low, the aim being to eliminate competitors, and refusals to supply. Infringement can result in consequences that are similar to those under Article 85.

Merger policy

In May 1988 a draft regulation was issued to give the Commission specific powers over merger controls. A similar proposal had been submitted by the Commission in 1973 but the Council had blocked its implementation. The 1988 regulation gives the Commission the power to vet mergers having a 'Community dimension', if the aggregate turnover of the parties exceeds £650 million, subject to certain exceptions. There was much debate about the Commission's powers to prohibit mergers and some argue that the threshold of £650 million is too low. The merger regulation adopted in December 1989 came into force in September 1990 and has a threshold of £3,259 million. This threshold is too high and is subject to review in 1996 at the latest.

State aids, for example regional incentives, can result in trade distortions, however, most state aids are now controlled by the EC to enable them to combat unfair competition issues.

Competition issues are illustrated in a number of the case studies contained in Part 2.

Technical standards

It was stated in Chapter 2 that technical barriers resulting from different product regulations and standards in different Member States are due to be removed as part of the Single Market programme. In some areas technical details must be harmonized, in others, where it is not thought to be necessary from an environmental health or safety point of view, the principle of mutual recognition will apply.

However, in areas where harmonization is thought to be necessary, legislation will set out essential health and safety standards. In these areas companies will not be able to sell their products unless they carry the CE mark (a European BS Kite Mark). Areas covered include: toy safety, construction products, machine safety, electromagnetic compatibility, gas appliances and personal protective equipment. In each of the areas in question it is the Commission that develops the directives, which cover the essential safety and other requirements, but it is CEN and CENELEC (the European standards organizations covering electrotechnical and other areas respectively) who provide standards that show how these requirements can be satisfied in particular products. It has been estimated that about 4,000 standards will be necessary. The British Standards Institute (BSI) is the UK member on both of these European bodies. EFTA members of CEN and CENELEC are co-operating with EC members in this work. The completion of the Single Market should see, as far as standards are concerned, a Single Market not only throughout the EC but throughout Western Europe.

A Single Market in standards will affect companies both large and small. It will mean European-wide distribution, marketing and production operations. In the sectors covered by technical harmonization, products will be required to carry the CE mark in most instances. For smaller companies the costs involved in complying with EC standards in order to qualify for a CE mark will not be insignificant. The Institute of Directors has stated that for smaller companies, especially those engaged in craft industries, the combined costs of monitoring equipment, inspection and certification could be high enough to threaten the continued viability of a business.

Public procurement

Many businesses, both large and small, benefit from the protected markets of supplying goods and services to the public sector. It has been estimated that public procurement within the EC is worth about 10 per cent of the Community's economic output. Public procurement has been used by all Member States to promote 'national champions' at the expense of foreign rivals. Clearly, this practice is a major obstacle to a European Single Market. For over 20 years the Commission has attempted to break this national favouritism but with only minimal success. For example, in 1989 fewer than 5 per cent of all central, regional and local public orders in the EC went to bidders from other countries and many were awarded on a non-commercial single tender basis.

Purchasers suffer because they get limited choice and poor value for money, while producers also suffer because they are increasingly victims of their closed home markets, which have fragmented European industries narrowly along national lines. For example, in areas such as telecommunications and boiler making, Europe has suffered from excess capacity and a surfeit of small manufacturers lacking the economies of scale available to their US and Japanese competitors.

Public procurement legislation

As part of the Single Market programme the Commission has attempted to tighten up existing public procurement legislation. The following changes are in force, or due to come into force by the mid-1990s. Defence procurement is excluded from this legislation.

Supplies and works

- The amended supplies directive has been in operation since January 1989. It affects regional and local goods purchases exceeding 200,000 ECU and central government contracts above 130,000 ECU. An amended works directive will take effect in the mid-1990s, covering contracts exceeding 5 million ECU;
- contractors must be able to justify use of methods other than open tender, for example, restricted competition between selected bidders;
- contracts may be awarded on price as long as criteria are spelled out in advance;
- procurement must normally be to European technical standards where they exist;

- calls for tenders must be advertised in the *Official Journal* of the EC in advance and the decision must be publicized in the same journal.

In addition, it is proposed that Member States will set up their own systems to monitor compliance and review infringements. Member States would have the power to correct violations, to set aside unlawful decisions and to award damages, subject to judicial review.

Other sectors

The previously excluded sectors of water, telecommunications, transport and energy have now been included in this process of opening up buying. Significantly, many of the organizations in these sectors are private companies.

A senior Commission official has said that 'the debate is not about "public" procurement any more. It is about breaking the long-standing incestuous relationships between national monopolies and their client suppliers.' Such developments have important implications for businesses that have benefited from protected markets. In the UK, for example, there has been a move towards awarding tenders for such services as refuse collection and cleaning to French, Dutch and Spanish companies.

Employment legislation

The social dimension of the EC is likely to have an increasing impact on the operations of business organizations as the Single Market comes into view. Social cohesion is viewed as a corollary to economic integration in the Community's drive to complete the Single Market. Chapter 2 outlined some of the rights included in the Social Charter such as the right to worker participation and the right to health protection and safety in the work place. The Commission is in the process of preparing 47 draft directives, which, if enacted, would add up to a comprehensive system of European employment law and few companies would be unaffected. Unfortunately, the UK Government has opposed virtually every employment initiative coming from the EC except those concerned with health and safety at work. This, in turn, has resulted in many employers giving inadequate thought to the implications of this area of legislation.

In the UK most areas concerned with employment relations have common law status, that means that such relations are largely unregulated, this is not the case in other Member States. Most of the proposed directives tend to follow the practice of continental Europe; therefore, the gap between existing UK practice and some of these proposed directives is wide.

In the area of flexible working patterns the UK, unlike other Member States, has reduced the level of regulation in order to encourage employers to take on more workers. In this sphere of employment legislation a number of directives have been proposed. For example, there are two draft directives which would require the pro-rata treatment of atypical workers such as part-time and temporary agency workers, regarding occupational and statutory benefits. A third draft proposal in this area proposes to impose an obligation on employers to be prepared to explain why they, for example, filled posts on a temporary rather than a permanent basis. A draft directive has been published on the adaptation of working time. If implemented, this legislation would set minimum rules on the maximum duration of work, rest periods, night work and weekend work.

It is important for employers to keep up to date with developments in Community employment legislation if only to give themselves time to develop and implement an appropriate response. It is clear that organizations relying on night shifts, part-time workers, temporary and female workers will be significantly affected if these draft directives are implemented.

Financial services

The European financial single market is an essential part of the frontier-free Single European Market, and encompasses not only the free movement of money and capital but also freedom of establishment and the freedom to provide services for brokers and financial undertakings. If a European financial single market is achieved, banks and insurance companies will be free to offer their financial products without restriction and securities will be quotable on all stock exchanges and issuable in all EC countries. Case 1 on Arthur Andersen examines the issues arising for accountancy organizations as a result of the integration of European financial services.

Banking

The Commission's proposals in the banking sector cover mortgage services, consumer credit, bank branch accounts, capital adequacy, electronic payments, and the licensing and supervision of bank services in general.

In the area of banking, the development of a Single Market began in 1977 with the First Banking Co-ordination Directive. This Directive harmonized the standards for licensing banks throughout the EC. This was a significant first step towards the aim of freedom of establishment.

In the context of the Single Market programme, the Council adopted the Second Banking Co-ordination Directive in 1989. The Commission views this Directive as the centrepiece for the integration of the European banking sector. At the core of the Directive is the principle of the single banking licence which allows every banking institution authorized to operate in one Member State to establish branches in all others without the need of obtaining eleven additional licences under eleven different regulatory regimes. This has been achieved by further harmonization of regulations concerning the criteria for granting a licence – for example, the level of initial capital, supervision of the bank's major shareholders and a limitation of participation in non-financial companies. In addition, the Directive introduces the principle of home-country control, by which the supervision of banks and their branches throughout the EC will be the responsibility of the home supervisory authorities who will have to ensure that the banks have adequate capital to support EC-wide business as well as sound administrative and accounting procedures. For example, the home-country authorities will have to give their explicit agreement whenever one of their banks wants to open a branch in any other Member State.

The Directive can only take effect if the other supporting directives, such as those concerned with own funds and solvency ratios, which are designed to harmonize the different standards of regulations in different Member States, have been implemented. The Second Banking Co-ordination Directive specifies that in areas such as the supervision of banking liquidity and implementation of monetary policy, where a considerable degree of harmonization has been achieved, the host authorities will continue to be responsible for supervision.

The Commission argues that the Second Banking Co-ordination Directive will make cross-border financial operations less expensive. The intensification of competition will increase the range of services and thus lead to a reduction in the cost of these services. The study of the Greek National Bank in Case 4 describes how one banking organization is responding to the challenges of the Single Market.

Insurance

The insurance industry in the EC is vast and highly significant in terms of the services it provides, the funds it makes available for investment, the people that it employs and the general impact that it has on the economies of Member States. Insurance is one of the largest in a series of markets which are of crucial importance for the functioning of the whole economy. It has great social importance requiring both a sense of security and stability; market failures have severe economic, social and political consequences to which governments are naturally very sensitive. The protection of the users of such services is an important issue for governments. They are responsible for ensuring that insurance undertakings remain solvent and are able to meet their financial commitments.

A major step towards the freedom to provide insurance services was taken with the adoption in June 1988 of the Second Non-Life Insurance Directive. The Directive, which came into effect in July 1991, allows Community insurance companies to cover the risks of potential policy-holders in any Member State, irrespective of where the insurer is established. As long as it complies with the rules of the country where the risk is situated, a company only has to have the authorization of the supervisory body in its home country. The extent to which it must comply with the rules of the country where the risk is situated is greater in the case of 'large' risks (group policies, commercial and industrial companies) than for 'mass' risks (individual consumers).

The Third Non-Life Framework Directive was adopted in July 1990. The aim of this Directive is to provide a single licence system for non-life insurance, whereby an insurer with a head office in an EC Member State can provide direct non-life insurance throughout the Community on its home state authorization. There will be a minimum harmonization of rules concerning assets permitted, their valuation and their diversification.

In 1990 the Second Life Co-ordination Directive was adopted and this introduced the right of an insurer to provide life insurance for group life and pension business, the equivalent of 'large' risks, and to individual residents in another Member State, but only where individuals seek the policy on their own initiative. Since active promotion of life products is not permitted, the scope of the Directive is rather limited. Indeed there are considerable impediments to the integration of European insurance sectors due to large differences in policies regarding policy-holders protection; this is particularly true if one compares the UK and continental Europe. For example, with regard to 'mass' risks the UK authorities do not impose any direct control on premium levels and policy conditions. While the continental countries regulate the premium rates and policy conditions in order to prevent excessive competition which they believe could undermine the financial stability of companies. In the UK there are no direct constraints on investment policy, and investment decisions are mainly governed by profitability expectations. In constrast, in most other Member States rules limit the freedom of investment by insurance companies. Without some harmonization of these approaches the granting of home country control would be deemed to constitute unfair competition against the companies located in continental countries.

Despite these difficulties, the move towards a common market in insurance is irreversible. The EC is attempting to reduce the level of economic protection which national supervisory authorities provide. The Commission finalized its proposal for a Third Life Insurance Framework Directive in March 1991. This Directive will allow companies to operate freely throughout the EC on the basis of the rules operating in their country of establishment. However, it will also provide a common set of prudential and consumer-protection rules which would apply to all Community life insurance companies. The proposed Directive sets out Community rules for the investment of the assets of life insurance companies, although they will be free to invest anywhere in the Community. The Directive includes a list of the different types of assets which can be acquired and the percentage of total assets which each can represent, so ensuring diversification. Member States will be able to limit this list and reduce the maximum percentages, but only for companies established in their territory.

Case 2 on the Olympic Insurance Company addresses some of the issues involved when a company attempts to respond to the threats and opportunities likely to result from the establishment of a single insurance market.

Transport policy

Article 3(e) of the Treaty of Rome states that one of the objectives of the Community is the adoption of a common transport policy. Transport was seen at the outset as both a means of achieving European integration and of accelerating economic development, it is one of the cornerstones of EC policy. Later it became equally significant in the thinking about regional development within the Community. However, by 1985 little had been achieved and the European Parliament brought to the Court of Justice a successful case against the Council of Ministers for the latter's failure to act. The White Paper *Completing the Single Market*, published in 1985, includes various transport measures. Under the SEA, all sectors of the common transport policy are subject to a qualified majority voting in the Council of Ministers.

In 1983 the Commission established a number of broad policy objectives which included:

- greater integration of national transport policies;
- a better climate of competition between and within different forms of transport;
- financial support for a series of major infrastructure projects of Community-wide importance;
- a co-ordinated approach to safety, technical harmonization, environmental protection and working conditions in the transport industry.

During 1987 and 1988 the Community's two policy objectives were freedom to provide services and the removal of distortions to competition.

Since the passing of the SEA, most areas of transport have assigned medium-term plans to take them up to the end of 1992:

Air. The Council has agreed new measures constituting the first step towards a common air transport policy. The main issues being deregulation, safety and a common approach to non-Member States.

Infrastructure. In 1988 a five-year transport-infrastructure programme, designed to upgrade the main intra-Community transport links up to and beyond 1992, was proposed.

Rail. It was decided to go ahead with the high speed network which is to link Brussels, London, Paris, Cologne and Amsterdam. The EC's rail policy aims to eliminate distortions in competition between different modes of land transport, make relations between governments and their rail companies transparent, promote co-operation between modes of transport, and develop the rail infrastructure. In June 1991 progress was made in the Council to 'open up the railway market', including a limited access to infrastructure for other Member States' railway companies.

Road. Many of the proposals on road transport are aimed at freeing the market, and the common transport policy seems likely to encourage greater use of road vehicles for international freight. Case 7 on National Breakdown looks at some of the implications of the likely great increase in car ownership in EC countries. Given the forecasted 40 per cent increase in road traffic by the end of the decade, the management of this traffic is a high priority. For example, the EC has adopted the EC-wide 40 tonne maximum weight for lorries. Figure 1.3.1 outlines the major policy initiatives in road transport.

Proposal for harmonizing national law regarding a weight limit of 40 tonnes for five-axle articulated or semi-articulated lorries.

The Community permits a certain number of long-distance hauliers to carry goods between all Member States without the need to obtain national authorization (cabotage).

Specification of maximum permitted driving hours per day and per week and the installation of a tachograph in heavy road vehicles.

Minimum levels of training for drivers.

Mutual recognition of national certificates and qualification so that hauliers can set up business in more than one country.

Community-wide driving licences and acceptance of national licences throughout Member States.

Fixing of rates for carriage of goods by road between Member States.

Fig. 1.3.1   Major common transport policy initiatives in road transport

Inland waterways. In terms of the Single Market this form of European transport has not received much attention from the Commission.

In 1988 the EP reported on the importance of the Channel Tunnel in terms of intra-Community trade and the free movement of workers. This point is raised in Case 7.

The real challenge for the common transport policy after 1992 will be to keep pace with developments in other areas of EC policy and to ensure that sufficient transport provision is in place before it is needed. A move away from cars and road transport to more environmentally friendly alternatives will be needed. Business-efficient transport is essential for growth and development.

Research and development

In addition to assisting the progress of the Single Market programme, the Single European Act also identified, '. . . strengthening the scientific and technological base of European industry as a major objective of the EC'. The main aim is to strengthen international competitiveness of European industry in high-technology sectors in the face of competition in global markets, especially from Japan and the USA. A general issue which is addressed in Case 9.

The core R&D activities supported by the EC are the enabling technologies; the information, communications, industrial and materials technologies; the management of natural resources and the management of intellectual resources. One of the major reasons put forward for collaboration is to pave the way for common European standards, which are essential for the establishment of a genuine Single Market.

One of the reasons for Europe's relatively poor showing in many high-technology sectors is the obvious one that the Continent is divided. The fragmentation of Europe's scientific and technological research environment is paralleled by the fragmentation of research policies and lack of coherence in long-range strategic objectives for research. Both Japan and the USA already benefit from a large Single Market with uniform standards and codes of practice and a common working language. By co-operation and the removal of various national barriers, fragmentation of effort can be reduced and European industry can take advantage of the Single Market potential to the full; the needs of European industry in the field of R&D are closely linked with the completion of the Single Market.

The Community sees its role in the area of R&D as that of a catalyst, giving support to companies, institutions of higher education and research institutes.

'. . . in their (research institutions, etc.) efforts to co-operate with one another, aiming notably at enabling undertakings to exploit the Community's internal market potential to the full, in particular through the opening up of national public contracts, the definition of common standards and the removal of legal and fiscal barriers to that of co-operation.' (SEA, Article 130F).

The Community encourages cross-border R&D projects by making extensive use of research teams and laboratories available in Member States. For the period 1990–4 the EC plans to spend around 5.7 billion ECU on collaborative research, with cost-sharing contract research being a major feature of the programme. EC funding under a range of programmes is open to competitive bids from companies, institutions of higher education and research institutes. Special efforts are made to enable smaller companies to participate in these transnational research programmes. The EC supports a wide range of R&D programmes which include: the European Strategic Programme for Research and Development in Information Technology (ESPRIT); the Advanced Communication Technology in Europe Programme (RACE); and the European Collaboration Linkage of Agriculture and Industry through Research (ECLAIR).

It is generally accepted that Community R&D must be confined to those activities which, for reasons of effectiveness and/or efficiency, are best carried out at the Community rather than at the national level. For example, the development of common standards and the funding of programmes that are too costly for individual Member States to support unaided. In the main, EC programmes are precompetitive in nature, that is research is necessary to underpin new developments, but does not itself have direct commercial application, although increasingly the Community is supporting research closer to the market.

Community R&D programmes provide organizations with research opportunities, and also enable many of them to benefit from the results of this research. To participate in these programmes, costs are involved, but the benefits are considerable; for example, participation in a Community R&D programme brings to an organization an additional badge of quality which it can carry to the market place.

There is a general agreement that much of UK industry needs to spend more on R&D, and the EC is now the largest organization through which the UK undertakes international collaboration in science and technology. There is likely to be increased emphasis on product innovation as pan-European R&D becomes a reality.

Vocational training

The completion of the Single Market raises a number of training issues as well as exacerbating others. Traditional employment and career patterns are changing and this will have a number of consequences for the skills required both to enter and stay in work.

The training issues include:

- the speed of economic and technological development will call for continually rising skill levels;
- the demographic downturn will place a premium on quantity as well as quality in the work force;
- the increasingly European nature of economic activity will mean that special value is attached to European expertise, including linguistic skills;
- new developments such as stricter environmental standards need specialist skills for their implementation.

From the late 1980s the Commission has given vocational training a high priority in a new Community-wide commitment to invest in people, thus encouraging Europe's capacity to innovate, compete and prosper. In a number of respects, the Commission acts as a catalyst in the area of vocational training providing financial support under a range of initiatives. For example, the LINGUA Programme was launched to encourage improvement in foreign language tuition, the COMETT Programme provides financial support for industrial training periods spent in other Member States, the PETRA Programme encourages Member States to raise the standard of initial vocational training, and the FORCE Programme aims to encourage greater investment in continuing training.

In the UK recent surveys have highlighted the relatively low levels of training achieved compared to the levels in other Member States. British companies spend about 0.15 per cent of their income on training compared to six times this figure in Japan, Germany and France. Thus, for example, in comparison to France and the former West Germany, few UK managers have degrees or professional qualifications, and a high percentage have little or no management training. Inadequate training affects many areas of the UK economy, for example, five times as many people in the building industry in the former West Germany gain vocational qualifications than in Britain; ten times as many sales and office staff are trained in France than in the UK.

For companies the Single Market raises three separate, but related, training issues. Firstly, the increased training requirements resulting from greater competition from other Member States. Secondly, the training needs relating more specifically to Single Market legislation; and thirdly, knowledge about business practices in other states of the EC. Participation in some of the EC training programmes could assist a range of companies to prepare for the Single Market.

In Part 2, Case 6 on The Greater Peterborough Training and Enterprise Council (GPtec) shows how one organization is developing a response to the training challenges of the Single Market. In addition, the studies of Arthur Andersen, Gates Hydraulics, the Greek National Bank and the Olympic Insurance Company, illustrate how a range of organizations view training as an important element of their Single Market preparations.

Conclusions

The completion of the Single Market will have a major impact on many areas of business. It is significant that in a number of areas, for example accounting practice and employment legislation, the gap between UK practice and that found in continental Europe is wide. Therefore, as much Single Market legislation has tended to keep closer to continental European practices, the impact on the UK is likely to be greater than on any other Member State.

To develop a defensive and/or offensive strategy in response to the challenges of the Single Market, a business organization ought to address three major issues:

- its competitive advantage in terms of price and quality in both the domestic and exporting markets;
- knowledge and understanding of appropriate areas of EC legislation;
- some knowledge of the business cultures in other Member States.

One of the prime objectives of completing the Single Market is to enable European business to compete more effectively with Japanese and US companies. But many global Japanese and US operations are already so strongly competitive that they could become the main beneficiaries of the Single Market. Japan's trading success has been based on exploiting the most favourable global opportunities open to it by concentrating on its competitive advantage in a limited number of key areas. In addition, Pacific Rim economies enjoy the double advantage of low labour costs and low tax charges, and have the fastest growth rate in the world. At the same time they have been casting their eyes overseas for new markets to conquer.

Businesses outside the EC, most notably in EFTA countries, are obviously concerned about the completion of the Single Market and the possibility of 'Fortress Europe' being established. As was stated in Chapter 2, a number of EFTA countries are implementing some EC directives in their laws to enable them to take advantage of some of the benefits of the Single Market. Developments in Central and Eastern Europe are providing businesses with some investment opportunities. All of these developments are having a major impact on the European business environment. Thus, it is becoming less relevant to view Europe as three blocks, i.e. the EC, EFTA, and Central and Eastern Europe.

Bibliography

El Agraa, A.M., *The economics of the EC*, 3rd Edition (London, Philip Allen, 1990).

Berwin, S.J., *Company law and competition* (London, Mercury Books, 1989).

Blue Arrow PLC, *Employment and Training* (London, Mercury Books, 1989).

Budd, S.A. and Jones, A., *The European Community: a guide to the maze* 3rd edition (London, Kogan Page, 1989).

Cecchini, P., *The European challenge – the benefits of the Single Market* (Aldershot, Wildwood House, 1988).

DTI The single market as part of the Europe open for business campaign, the DTI has issued a range of useful booklets on subjects as diverse as EC standards, public purchasing and intellectual property.

Dewhurst, J., *Your business in 1992* (London, Rosters, 1989).

Dudley, J.W., *1992 strategies for the Single Market* 2nd edition (London, Kogan Page, 1990).

Leighton, P., *European Law and its impact on UK employers* (IMS, Sussex University, 1990).

Lodge, J., (ed.) *The challenge of the future* (London, Pinter, 1989).

Lynch, R., *European business strategies* (London, Kogan Page, 1990).

Nugent, N. *The government and politics of the EC* (London, Macmillan, 1991).

Pelkmans, J. and Winters, A., *Europe's domestic market* (London, RIIA/RKP, 1988).

Preston, J., *EC education, training and research programmes – An action guide* (London, Kogan Page, 1991).

Quelch, J., *The marketing challenge of 1992* (Wokingham, Addison-Wesley, 1990).
Steiner, J., *Textbook on EEC Law* 2nd edition (London, Blackstone Press, 1988).
The Times Guide to 1992 (London, 1989).
Venturini, P., *1992: the European social dimension Commission of the EC* (Luxemburg, 1988).

Note: Those people wanting a deeper treatment of the issues raised in Part 1 are referred to *European Business* by Richard Welford and Kate Prescott (Pitman, 1992).

Part 2
The case studies

Case 1
Arthur Andersen & Co. SC – A UK practice in an international context*

Jill Preston

Advice to readers

In general terms, there are two accounting traditions within the EC; the Anglo-Saxon tradition of common law which has evolved into the emphasis upon commercial substance predominating over legal form, and the more codified systems based upon rigid accounting rules found in most other EC States.

In many Member States annual public accounts are produced to satisfy the tax authorities and in Germany the major financial institutions. In Britain the emphasis is on a true and fair view from which auditors form an opinion; audit and tax are separate branches of a large accounting profession, whereas the accounting profession in most continental countries is divided between a small body of auditors and a larger body of bookkeepers.

The harmonization of accounting standards is imperative for cross-border comparisons to have any meaning, and for acquisitions and mergers between companies in different Member States to be anything other than a leap in the dark. In 1978 the EC commenced the process of accounting harmonization, and the Single Market programme (most notably the Fourth and Seventh Company Law Directives) provides a foundation for the progress of harmonization at the European level, although the process of implementing these directives does vary greatly between Member States.

* I should like to express my gratitude to David Oliver, Conor Boden, and Marguerite Deliege-Sequaris of Arthur Andersen for the advice and assistance that they have given during the development of this case study.

It is suggested that readers consider three general issues as they study this case: firstly, to examine whether the pride that the firm has in its international approach is justified; secondly, the extent to which other organizations could benefit by following this approach. And finally, to consider the more general issue of whether EC directives alone are likely to eliminate the problems of cross-border reporting.

Current situation

'To provide quality professional services that meet the information needs of the global market place.'
Arthur Andersen's Mission Statement

The Arthur Andersen worldwide organization covers not only Europe but the Americas, Africa and the Middle East as well as Asia and the Pacific Rim area. The firm provides a range of services related to the completion of the Single Market and it is taking advantage of the opportunities presented by the developments in Eastern and Central Europe. Arthur Andersen prides itself on its international approach to services provision and the training that it gives to its personnel.

The Arthur Andersen worldwide organization has 299 offices in 66 countries and through a network of representative firms serves cities in 25 additional countries. During the 1980s the growth of the organization was dramatic. In 1981 it employed 21,400 people, by 1990 this had increased to 56,800. The firm has over 15,000 professional staff in almost 100 offices across Europe, it has ten offices in the UK.

Figure 2.1.1 shows Arthur Andersen's fee income in comparison to other international accounting firms.

Each member firm is privately owned and controlled by the partners in the country of operation, for example, personnel are recruited and promoted locally, but training is a constant across the firm. This is illustrated by the fact that the level of expertise in, say, international taxation is as high in the regions as it is in London, so that clients do not have to be passed 'onto London' for more specialized advice, as is frequently the case in other similar operations.

The firm operates a tightly-knit network around the world, offices share practice methodologies and technology, and co-ordinate their operations to eliminate barriers to serving clients, as far as national laws and professional regulations allow.

Rank firm	Fee income Total 1990/1 (£m)	Change 1990/1(%)
1. Coopers & Lybrand Deloitte	588.0	11.1
2. KPMG Peat Marwick McLintock	467.1	18.2
3. Price Waterhouse	377.4	25.8
4. Ernst & Young	358.3	6.2
5. Touche Ross	294.9	17.9
6. Arthur Andersen	268.8	32.2
7. BDO Binder Hamlyn	119.7	13.5
8. Grant Thornton	115.3	12.5
9. Pannell Kerr Forster	84.6	11.0
10. Stoy Hayward	66.6	13.3

Fig. 2.1.1 Arthur Andersen's fee income in comparison to other international accounting firms

The organization targets its services to the quality end of the market and services are provided through two business units: Arthur Andersen, for audit and business advisory services, as well as tax and corporate speciality services, and Arthur Andersen Consulting for strategic services, information technology consulting and change management services.

Figure 2.1.2 illustrates the fee income of Arthur Andersen 1980–90.

Growth of the consulting business

In the early 1980s the consulting business grew, so that it stopped being purely an adjunct to accounting. This development resulted in a number of internal difficulties.

'Consulting partners began to resent their second class status within the firm. As they regularly chalked up higher growth rates and higher profit margins, they also began to resent the fact that the accounting partners continued to take most of the spoils at the end of every year.'
The Economist 17/8/91

After much internal debate the firm was split into two business units in 1989, Arthur Andersen Consulting and Arthur Andersen, each with almost complete financial autonomy. The new group Board contains eight consulting partners out of 24. Partners on both sides of the business say the new structure has helped with boosting the firm's performance. For the fiscal year to August 1990 total revenue was $4.2 billion, up 23 per cent from 1989, by 30 per cent in consulting and by 18 per cent in accounting.

The growth in accounting is surprising because this business had been hardest hit by the recession of 1990–1.

In line with most international firms of accountants Arthur Andersen were unwilling to provide information on their pricing policies.

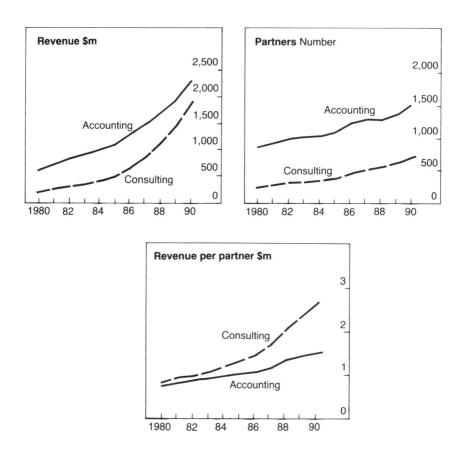

Fig. 2.1.2   Fee income of Arthur Andersen 1980–90. Years ending August 31st
Source: Arthur Andersen

Audit, business advisory and tax services

In supplying audit, business advisory and tax services, Arthur Andersen seeks to offer clients a co-ordinated seamless approach. For example, in the area of tax advice the Andersen approach is first to obtain an understanding of an organization's overall position, rather than providing advice in an isolated way. A major aspect of this whole approach is that resources and expertise are available between one office and another both nationally and around the world when necessary. In addition, the annual audit diagnostic process assists clients to improve their operations and, with Andersen Consulting, the firm can assist clients to implement this advice.

Andersen Consulting

Andersen Consulting has market dominance in the USA and in the major markets of Europe; further expansion is planned in the Asian/Pacific area. This operation provides technological solutions for clients to enable them to view technology as a competitive weapon, tying their information systems directly to their corporate strategy. The emphasis being on the concept of 'Total Business Integration', which involves a seamless approach to integrating strategy, people, operations and technology.

The strategy of Andersen Consulting is to pursue national markets aggressively, at times on the heels of Arthur Andersen's audit penetration, and sometimes independently. It tends to concentrate on the top 100 companies in each country. More recently the Government services market – most notably defence and security, healthcare and telecommunications – have been targeted.

In 1974 Arthur Andersen & Co. SC established its first Public Review Board. The major role of the Board is to advise the organization on how best to meet its responsibilities to the general public; it concentrates on the scope of its practice and quality control procedures. The Board has full access to information and may visit any office and talk to any employee in pursuit of these functions. Edward Heath, a former British Prime Minister, is a Board member, along with Gaston Thorn, both a former President of the Commission of the EC and a former Prime Minister of Luxemburg.

Despite the global nature of Arthur Andersen's business, the case study concentrates on the UK operations of Arthur Andersen & Co.

Organizational response to 1992

Arthur Andersen is a global entity and has been for many years. The firm feels that it has been living the spirit of 1992 for some time.

'We look to our one firm concept and the lack of barriers between national practice teams to provide a unique source of competitive advantage.'
David Oliver, Tax Partner, Cambridge

The 1992 Office

In 1988 Arthur Andersen established a 1992 Office in Brussels. The origins of this development go back to the mid-1970s when the UK joined the EC and some partners felt that there was a need for closer involvement in Community matters. They felt that it was important for the firm to identify some of the implications of EC developments both for itself as well as for its clients. The need to try to influence EC policy developments was also identified at this time. For example, by the beginning of 1980 the Commission was working on the Fourth Directive on the Annual Accounts of Firms and Arthur Andersen began to provide some policy advice. But it was only in 1988, mainly as a result of client enquiries, that the firm began to view Single Market items as a major issue.

During the 1980s a number of partners within Arthur Andersen felt that the firm should explore a range of specific issues and target its contacts with EC institutions in a more systematic way. A major aim being to build up the credibility of Arthur Andersen within the main Community institutions. One important issue that concerned the firm at this time was the possibility that the accounting standards being developed by the EC would be lower than those in the UK. In addition to accounting policy developments, the firm was interested in a wide range of EC developments which were affecting either itself or its clients, including company law, competition law, indirect taxation and public procurement.

In 1982 a partner was appointed in the Brussels office to develop a network of contacts within EC institutions. And in 1983 a lawyer was appointed to deal with EC matters, on a full-time basis. One of his responsibilities was to identify sources of funding available from the EC. During 1983, EC issues were introduced to the various training programmes run by the firm, for example, the issue of using Community law as opposed to national legislation in cross-border disputes was integrated into these programmes at an early stage.

With the launching of the Internal Market Programme in 1985, the firm decided to reinforce this group of EC experts in Brussels and in 1988 another partner, Mr Iain Stitt, a former President of the Institute of

Taxation, was transferred to Brussels to manage the newly created 1992 office. By this time a Single Market policy was being developed at a senior level within the firm and a network of EC co-ordinators was being set up throughout the world.

Structure

In terms of people recruited to the 1992 Office, the aim has been to develop a multinational team which can deal with the full range of EC languages and also have knowledge of the governmental structures and business cultures in the different Member States. The 1992 Office has a full team of accountants, economists and lawyers and, with the appointment of a Greek national in 1990, every EC nationality is represented within this team.

Objectives

The main objective of the Office is to inform partners and managers about developments in Europe, thus enabling them to assist clients to identify and respond effectively to the demands of the Single Market and developments within the wider Europe. In line with the integrated seamless service that the firm has developed, the local office which deals with the European needs of clients but it has the expert back-up from the 1992 Office. Arthur Andersen decided against the option of providing a centralized European service for clients. The argument being that it is the partners and managers in the local offices who know their clients' needs and therefore they are in the best position to provide assistance in identifying appropriate Single Market issues. The organization views itself as a pro-active business adviser dealing with the whole range of business issues; developments within Europe are viewed in this context.

In the early years of the 1992 Office, some concern was expressed within the organization that this system was not working as well as it might, in that many local partners and managers were not using the services of the Office to best advantage. Partners and managers were often hard pressed to keep up to date with such topics as taxation legislation, therefore keeping abreast with the broad range of European issues was sometimes a problem. Perhaps in some areas insufficient emphasis was being given to Single Market and related issues. By mid-1991 the organization felt that this problem, where it did exist, had largely been overcome.

Functions

The 1992 Office provides a range of services for local offices and their clients, including:

(a) The provision of an updating service on a weekly basis, giving some idea of the thinking behind legislation and proposed legislation as well as the legislation itself.

(b) The production of a monthly *European Review* aimed at staff members as well as their clients. The *European Review* covers general news on such issues as proposed tax changes, rules of origin, and R&D developments.

(c) Details of the EC policy-making process and advice on how and who to lobby are also provided. For example, the Office can introduce clients to appropriate EC officials if an issue is particularly complicated. The EC Commission tends to welcome this approach as it gives them expert feedback on policy developments.

(d) The Office provides short briefing documents on specific European topics, for example, EC competition policy.

(e) The Office also responds to individual queries coming from clients via the local offices, for example, on the progress of individual directives. The 1992 Office has a comprehensive database to assist in this work.

(f) A major guide on the Single Market programme (*'1992' A Guide for Clients*) was produced in Brussels as a reference book and distributed to all partners.

(g) In addition, the staff within the 1992 Office have developed a system by which partners and managers in the local offices can assist clients to develop a Single Market strategy. This is called the Initial Assessment Review (IAR) and is divided into five phases in a continuing process as shown by Fig. 2.1.3.

Phase one · Identify the relevant proposals from the Single Market programme for a specific client.

Phase two · Evaluate the business implications. For example, which of the proposals are of fundamental importance to a particular business.

Phase three · Develop strategies and detailed plans. For example, markets, mergers, sources of finance and personnel policies.

Phase four · Implement plans at appropriate times. For example, information is often required about when a specific proposal is likely to be implemented and whether any amendments are likely to be made.

Phase five · Follow up review. For example, a business must be aware that many proposals will change before they become legislation. In some instances a quarterly briefing is involved, in others in-house seminars are provided on specific issues, for example, R&D opportunities.

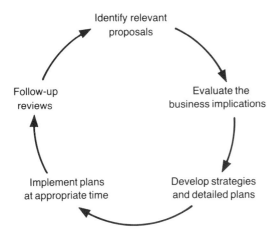

Fig. 2.1.3   The five phases of the IAR process

This phased process is carried out at two separate and distinct levels: strategic and operational. Clients are encouraged to involve all areas of their organization in this review process, not just one or two senior managers. This approach also provides local offices with an additional opportunity to market complementary services to clients. This point is viewed as a major benefit of the whole procedure.

In late 1991 it was decided to close the separate 1992 Office and integrate its staff within the main Brussels operation, the argument being that partners and managers within the local offices had sufficient Single Market expertise, therefore a separate 1992 Office was no longer required.

Training

From its earliest days Arthur Andersen have had a major commitment to training and staff development: about 7 per cent of fee income is spent on training. One unique aspect of this training is that people throughout the world train together. From the time of joining the organization graduates are encouraged to think internationally. The organization gives them a common training programme, including uniform procedures. This approach also enables a wide range of informal cross-border links to develop from a very early stage in a young graduate's career.

> 'I can always call on a colleague in another country if necessary to assist with cross-border companies and in most cases it's someone I know quite well.'
> David Oliver

Professional training within Arthur Andersen focuses on technical issues but it is also concerned with the wider aspects of industrial and management topics. The firm has a worldwide training college on a 145-acre campus at St Charles, Illinois and most of the academic staff there are professional educationalists. In addition, the firm has training facilities in Veldhoven, in the Netherlands; Segovia, in Spain; and in Manila, in the Philippines. New tax recruits spend two weeks at the training centre at Veldhoven. And for audit staff, methodologies are developed on a world-wide basis so that a manager could walk into any Arthur Andersen office across the world and feel at home. Most graduate recruits are managers after five years with the firm. Training and staff development is seen as a continuous process for professional staff.

With the establishment of the 1992 Office in Brussels, training on EC issues became more targeted and systematic. In its first 18 months of operation, Iain Stitt from the Office spent up to three weeks each month giving presentations on EC issues to partners and managers around the world.

New market identification

Arthur Andersen has identified both new markets and new services for existing clients as a result of the Single Market programme and develop-ments in Central and Eastern Europe. To take two examples, the Bristol (UK) office helped an existing client in the health care industry with an internal group re-organization valued at £12 million. The task was to achieve a step up in value of the client's Italian subsidiary, with subsequent additional tax deductions of about £10 million. This opportunity arose from a multinational tax-planning meeting with the client, involving several of the firm's European offices. The Bristol office supervised the project and provided liaison between the client in the UK and the USA, and the firm's offices in Rome and The Hague.

The second example is of a client of the firm's London office who wanted to increase its European presence by expanding its operation throughout continental Europe. A deal was put together by its holding company to sell one subsidiary to a French company and use the funds to implement its European strategy. This involved the acquisition of a majority interest in a Finnish–French joint venture and the creation of a new manufacturing and distribution operation in Portugal. Using the firm's pan-European network, the London office devised a tax structure that helped the client successfully implement its European strategy.

The introduction of the Initial Assessment Review has provided the firm with an additional opportunity to market its other services, although significantly very few non-clients have used this service, and some concern has been expressed within the organization about the take-up rate of services as a follow-on from an IAR.

Central and Eastern European markets

Offices located in the former West Germany are focal points for thrusts into the opening economies of Central and Eastern Europe. Arthur Andersen have established operations in the former East Germany, Czechoslovakia, Hungary, Poland, the Soviet Union and Yugoslavia. It is actively recruiting nationals to these offices.

In Central and Eastern Europe the firm provides a range of services. For example, it has assisted in the development of joint ventures between local and foreign companies and it has also carried out work in the area of the privatization of State-owned enterprises in Hungary and Poland. Arthur Andersen have organized conferences in Moscow, Prague and Vienna to disseminate ideas about business opportunities available in Central and Eastern Europe.

Andersen Consulting has opened offices in the former East Germany, Hungary, Poland and Czechoslovakia. In this respect the firm is responding to the transnational needs of clients. The primary impetus has come from the multinationals but there is an increasing need to move ideas and skills across borders to meet national client requirements.

The 1992 Office keeps an eye on the developments between the EC and Eastern and Central Europe and advises the Commission on a range of issues in this area.

Andersen is investing considerable resources, in terms of personnel as well as capital, into countries of Central and Eastern Europe and these are likely to run at a loss 'for a year or two'.

Marketing

When during 1988 it became apparent that clients were increasingly requesting advice on the moves to create a Single European Market by 1992, Arthur Andersen responded not only by setting up a specialist office in Brussels but also by developing a more focused and concerted strategy to market its European services.

Recognizing that the key marketers of any service line are the local partners and managers with daily client contact, the firm first set about educating its staff about '1992' and the opportunities that could develop for clients as a result of the completion of the Single Market. In 1989, it developed *'1992' A Guide for Clients*, 20,000 copies of which were subsequently distributed to clients and contacts worldwide. Following the publication of this guide, the firm has sought to update clients on the latest developments by issuing a range of newsletters, booklets and brochures. Where appropriate, these have focused exclusively on European issues. In general terms, the firm continues to position its European services as being merely a part of the full range of skills which it can provide to clients.

'Though potentially very important, the European perspective should never be viewed in isolation. At Arthur Andersen we prefer to see it in the overall context of our clients' operations and we advise them accordingly.'
Conor Boden, Marketing Manager

This approach is reflected in a recent pan-European advertising campaign conducted by the firm where, rather than focus on 1992 *per se*, it demonstrated European expertise by featuring a client which it had helped expand into new markets across the Continent. See Fig. 2.1.4 for an illustration.

Fig. 2.1.4 (opposite)   Arthur Andersen's pan-European advertising campaign

When Autoglass wanted to expand, we offered them a clear view.

Autoglass is the leading automotive glass replacement business in the whole of Europe.

Being mindful of 1992, Autoglass wanted to increase their European presence by expanding their successful UK operation throughout the Continent. A deal was put together by their holding company to sell its building glass subsidiary to a French company and use the money to fund Autoglass' expansion throughout Europe.

Using our pan-European network, we were able to devise a tax structure that successfully addressed the tax issues arising from the implementation of the company's European strategy.

Proof that when it comes to the complexities of cross-border taxation, there's one firm that doesn't glaze over at the challenge.

ARTHUR ANDERSEN & CO. S.C.

ARTHUR ANDERSEN TAX AND LAW* CONSULTANTS
Arthur Andersen & Co is authorised by the Institute of Chartered Accountants in England and Wales to carry on investment business (*in countries where professional regulations permit.)

APPENDIX – Coppelia SA

1.   Name and domicile of parent company

Name: Coppelia SA
Nationality: Registered in Lille (France)

2.   Products

Coppelia SA and its subsidiaries manufacture and market toys (products and materials designed or clearly intended for use in play by children under 14-years old); most toys are controlled by microchips.

3.   Structure

The French parent company has wholly-owned subsidiaries in the UK, West Germany, Spain and the USA. There are two manufacturing plants: one in Belfast (Northern Ireland) and the other in San Erico, California (USA).

   Coppelia SA has a European Distribution Centre (principally warehousing) in Werchter (between Brussels and Antwerp). It is a branch of Coppelia SA. Sales are carried out by a worldwide network of wholesalers; most are independent third parties, but in the former West Germany and Spain the group has its own companies who in turn sell to retailers. Coppelia SA is currently trying to dictate a pricing policy to its wholesalers.

4.   Sourcing

(a) *European plants*
     30 per cent of the components, mainly electronic, are imported from the Far East.
     60 per cent of the components are purchased in the EC.
     10 per cent of the components are imported from various countries (EFTA, Eastern Europe, etc.).
(b) *US plants*
     30 per cent of the components are imported from the Far East.
     50 per cent of the components are imported from North American sources.
     20 per cent of the components are imported from the EC.

5.   Shipping

Toys manufactured in Belfast are shipped to Antwerp and then carried by road to the Werchter Distribution Centre.

Toys manufactured in San Erico are sold only in the North American or Far Eastern markets.

6.   End users

Most retail customers for the group's products are individuals. In addition, Coppelia SA has developed a range of educational toys and sells almost 10 per cent of its production to public bodies, mainly schools in France. So far attempts to sell to public authorities in other countries have not been successful; however, efforts are continuing.

7.   Competitors

Coppelia faces tough competition in its sector. As a response to the growing threat of Far Eastern competitors Coppelia has opened negotiations with its main European competitors in the hope of finding solutions which will enable it to preserve and enlarge its market shares and profit margins.

Coppelia also plans to initiate a careful review of legal instruments available to fight unfair trading practices (misleading advertising, counterfeit products, etc.). It also envisages increasing the legal protection of its products and seeks information thereon.

8.   Strategy

As part of its strategic planning, the group anticipates that, in the next four years, it will:

- carry out joint research activities with other toy manufacturers;
- strengthen the sales and distribution network and expand market share by taking over smaller toy companies;
- review the benefits of re-organizing the group or adopting a new legal structure;
- emphasize its products' safety in line with EC technical standards;
- participate in Europe-wide public procurement tenders;
- increase the level of qualification of its personnel through training schemes, co-operation with universities, language courses, recruitment of non-nationals, etc.

At the moment, each subsidiary has a range of various banking and insurance arrangements. The parent company thinks there is scope for considerable costs savings in these areas.

9.   Personnel safety

Coppelia has 4,500 employees worldwide, three-quarters of whom are based in Europe. The Belfast plant is equipped with sophisticated machines, some of which could endanger the workers' safety if not properly used. (There have been ten minor, and two serious, accidents in three years.)

Question/discussion topics

1. To what extent is Arthur Andersen living in the spirit of 1992?

2. Evaluate Arthur Andersen's decentralized approach to providing European advice services as opposed to the provision of a centralized European Office.

3. What advantages and disadvantages do you see in an organization such as Arthur Andersen having a 1992 Office in Brussels? How would you view their decision to amalgamate this unit with their main Brussels Office?

4. Carry out a SWOT analysis on Arthur Andersen, focusing most specifically on its EC and Eastern European activities.

5. Using the information contained in the Coppelia SA mini case study found in the Appendix to this Case, and additional information found in Part 1 of the book, prepare an Initial Assessment Review of the impact of 1992 on Coppelia's activities using the procedure developed by Arthur Andersen. How would you evaluate this procedure for determining the impact of the Single Market on an organization?

Case 2
The Olympic Insurance Company, Greece – A study in European collaboration

Theo Kiriziadis

Advice to readers

This case study illustrates the response of a small insurance company, in one of the less developed Member States, to the integration of the European financial market. The inability of the Olympic Insurance Company in Greece to compete with the large multinational companies led to it signing an agreement of collaboration with the Victoria Insurance Group, the fourth largest Insurance Group in Germany. The study looks at this development and takes the story up to the end of 1990.

Introduction

The Olympic Insurance Company provides a full range of insurance services. The company's head office is in Thessalonika and its sales network covers the whole of Greece. (The Appendix to Case 2 provides information on the network.) In 1990 the share capital of Olympic accounted for more than £3 million and it had a premium income of around £4.5 million; the company employed approximately 200 people.

As far as re-insurance* is concerned, Olympic co-operates with the biggest re-insurance companies in the world, such as Munich Re, Union Re, Great Lakes, Victoria, Ina Re, Cologne Re, Union des Assurance de Paris Re, and Winterthur.

---

* Reinsurance is an arrangement between insurers to insure the risks they have entered into in their direct insurance business. It is a type of risk-spreading which has become increasingly important as the increasing size of risks have caused insurers to go to reinsurance as additional protection.

The move towards the Single Market

As the Greek economy advances towards the Single European Market, there is a growing realization that this development will herald the beginning of a major restructuring of the Greek insurance sector. The EC Commission's programme for the completion of the internal market pays considerable attention to the financial services sector not only because it is large (7 per cent of the GDP of the EC), but also because it is very important for the development of other sectors of the European economy.

Insurance is at the forefront of the changes which are taking place in Europe. The development of the Single Market is encouraging the growth of service industries and rapid technological changes have led to the internationalization of the insurance industry. For example, the number of cross-border operations has increased significantly since 1987. In 1973 and 1979 respectively, two Directives on the co-ordination of direct non-life insurance and life assurance were adopted by the Council of Ministers. The main objective of these Directives was to start the process of dismantling the barriers to intra-Community insurance transactions.

Insurance is a highly regulated activity; both stability and security are required within this market. Failures within the insurance sector have severe economic, social and political consequences to which governments are naturally very sensitive. To protect the users of these services, governments have a responsibility to ensure that insurance undertakings remain solvent and are able to meet their financial commitments. Furthermore, the importance of insurance companies as channels for savings and investment are important factors in national economic growth.

As part of the Single Market programme, the Council of Ministers adopted the Second Co-ordination (Services) Directives in the late 1980s. The object of these Directives is to lay down special provisions relating to the freedom to provide services. That is the right of an insurance company authorized in one Member State (the home state) to provide insurance in another Member State (the host state). The Second Non-Life Directive, adopted in 1988, introduced this freedom, subject to specific notification requirements, for 'large risks', i.e. major commercial contracts. The Second Life Directive, adopted in 1990, has introduced the right of an assurance company to provide life insurance for group life and pensions business (the equivalent of 'large risks'). The Second Co-ordination Directives will allow large insured companies in Greece and group life and pension business to be insured abroad, while the Greek insurance undertaking will be able to provide specific insurance services in other Member States. Greece, Portugal and Spain will not have to implement these directives until 1995, whereas other Member States will be expected to implement this legislation by the end of 1992.

The Second Co-ordination Directives are only an interim step since they provide freedom of intra-EC insurance transactions for large risks. It is the Third Co-ordination Directives which should complete the single insurance market and cover all risks and all insurance classes. The Third Co-ordination Directives will eliminate the barriers to the freedom of insurance services for all areas including small businesses and individuals.

The Greek insurance sector

The implementation of the EC directives is already bringing considerable changes to the Greek insurance sector, as eventually these directives will eliminate the restrictions on the type of services that can be offered and on the range of activities in which private insurance concerns can engage.

Of the 140 insurance companies operating in Greece, seven belong to the public sector and their share capital is controlled by at least one State-owned commercial bank. These companies hold a substantial market share; on aggregate, they account for more than 40 per cent in terms of premium income. It is generally acknowledged in Greece that the public sector insurance companies are not as efficient as their dominant position in the market may suggest. These companies are allowed to use their links with State-owned banks and the national authorities in order to attract business away from private insurance concerns and to attain (or sustain) a large market share. The State-owned banks strongly recommend State-controlled insurance concerns to their clients. In addition, the State insures all its property with these companies. The implementation of the EC insurance directives will eliminate these practices in Greece, so that private sector companies will have the opportunity to attract a significant amount of business away from the State-owned insurance concerns.

Furthermore, the Greek authorities control premium levels and insurance contracts of all insurance companies. In the case of life assurance the premium levels have to be approved by the Ministry of Trade. The Ministry sets indicative rates which are almost compulsory since they must be taken into account by the insurance companies if they wish to obtain approval. As a result, the life assurance companies have almost equal premium rates. The premium rates in the fire, motor and almost all the lines of accident insurance are fixed by the Ministry and are not allowed to fluctuate.

In all Member States there are controls over premium rates and policy conditions in order to avoid excessive competition which could undermine the stability of insurance companies and thus the security provided to policy holders. However, in Greece these controls are very rigid, protecting the large market share of State-owned insurance companies and drastically reducing competition. The rigid system of controls on contracts and rates severely restricts the freedom of private insurers to determine the terms and conditions of their policies. The loosening of these controls, which will take place after the implementation of co-ordination directives, will thus increase the ability of private sector companies to adapt to the changing market. It will enable them to extend their range of products and improve their service delivery.

The situation in the different lines of insurance is as follows.

Fire insurance

In 1989/90 fire insurance represented more than 20 per cent of the insurance market in Greece. The implementation of the Freedom of Services Directive, covering large risks, will open the domestic market to foreign insurance concerns. This will increase competition and result in the liberalization of the premium rates.

Motor insurance

In Greece motor insurance is compulsory and the premiums are set at a very low level by the national authorities. Some fear was expressed that if premiums were set at a more realistic level 'this would affect the level of inflation'. A major result of this restriction is that all the insurance companies engaged in this branch of insurance suffer substantial losses.

Life insurance

Life insurance is definitely the sector which offers the best opportunities for the private sector, including companies such as Olympic, although competition will be intense. In the mid-1980s life insurance represented only 10 per cent of the national insurance market. By 1990 this had increased to almost 40 per cent. Despite this high level of growth, only one-fourth of all insurable individuals are covered by life assurance.

Traditionally, Greeks do not enter into long-term contracts to acquire additional capital on retirement because of the very high level of inflation in Greece. In most European countries more than half of the assurance companies' activities concern pension insurance, while in Greece this type of insurance is undertaken only to a very limited extent. Greece appears to be under-insured and there is much room for growth.

Size of Greek insurance market

The Greek insurance market is small. Table 2.2.1 shows that in terms of premium income, this market is the eleventh in the EC.

Table 2.2.1   Expenditure on insurance ($) – EC ranking

Country	Total Premium	% EC Premium	Life Insurance	% EC Premium	Non-Life Insurance	% EC
West Germany	59 685	32.15	25 304	31.56	34 381	32.59
UK	45 804	24.67	27 201	33 93	18 603	17.64
France	36 440	19.63	14 108	17.69	22 260	21.20
Italy	14 452	7.78	2 641	3.29	11 811	11.20
Netherlands	11 474	6.18	5 234	6.53	6 240	5.92
Spain	5 319	2.87	1 088	1.36	4 231	4.01
Belgium	5 057	2.71	1 400	1.75	3 657	3.47
Denmark	3 806	2.05	1 579	1.97	2 227	2.11
Ireland	2 180	1.17	1 283	1.60	897	0.85
Portugal	783	0.42	76	0.09	707	0.67
Greece	461	0.25	14	0.18	320	0.30
Luxemburg	192	0.10	46	0.06	146	0.14
Total EC	**185 653**	**100.00**	**80 173**	**100.00**	**105 480**	**100.00**

Source: Sigma 1987

Table 2.2.2 gives details of per capita expenditure on insurance, which is a more realistic indicator of a market's development since it takes into account population differences. This table reveals that the level of insurance per capita in Greece is the lowest in the EC. Such a low level is due to strict State controls on premium levels and insurance contracts that do not allow insurance companies to offer attractive products to the public. Thus, while the size of the market is small, the low level of insurance per capita makes the potential for insurance high once these restrictions have been removed.

Table 2.2.2 Per capita expenditure on insurance ($) – EC ranking

Country	Total	Life	Non-Life	Total	Life	Non-Life
West Germany	978	415	563	1	2	1
UK	807	479	328	2	1	7
Netherlands	788	359	429	3	4	3
Denmark	743	308	435	4	5	2
France	658	256	402	5	6	5
Ireland	616	326	253	6	3	8
Luxemburg	533	128	406	7	8	4
Belgium	510	141	369	8	7	6
Italy	253	46	205	9	9	9
Spain	183	28	109	10	10	10
Portugal	76	7	69	11	12	11
Greece	46	14	32	12	11	12
EC average	576	248	327			
US average	536	621	915			

Source: Sigma 1987

The opportunities available

The Olympic Insurance Company views Greece as an untapped market and believes that the insurance companies which develop a modern and efficient organization, and products at the right price will be in a strong position to take advantage of these opportunities.

> 'If we are successful in developing the right products we shall be in a strong position, to take advantage of deregulation in Greece, as well as the opportunities arising from the completion of the Single Market.'
> George Anagnostou, Managing Director of Olympic

Equally, those insurance companies that are unable to adapt to this new competitive position are likely to lose substantial sections of their markets.

Competition

In this new competitive environment insurance companies in Greece are likely to face competition from the large multinational insurance companies. In comparison to the smaller domestic operations in Greece, these multinational organizations enjoy a wide range of advantages, including:

- they enjoy the benefits of scale from their extensive global operations;

- they are in possession of a large amount of investment capital; therefore they are in a position to invest in Greece at a level which would ensure a significant market share;
- they possess considerable experience and know-how of markets across the EC and beyond;
- they employ highly-skilled labour; insurance is a labour-intensive industry requiring high levels of expertise;
- they have easy access to international re-insurance and capital markets, which means that they can re-insure and raise capital at relatively low costs, this in turn can be reflected in lower premium rates.

Given these advantages, the large foreign insurance companies will be in a position to provide better services and at lower prices in Greece than their rivals among the indigenous insurance concerns. For example, the Greek insurance companies lack staff in sufficient number with advanced technical skills.

Greek companies have a limited number of investment options and the existing national restrictions imposed on these options put them in a highly disadvantageous position. The foreign exchange controls at present in operation prevent companies established in Greece transferring funds abroad and investing in the international financial markets which offer higher expected yields. Moreover, the indigenous insurance companies are forced to invest a considerable proportion of their funds in public sector organizations. Obviously, these controls substantially restrict the ability of indigenous insurance companies to pursue independent and profitable investment policies and to compete on an equal footing against large companies from other Member States. In this situation Greek companies not only face major challenges to their domestic market share but also to their foreign business activities.

Of course, all these restrictions will be eliminated when Greece integrates its financial services market with the rest of the EC. The Capital Movement Liberalization Directive of 1988 will bring to an end the restrictive foreign exchange controls. And as Greek insurance companies obtain access to the foreign capital and money markets, they are likely to convert their funds to other forms of investment which provide a better yield.

However, investing in international capital and money markets requires a high degree of financial expertise, which at present is lacking in Greece.

To some extent this problem can be overcome by commissioning international consultants such as Arthur Andersen.

In spite of the competitive advantages that international insurance companies enjoy, Olympic feels that it can compete in this market because the growth potential is large and it will gain from deregulation in Greece, which is being implemented in parallel with Single Market legislation.

Organizational developments within Olympic

At the end of the 1980s the management at Olympic adopted a comprehensive long-term development programme. A major aim of this plan was to increase the size of its operations, as well as to modernize processes and enlarge its portfolio of products.

Acquisitions

Macedonia Non-Life Insurance Company was acquired in 1988. Macedonia operates as an affiliated company and provides the full range of insurance services in the non-life sector. The premium income of the company (net premium and policy fees) for 1989 amounted to £296,411 approximately, an increase of 30 per cent over 1988. The premium income experienced a major increase of 147 per cent in the first five months of 1990 in relation to the same period in 1989. In part, this success was due to the changed nature of the company's portfolio, with a considerable decline in dependence on motor insurance. During this period its income from motor premiums dropped from 68.44 per cent of all premium income in 1988 to 49.05 per cent in 1989. During the same period, income from fire premiums rose from 26.8 per cent in 1988 to 42.51 per cent in 1989.

Macedonia operates independently from Olympic, but it does use the latter's marketing network. It tries to find a niche in the market of the so-called 'simple risks' sector, such as small business cover, where local knowledge and contacts can be vitally important. At the same time, it is developing new products such as 'loss of profits' cover, which is virtually unknown to the insured public at large.

Development of non-life insurance

In 1989 Oylmpic Non-Life was established and started its operation on 1 January 1990. Its scope was to take over and develop the existing non-life portfolio.

'The separation of life and non-life portfolio was considered necessary by the management in order to create the necessary specialization so that it can face the challenge of the Single Market.'
K. Papadopoulos, Economic Adviser, Olympic Insurance Co.

In all classes of insurance business there is a time lag between the payment of premiums and the settlement of claims. While non-life policies are usually written on an annual basis, life insurance is long term in nature – for example, the settlement of claims may take place 20 years or more after the payment of premiums. A major operation of the life insurance industry involves the large-scale accumulation and investment of funds. This includes the management of funds on behalf of other institutions, for example, pension funds, unit trusts, and investment trusts. The life insurance industry has become a major part of the capital market transforming individual savings into interest bearing capital and providing a wide range of financial services to its customers.

The separation of the life and non-life portfolio, and the establishment of Olympic Non-Life created the necessary specialization to respond to the challenge of the Single Market. In effect, the separation of the two portfolios was imposed by Community law; for the Second Life Directive refers to the problem of composites, i.e. companies undertaking both life and non-life insurance. According to this Directive, newly-formed companies should no longer be authorized to carry on both life and non-life activities. Pre-existing companies which transact both life and non-life business may continue to do so provided that they observe strict rules on separate management and financial obligation, so that the respective interests of life policy holders and non-life policy holders are safeguarded. There were fears that without this safeguard, life insurance funds might be used to support the risk of other insurance operations.

The ending of composites by the EC

The question over composites will possibly be reviewed again by the EC Commission because it will arise again in the context of the Third Co-ordination Directives for life assurance. Most European countries have adopted the principle of specialization, by setting rules which provide that the same undertaking cannot carry on both types of activities. These countries will be unwilling to allow composites from other Member States to offer services in both classes in their countries, while their indigenous companies cannot. It is likely that a freedom of services directive for life assurance would adopt the 'principle of specialization' and gradually end the existence of composites.

The expansion of Olympic Insurance

In the early and mid-1980s the main aim of Olympic's management was internal modernization and expansion. The company had adequate resources to purchase and furnish new office accommodation and to train staff. However, it soon became evident that the strong premium growth of recent years, plus the completion of the internal market for financial services in the years to come was encouraging insurance companies in other Member States to take an interest in the Greek market. For example, branches of international companies have recently been established in Greece. Olympic felt the necessity to take further action to defend and enlarge its market share.

The collaboration with Victoria

The management at Olympic felt that the integration of the European insurance industry would result in fewer companies operating, and smaller companies that do not find a niche in the market or a 'big brother' will find it difficult to grow or even continue their operation. In this situation Olympic felt that it had little option but to find a large insurance group with which to co-operate. Capital availability was also a major consideration; even if the company had the adequate capital to expand at the first stage, a rapid growth in a market which is under-insured would create great demands and would mean that Olympic would have to turn to foreign capital.

On 30 November 1989 the Olympic Group signed an agreement of collaboration with the Victoria Insurance Group, the fourth in size in Germany. Victoria's roots stretch back to 1953 when the General Railway Insurance Group was formed in Berlin; in 1990 it had an annual premium income of about £5 billion. The Victoria Group, with the Victoria Companies, the Deutsche Automobil Schutz, and numerous foreign affiliated companies operating in most West European countries, offers its clients coverage in all sectors of insurance and also a comprehensive range of other financial services. The characteristic elements and advantages of Victoria are its significant status, experience, technical expertise and modern organization and processes. Victoria obtained 60 per cent share capital of Olympic.

The negotiations leading to the agreement lasted three years and were complex because Olympic wanted to keep its own style of management. To a large extent, it succeeded in achieving this aim, for example, only two of Victoria's officers participate in the management of Olympic.

By collaborating with Victoria, Olympic not only increased its resources but it also improved both its credibility and security for policy holders, a fact which is very important for all types of insurance, but especially life insurance which tends to be long term.

Victoria is a powerful partner which, due to its size, can exploit increasing economies of scale. It has developed highly-efficient production and marketing systems and possesses huge capital, skilled labour, sophisticated managerial capacity, expertise and technology. All these benefits are expected to be passed on to Olympic.

At present, the foreign exchange control regulations prevent Olympic from transferring funds abroad and to use the services of the international capital and money markets for more profitable investment operations. However, after the elimination of foreign exchange controls Victoria, through its international network of branches and associated companies, will provide Olympic with good links to the international capital and money markets.

Training for the Single Market

One reason for the low quality of insurance service in Greece is the low level of technical and managerial expertise. Part of Olympic's long-term plan is to improve skill levels by implementing a comprehensive training programme. In 1988 it established the Centre of Insurance Studies, which provides training for the whole Olympic Insurance Group. Training courses include new developments within the EC as well as more technical subjects. Programmes at the Centre have obtained support from the European Social Fund and the Greek Manpower Employment Organization. In its first year of operation it provided training for 250 employees. In addition to full-time courses, the Centre also runs seminars on a wide range of subjects for staff at all levels, including senior managers. Employees are encouraged to attend staff development activities run by other organizations such as the Association of Greek

Insurance Companies (AGIC). Many of these events are supported by the European Social Fund.

Distribution

One of the objectives of collaborating with Victoria is to 'outrun' the insurance limits in Greece and develop resources to allow better access to the wider European market. With the completion of the Single Market in financial services, Olympic is hoping to establish offices in other Member States. It is of the opinion that only through establishing such offices can it compete effectively with indigenous companies. Individuals are reluctant to enter into a contract with an insurer who lacks a domestic establishment. Olympic intends to use Victoria's extensive network of branches and associated companies to promote and sell its products.

Product development

The completion of the internal market as well as the undergoing expansion of the domestic insurance market requires more flexible and sophisticated insurance products than the domestic industry is able to supply. However, the development of these kinds of products demands a high degree of financial and marketing expertise that at present is lacking in Greece.

One of the reasons why Olympic went into partnership with Victoria was to increase the quality of services and the range of product choice. For example, in the non-life sector Olympic is developing new products such as coverage of electronic equipment, loss of profit insurance or business interruption insurance, insurance of financial risks and product liability. Olympic appreciates that to develop a competitive advantage it must continuously develop new products.

Without the collaboration with Olympic, Victoria would be less able to penetrate the Greek market, for the German organization has little knowledge of local needs and the peculiarities of the Greek financial sector. Most of the policies offered directly by Victoria would be unsuitable for this market. Therefore, the company would have had to concentrate its sales effort on specific segments of the market. A major advantage of the Olympic–Victoria partnership is that it brings together extensive knowledge of both local markets and a high level of technical expertise and experience.

Appendix – The Olympic Insurance Group

The organizational network comprises:

- three branches in Thessalonika which were established in 1988 in order to strengthen the presentation of Olympic in its city of origin and to satisfy the growing operating needs of the company;
- ten branch offices covering the cities of Athens, Alexandroupolis, Veria, Volos, Katerini, Kilnis, Kojani, Larissa and Serres. All branch offices are housed in privately-owned premises;
- five offices in the towns of Drama, Didimotiko, Xanthi, Orestiada, Giannitsa;
- 150 agencies established all over Greece;
- 100 insurance brokers.

Questions/discussion topics

1. How will the implementation of the EC insurance directives affect the Greek insurance sectors?

2. Evaluate the strategic response of the Olympic Insurance Company to the completion of the European financial market.

3. In the light of current European developments, carry out a SWOT analysis on the Olympic–Victoria partnership.

Case 3
Labsworth World Wide PLC – European brand pricing issues*

James W. Dudley

Advice to readers

Readers should try to use this case study to identify some of the issues involved when a medium-sized international company is examining the advantages and disadvantages of regionalizing its pricing policy in response to the needs of the Single Market.

Introduction

Labsworth World Wide PLC ended 1989 with yet another year of record profits and earnings per share. Results had been consistently good since the beginning of the 1980s.

Labsworth is a medium-sized international pharmaceutical company headquartered in the UK. In 1979 the company posted its worst ever results. In the 20 years since it was founded it had become over-diversified and had too great an exposure in developing countries. Furthermore, it also had a large chemical business which in the late 1970s was suffering a cyclical downturn.

In 1979 a new Chairman and Chief Executive, George Redding, was appointed and charged with turning the company around. His strategy was to mount a five-year restructuring programme which included:

- selling off the chemicals business;
- reducing exposure in lesser developed countries;
- making strategic acquisitions in the USA and Europe;

---

* Please note that this case has been both simplified and disguised to hide the identity of the company and brands involved.

- divisionalizing the company into three core strategic business activities, i.e. pharmaceuticals, agricultural products and biotechnology.

Furthermore, Redding was conscious of the fact that many senior managers were not up to the mark. Therefore, he introduced a policy of recruiting 'high flyers' to spice up the management team at middle and lower senior levels. In his view the company, in 1979, was not an attractive proposition for graduate intakes and the company simply could not afford to take on top managers from outside. He was convinced that an intake of 'high flyers' would make their way up the management ladder and be in the right position by the mid-1980s to take the company forward once the turnaround had been achieved. Extracts from the company's reports follow.

Table 2.3.1 Company sales and profits 1980–9 in $ million

	1989	1988	1987	1986	1985	1984	1983	1982	1981	1980
Sales	2040.0	1650.0	1522.0	1400.0	1300.0	1105.0	728.0	702.0	985.0	908.0
Profit/BT	340.0	260.0	220.0	172.0	142.0	94.0	62.0	42.0	18.0	8.0
Dividend	16.6	13.4	10.8	9.0	7.8	6.4	5.4	4.4	3.6	3.6
Ratios	%	%	%	%	%	%	%	%	%	%
EPS	22.0	19.5	17.0	13.5	11.9	9.1	6.5	4.3	1.2	nil
Profit/AS	33.0	30.0	28.0	26.0	24.0	21.0	16.0	14.0	9.5	6.3

Table 2.3.2 Markets and activities – turnover by region in $ million

	1989	1988
UK	318.0	308.0
Europe	456.0	356.0
Africa	24.0	28.0
USA	900.0	800.0
Other	342.0	158.0
Total	2040.0	1650.0

Table 2.3.3 Turnover and profits by activity in $ million

	Sales by activity		Profit activities	
	1989	1988	1989	1988
Agriculture	904.0	824.0	62.0	40.4
Biotechnology	176.0	20.0	18.0	2.0
Pharmaceuticals	960.0	806.0	259.0	217.6
Total	2040.0	1650.0	339.0	260.0

Labsworth Pharma is the major division of the company accounting for 40 per cent of sales and 80 per cent of profits. The division is split into two areas of activity, namely:

- Labsworth Pharma producing prescription medicines and accounting for 70 per cent of total divisional sales and profits;
- Labsworth Consumer producing consumer pharmaceutical products, i.e. products sold to the consumer without a prescription being necessary.

Labsworth Consumer

Labsworth Consumer evolved as a semi-autonomous, major business unit following the restructuring processes which occurred in the late 1970s and early 1980s. Before that, the company's consumer products were not taken seriously by management or sales staff. The company did, however, have a small and robust range of products including 'Gina Vita', a vitamin-based sore throat remedy, and 'PK-Dailyvit', a multivitamin range. These were sold in the UK, France, Germany, Italy and Spain through distributors, and in the USA by Labsworth Inc. In 1980 the company created the consumer products business centred around these two vitamin products plus a number of others which had previously been sold through doctor prescription, although they were in fact legally registered non-prescription products.

In 1986 the company acquired J.B. Stone Inc. in the USA. Although the primary reason for the purchase was Stone's presence in the prescription sector of the market, it also had a large portfolio of consumer medicines. Some of these medicines were sold in Europe.

By 1988 Labsworth Consumer had world sales of $167 million from:

	$ million
USA	98.0
UK	12.6
Europe	40.2
Rest of the world	16.2

These sales had been largely achieved through organic development and minor acquisitions in Spain and Italy.

In late 1988 Labsworth World Wide PLC acquired Splendix Artzniemittel, a German consumer products company, for $117 million. This added about $66 million to the consumer division's annual sales and doubled the size of its European business. Splendix worldwide sales in 1988 were as follows:

	$ million
USA	Nil
UK	5.0
Europe	45.0
Rest of the world	16.0

With the growing strength of consumer products within the group, Redding decided to split the business centre into three divisions with sales expected for 1989 as follows:

	$ million
North America	104.0
Europe	137.0
Rest of the world	35.0

Redding was also conscious that, like the prescription sector, consumer products were becoming much more global. The need for larger advertising budgets and opportunities for economies of scale were driving companies to develop brands regionally, and in many cases globally. Whereas it was not his intention to make every brand a global 'Coke', as he put it, he did believe that the European part of the company could be better co-ordinated and that both marketing and production synergies could be found. With the gradual unfolding of the Single Market he was convinced that more could be done, especially with the newly-acquired Splendix Artzniemittel cold-remedy range. He decided that Jack Z. Johnson, one of the 'high flyer' recruits of 1979, would be just the person to carry out his wishes.

The European market

The non-prescription sector of the pharmaceutical industry was estimated to be worth just under $7 billion in 1989 and is forecast to grow to almost $21 billion by 1995. However, smaller companies are coming under increasing pressure from both larger European and multinational enterprises and, more importantly, from a new breed of transatlantic organizations. This latter group has been created by either mergers or strategic alliances between US companies and major European players. Players for which global competitiveness is a strategic goal.

Europe's top twelve self-medication companies account for just under 20 per cent of sales in six major markets, namely France, Germany, Italy, the Netherlands, Spain and the UK. The sales figures for these ten companies are shown in Table 2.3.4.

Table 2.3.4 Top ten European self-medication companies' sales in Europe, 1990

Company	$ million
*Rhône-Poulenc Rorer	280
*Sanofi/Sterling	280
Roche	220
Bayer	210
*SmithKline Beecham	170
Procter and Gamble	170
Boehringer Ingelheim	150
Boots	150
*American Home Products	140
Warner Lambert	110
Total	**1880**

* Major mergers, acquisitions or strategic alliances since 1989

Labsworth Consumer Europe

Jack Z. Johnson took over as Vice President Non-Prescription Medicine Division at the beginning of September 1989. He had returned to the European Headquarters in London after a three-year tour in the USA as Vice President, marketing over-the-counter (OTC) products. He had been in the pharmaceutical industry for 20 years; he was a graduate in biosciences and had an MBA from a leading UK management school. Since leaving university, he had worked as a brand manager with a major US company. In 1979 he joined Labsworth Laboratories as International Product Controller, bringing with him a high quality of consumer marketing knowledge and considerable expertise. He was, from the outset, different in both background and style from the majority of his colleagues who were steeped in conservative pharmaceutical marketing, a feature of the UK industry at that time.

After two years in the UK, Johnson was transferred, first to France, then Germany and Italy, in a series of short tours. In 1985 he was given a one-year sabbatical to take an MBA. In 1986 the company acquired J.B. Stone Inc. in the USA. Johnson was assigned to integrate the consumer products of the newly-acquired company into Labsworth's small, but robust, consumer division. He became Vice President marketing six months later.

Splendix Artzneimittel's products

In 1988 the company acquired Splendix Artzneimittel, a European subsidiary company of a major German chemical manufacturer. Splendix Artzneimittel was a medium-sized company selling a range of oral hygiene products, eye-care products and remedies for coughs, colds and respiratory infections. Its leading brand was Nasalvine, a range of cold remedies which were sold over the counter in every country in Europe except France. Splendix Artzneimittel operated through marketing subsidiaries in Germany, Italy, Spain and Holland. In all other countries except France, the product was handled by distributors. In France, Splendix Artzneimittel was handled by its previous parents, Pharma Division, and was transferred to Labsworth. Nasalvine had been half-heartedly introduced in France by Splendix Artzneimittel, as a prescription product, on the basis that after a couple of years the product could be launched onto the consumer market. This strategy allowed patients to become aware of the product range through doctor prescribing, thus providing a 'doctor-endorsed' heritage to the brand. In the event, insufficient effort or investment was put behind the brand.

The merger between Labsworth and Splendix Artzneimittel in Europe doubled the size of the European Consumer Products business. Nasalvine became the largest single product group in the new division and accounted for 13 per cent of sales. Furthermore, Nasalvine was the only product sold in all the EC countries (if the minute share of the French market was included) and, as such, joined a small club of only ten other fully regional OTC pharmaceutical brands among more than 5,000.

Structures

Until the merger in Europe, Labsworth was managed on a matrix system in which the subsidiary companies reported functionally to a European regional controller and the international brand management was co-ordinated in terms of strategy, policy and planning by UK product group managers across the region through local marketing teams. Surprisingly, the system worked well and provided a degree of unity and common policies for six major brands in Europe. Furthermore, new product development was driven from the centre to clear development targets. Labsworth was a major advertiser in the sector in all its European markets.

Splendix Artzneimittel had, in financial terms, been managed centrally but subsidiary companies had been allowed to pursue very independent branding, product development and pricing policies. Thus, for brands such as Nasalvine, there was little regional uniformity except for that dictated by production economies, i.e. a common container and a uniform-size, but not design. Furthermore, Splendix Artzneimittel spent little on advertising and had (successfully) created its market by promoting its products to doctors, even though they could be acquired without a prescription. Such products are described by pharmaceutical manufacturers as 'semi-ethical products'.

The changing European market

Since 1983 the OTC market in Europe has been undergoing a series of changes. The creation of Europe's single internal market will, it seems, exacerbate the pace of these changes.

In continental Europe, unlike the UK and USA, nearly two-thirds of all pharmaceutical brands bought over the counter are also prescribed, i.e. 'semi-ethical' products. In nearly all cases, the OTC purchase decision for a semi-ethical is based on downstream self-medication of a prescribed product. However, until 1983 few doctors prescribed products which were advertised to the general public. Therefore, brands which are deemed semi-ethical were promoted to doctors and pharmacists, whilst those aimed solely at the consumer were heavily advertised.

The promotion of brands via the doctor had a number of advantages namely:

- most medication prescribed by a doctor was re-imbursed either in total or in part by the State;
- a doctor's prescribing of a product endorses it as an ethical product in the consumer's mind;

- the manufacturer enjoys two sources of business, namely prescription sales and downstream self-medication by patients;
- promotional costs were lower in that direct charges were for samples and doctor communications literature, and in that brands shared the costs of sales forces who visited doctors. Thus such brands enjoyed considerable endorsement to patients from doctors without the high costs of public advertising.

Furthermore, this method of marketing had become very much embedded in the culture of many European manufacturers. However, companies marketing their products as semi-ethicals worked under three major constraints, namely:

- prices were controlled as long as drugs were on prescription;
- advertising was not permitted for prescription brands;
- prescription products could not be marketed outside pharmacies.

Since 1983, all the leading pharmaceutical markets except Spain have been hit by government legislation aimed at reducing the cost to the State of this practice. In Germany in 1983, the UK in 1985, France in 1985 and Italy in 1987, governments either issued negative prescribing lists (Germany and the UK) or reduced the level of price reimbursement to the patient (Italy and France). By 1989, Spain had not introduced either policy but it was clear that it would only be a matter of time before it did so.

At the same time, pressure to prevent manufacturers raising prices on products 'for which the State paid' was intensified. In Germany and Holland, manufacturers introduced voluntary controls, in other markets State price control of one sort or another held down prices. In 1990, Germany set new price contracts (*Festbetrag*) with manufacturers, which were based on ingredients and were to be implemented in 1991. Thus effectively reducing prices by as much as 30 per cent for many suppliers.

The combination of these pressures led manufacturers to switch from semi-ethical doctor-based marketing to consumer advertising; in some cases they had little choice if their brands were to survive. In others the move was pre-emptory to escape price control and future prescribing restrictions. A few enlightened and progressive companies, however, saw an opportunity to exploit the power of advertising. Others, including Splendix Artzneimittel, made the switch reluctantly.

Labsworth had been, like many major consumer-orientated organizations, such as American Home Products, Procter and Gamble, Warner ·Lambert, Bayer and Boehringer Ingelheim, consumer-driven advertisers. Their popular brands were not prescribed and demand was based entirely on the consumer's own buying decisions and not their doctor's.

By 1987, the market had begun to move rapidly from semi-ethical to advertised products with over half the sales being derived from consumer purchase decisions, thus benefiting more consumer-orientated firms. Figure 2.3.1 shows the growth of the European self-medication market. Since 1987 the market has accelerated as a result of intense competition for consumer choice through increased advertising. However, it was beginning to be seen that doctors in Germany were continuing to prescribe some of the consumer-advertised (switched) products, especially for children's illnesses where these were exempt from prescribing restrictions. Thus, firms faced painful decisions in Germany in 1991. They either had to reduce their prices or abandon the prescription market altogether. Yet, they were also aware that brands which did not leave the prescription market would create a low-priced sector capable of under-cutting the prices of advertised brands which did leave the market.

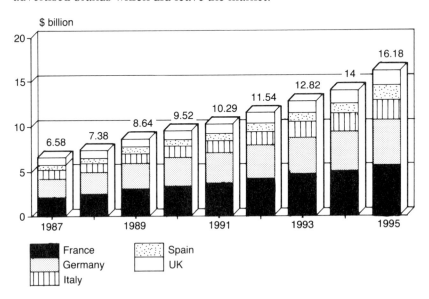

Fig. 2.3.1   European self-medication sales 1987–1995, advertised brands RSP
Source: *Self-medication in Europe*, James Dudley Management, 1991

Nasalvine development

Nasalvine was one of those semi-ethical brands which had either been forced to switch to being an advertised product (Germany and UK) or had done so pre-emptively (Italy, Spain and Holland).

Jack Z. Johnson believed that the integration of the EC's Single Market would give Nasalvine the same sort of advantage enjoyed by brands such as Nicholas's Rennies and Crooke's Strepsils if it were to be marketed as a regional brand.

In effect, Splendix Artzneimittel subsidiaries were merged with Labsworth's, with the latter's management taking over control in all countries except Germany where Splendix Artzneimittel was stronger. After a shake-out of managers from both companies, the ratio of Labsworth personnel to Splendix Artzneimittel was about 60–40 in all markets except Germany where it was 100 per cent Splendix.

Nasalvine European project

Tony Chase, the Marketing Director of Labsworth UK, was selected to head up a team consisting of Nasalvine country marketing managers to examine the European opportunity to make Nasalvine a regional European brand. Germany, Italy, Spain and the UK (80 per cent of European brand sales) were to form the nucleus of the project. The aim was to pursue the exercise and not to execute a foregone conclusion, as Jack Z. Johnson had said to Tony Chase:

> 'I want us to be in a position where we have thoroughly exhausted the options available to us. If the brand presents a strong candidate for regionalization then that's the way we'll go – if it doesn't then we have carried out the exercise should somebody start trying to push us along that route – keep an open mind but be objective'.

The team met and created a work programme to audit the brand's position in each country. A series of workshop retreats followed. In early 1990, Tony Chase was ready to present the audit.

A summary of Tony Chase's presentation

Tony Chase's first conclusion was that of the leading brands in each market, three, including Nasalvine, were available in all four markets under review. Both Vicks and Otrivin were, it appeared, marketed as regional brands with common marketing features in each market. Respective brand positions in each territory are shown in Fig. 2.3.2.

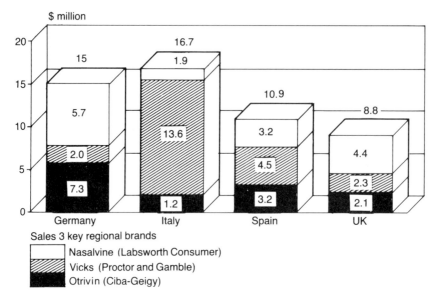

Fig. 2.3.2   Cold remedies 1989 – four key markets

Tony Chase then provided the basic model for pursuing the regionalization project (see Fig. 2.3.3). It bases key activities on gains to both the brand's competitive advantage and economies of scale.

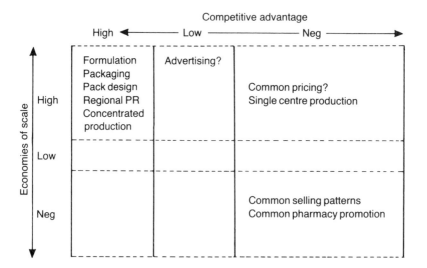

Fig. 2.3.3   Competitive advantage

Harmonization

It was evident that considerable competitive advantages and economies of scale could be achieved with common formulation, packaging (which already existed) and from a common pack design. This latter activity was, however, based on the fact that research showed that in all countries both consumers and pharmacists disliked the existing four different designs and that none stood out at points of sale. Regional PR also provided scale economies and would provide competitive advantages if regionalized. Concentrated production from four factories to three provided the optimum in terms of costs.

Centralized production, whilst providing (theoretically) high economies of scale would, it seemed, create a negative advantage competitively (based on a set of logistics exercises modelled by the company). Trying to achieve common trade-selling platforms or common trade promotions could provide little scope for economies of scale and would be so inflexible as to create a negative competitive advantage.

Harmonized advertising provided attractive economies of scale, especially in terms of film production where there were considerable and increasing opportunities to overlap advertising through pan-European and cross-border media. Furthermore, many of the smaller territories and export markets around the rest of the world could access high quality commercials. However, the UK, Germany and Spain had long-running, but very different, advertising themes and, therefore, it was felt that there would be little competitive advantage from complete regionalization of the 'message content' in the short term. A project was set up to investigate further how media economies could be achieved.

Pricing – the final barrier

Pricing remained the only outstanding and contentious issue. Each subsidiary company set its own prices on the basis of:

- a minimum gross contribution of 80 per cent (achieved in all countries); however, ingredient transfer prices were controlled at the centre and were scaled to allow subsidiaries to achieve their criterion gross profit. Historically ingredient transfer prices were set at levels for both tax purposes and price increase submissions to government;
- what each company believed was a competitive level of pricing versus competition.

No studies had actually been done to ascertain price elasticity, and pricing decisions were argued through at subsidiary level on the basis of financial targets and what the marketing manager believed the market would take. Yet the power of the finance department in pricing decisions was deeply imbedded.

In effect, pricing decisions were largely carried out by the finance departments at subsidiary company level. This was mainly for historical reasons, because when Nasalvine was a prescription product it was largely government price-controlled. This meant that a group within the finance function in each market was continually preparing and submitting lengthy pricing proposals to national health controllers. After Nasalvine became an advertised product, the finance function simply continued to do the pricing work. However, the pricing groups had never become close to the market. In the old days they strove to get as much as they could. The only difference between the pre-advertising days and now is that the pricing department was not required to justify price increases to government departments.

However, the initial audit indicated that pharmaceutical brands were subject to what is called 'parallel importation'. This is the practice among wholesalers to shop around the EC and buy pharmaceuticals where they are least expensive and resell them where the selling prices are highest.

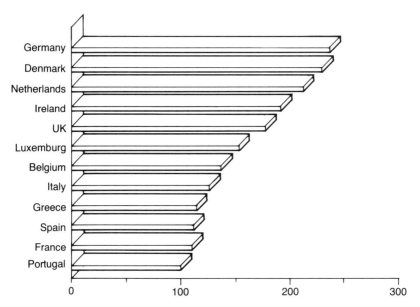

Fig. 2.3.4   Price differences in the EC markets (using Portugal as an index)

This practice was not only common but it was also advocated by health authorities in Germany. Furthermore, any manufacturer who tried to prevent parallel importation would be indictable under Article 85 of the Treaty of Rome.

Target markets for 'parallel imports' were the UK, Holland and Germany where prices were generally higher. Italy largely escaped 'parallel imports' because of hidden barriers to trade. Spain's pharmaceutical prices were generally lower than the rest of Europe making it unattractive as a target market but attractive as a source of lower-priced brands (see Fig. 2.3.4).

Nasalvine was subject to limited 'parallel imports' from the UK to Germany but largely escaped because its packaging was different in each market. As a consumer product it was an unattractive prospect for 'parallel imports'. However, where it was prescribed i.e. in the UK, Germany and Holland, wholesalers could exploit 'parallel imports' to profit from price differentials.

Tony Chase used Fig. 2.3.5 to explain how the threat of 'parallel imports' builds-up for regionalized brands.

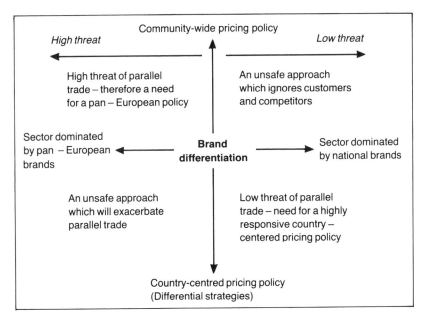

Fig. 2.3.5 Pricing analysis
Source: James W. Dudley (1990) *1992: Strategies for the Single European Market* p.270 © James W. Dudley (London, Kogan Page)

As it stood, 'parallel imports' were not a problem of any great significance. Regionalization of the brand could, however, trigger parallel
imports where:

- the product packaging was similar across all markets;
- raised levels of advertising would raise awareness of the product
  among parallel importers;
- significant increases in the brand's value within the market would
  make it a target for 'parallel imports'.

Country marketing managers from the four territories began expressing
reservations about pursuing the regionalization project lest it triggered
parallel imports. So, Tony Chase went to see Jack Z. Johnson with the
pricing information contained in Fig. 2.3.6.

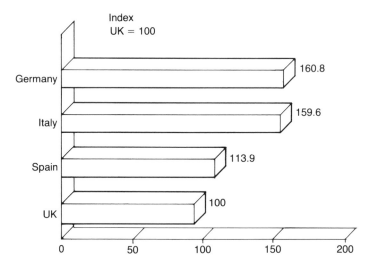

**Fig. 2.3.6 Price comparisons of Nasalvine in Europe (1990) (Based on the UK
manufacturer's selling price)**

Jack Z. Johnson thought for a moment and said:

'What you are telling me is that the whole of our regionalization project is
jeopardized by the threat of parallel importation and that country managers
are reluctant to go ahead with the project for fear that they will lose profit if it
happens?'

Tony Chase agreed. Jack Z. Johnson rounded on Chase:

'What you are saying is that progress in this business is based on the off chance that one manager in this company is going to have to explain away a year's drop in profits because of the threat of parallel importation. I thought we were seeking scale and competitive advantage gained through regionalization. What I want from you is a cost benefit analysis of what we might gain, against what we might lose if we go ahead with the regionalization project. What's more I am not interested in trading off margins between markets because of parallel imports. I want to know how our pricing decisions are going to affect our competitive position.'

Tony Chase's conclusions

For the April 1990 meeting of the Nasalvine regionalization group, Tony Chase decided that he had three options:

(a) Recommend a standard pricing system which would prevent parallel imports but no doubt would not be market responsive. What, therefore, would the brand gain or lose?
(b) He knew that other company divisions used a reference price system by which a European reference price was set and countries were permitted to charge price, plus or minus 5 per cent of this price. This, he felt, was really not much better than standardized pricing – unless he could work out how much latitude he could offer. Ten per cent would be neither here nor there across Europe when the accounts were consolidated. Industry estimates put the trigger point for parallel imports at between 12 and 18 per cent.
(c) His last option was to ignore the 'parallel imports' issue and go for differentiated pricing on the basis of local price competitiveness. Again, he needed to know more about consumer price expectations and competitive levels of pricing.

He therefore asked the country managers to supply comparative pricing data. He then thought for a moment about currency movements. This might present yet another factor. He telephoned the company's corporate treasurer and put the issue to him. The answer put his mind at rest. He was assured that by the time that he came to introduce any decision regarding pricing, all the countries he had listed in the project would be members of the Community's Exchange Rate Mechanism. This would hold currencies relatively stable against the ECU but there could be very minor fluctuations between Member States' individual currencies.

Comparative data

A week before the April meeting Tony Chase had Tables 2.3.5 – 2.3.9 on his desk.

Table 2.3.5   Basic data

Germany Average price per pack	Manufacturers sales prices	Retail sales (DM)	Share ot market by value 1990 (%)	Average growth 1987–9
Nasalvine	2.8	6.2	13.0	-2.0
Otrivin	2.8	6.2	16.5	3.0
Wicks	2.8	6.2	4.6	22.0
Olynth	2.8	6.1	16.0	11.0
Ratiophai	2.0	4.3	4.0	31.0
Others	2.5	5.6	45.9	11.0
Italy	*Manufacturers sales prices*	*Retail sales price (L.)*		
Nasalvine	2095.2	4400.0	5.0	4.0
Otrivin	2023.8	4250.0	3.0	4.0
Vicks	2571.4	5400.0	35.0	9.0
Rinazina	1857.1	3900.0	20.0	1.0
Others	2119.0	4450.0	37.0	7.0
Spain	*Manufacturers sales prices*	*Retail sales price (Pta)*		
Nasalvine	188.2	320.0	15.0	4.0
Otrivin	182.4	310.0	15.0	9.0
Vicks	223.5	380.0	21.2	1.0
Nedulcina	121.2	206.0	20.0	9.0
Others	152.9	260.0	28.8	7.0
UK	*Manufacturers sales prices*	*Retail sales price (£)*		
Nasalvine	0.6	1.2	21.8	19.0
Otrivin	0.7	1.4	42.1	19.0
Vicks	0.7	1.4	21.9	1.0
Own label (Boots)	0.9	1.8	7.1	1.0
Others	0.6	1.2	7.1	1.0

Source: Trade estimates 1990

Table 2.3.6   Nasalvine sales consumer OTC v Doctor's prescription (%)

Country	Consumer	Doctor's prescription
Germany	70	30
Italy	100	nil
Spain	100	nil
UK	82	18

Table 2.3.7   Nasalvine gross profit

Country	GP
Germany	79.1
Italy	81.2
Spain	78.3
UK	80.1

Table 2.3.8   Nasalvine advertising

Country/Currency	Advertising $ million	Average promotional allowance trade (%)
Germany (DM)	2355.6	15%
Italy (L.)	492.0	16%
Spain (Pta)	nil	16%
UK (£)	334.4	7.5%

Table 2.3.9   Nasalvine sales Europe 1989

Country	Sales $ million	%
Germany	5720.0	24.5
Italy	1950.0	8.4
Spain	3150.0	13.5
UK	2229.0	9.5
Other	4225.3	18.1
Total	**17274.3**	**74.0**

Germany comes to the rescue, or does it?

Two days before the April meeting, Hans Smidt, Marketing Manager Splendix Artzneimittel Gmbh, Germany, telephoned Tony Chase to inform him that the German Government had offered a supply contract to manufacturers on a take it or leave it basis. The *Festbetrag* as interpreted by Splendix Artzneimittel Gmbh finance directors suggested that Nasalvine's prices would fall by 32 per cent if the brand was to retain its prescription element (i.e. 30 per cent of sales). Hans Smidt said 'We are inclined to go along with the *Festbetrag* – we could lose nearly a third of our sales if we don't. What's more, that would bring German prices into line with the lower-priced markets'.

Tony Chase considered the discussion. Dropping Germany's prices was not something he had in mind. Germany was Nasalvine's second most important market. Going to a government-imposed price decrease would solve many of his problems of pricing harmonization but the loss of Germany's profit contribution would mitigate the benefits of the whole project. 'We are back to reactive marketing' he said to himself. He also thought about what Jack would say, 'Local managers clinging to what they've got rather than driving their brands'. He pulled out the German profit and loss account shown in Table 2.3.10.

Tony Chase wrote down a checklist he needed to go over before he made his recommendations to the project team:

- transfer prices are a key ingredient cost; can we control them? – yes;
- do we cost to market or market to cost, can production synergies be achieved? – yes;
- can we set our gross margin criterion on the basis of efficiencies rather than on a cost-plus basis – what are the issues, market share or production location?
- how competitive are our local pricing arrangements in real terms?
- are we organized properly to market a regional brand?
- what do we do in Germany? If we go along with the *Festbetrag* we lose all the gains of harmonization, if we don't, we could still lose to parallel imports;
- time is the key. Do we bite the bullet and do everything at one go or can we phase things?
- the problem is remaining objective – what are the hidden agendas of country managers?

Table 2.3.10 German profit and loss account

	1989	1988
Sales		
Nasalvine	5720.0	5834.4
Artz PR	2110.0	1980.0
Oraltex	1534.0	1510.0
Other	1112.0	1009.0
Total sales	**10476.0**	**10333.4**
Gross profit		
Nasalvine	4518.8	4609.2
Artz PR	1666.9	1564.2
Oraltex	1211.9	1192.9
Other	878.5	797.1
Total GP	**8276.0**	**8163.4**
Advertising	744.8	744.8
GP *less* advertising	7531.2	7418.6
Key costs		
Selling	1990.4	1963.3
Distribution	1152.4	1136.7
Administration	942.8	930.0
Total costs	**4085.6**	**4030.0**
Contribution	3445.6	3388.6
Ratio: contribution/sales	32.9	32.8

Questions/discussion topics

1. Taking Tony Chase's agenda, what are the two underlying features of the business environment likely to impede the Europeanization of the company?

2. Is the company being too ideological in its approach to branding across several markets – or is there a true economic benefit?

3. Provide a brief for the meeting based on Tony Chase's agenda.

4. Set out the next step of the plan including a detailed market research brief.

Case 4
The National Bank of Greece (NBG) – a case of a State-controlled bank preparing for the Single European Market*

Theo Kiriziadis

Advice to readers

This case study illustrates how a major State-controlled banking organization is responding to the challenges of an integrated European banking
market. The bank will have to pass through a phase of major change to
meet the demands of the new competitive conditions. However, any effort
towards the achievement of this goal is being very seriously impaired by
State controls in Greece.

Introduction

The National Bank of Greece (NBG) is a State-controlled banking organization that offers a full range of banking services and holds a dominant
position in the domestic financial market. It is the largest bank in Greece
and plays an important role in the accumulation and allocation of savings.
Through its operation, it absorbs something in the region of 55 per cent of
total deposits in Greece and finances most sectors of the economy.

The NBG has a number of branches abroad to serve the Greek Community. It also has a large number of affiliated and subsidiary companies.
Appendix B gives a list of the most important companies in this network.

* The author would like to acknowledge Mr I. Angelides, Economic Adviser of NGB,
  for his assistance in the development of this case study.

The European business environment

The completion of the Single European Market will present considerable opportunities for the NBG to expand into other Member States, especially those containing a significant number of Greek nationals. However, the integration of the European banking market will also threaten the NBG's large domestic market share.

At present the entry and establishment of foreign banking organizations in Greece is severely restricted by national regulations. These restrictions concern items such as licensing, requirements for minimum earmarked capital, provisions with respect to competence of personnel, as well as the restrictions on the type of services that can be offered.

The completion of the internal banking market is based largely on the implementation of the Second Banking Co-ordination Directive which involves the principles of the single banking licence and home country control. The principle of the single banking licence allows a banking institution licensed in one Member State to establish itself in all others without the need of eleven additional licenses, issued under eleven different regulatory regimes. The principle of home country rule means that any banking institution established in one Member State will be allowed to operate, and offer its services, in all others, while its operations will be governed by the supervisory authorities of the country where the head office is located.

The Second Banking Co-ordination Directive has been adopted by the Council of Ministers and is due to to be implemented by the end of 1992. However, there is some uncertainty as to the exact timing of the implementation which will eliminate discriminatory treatment against the establishment of foreign banking organizations that arise from national regulations. For example, the Greek authorities will not be able to impose any restriction on the type of services that can be offered or on the range of activities in which banks from other Member States can engage.

Multinational banking institutions enjoy benefits of scale from their extensive global operations, they have relatively easy access to international capital markets and operate under favourable supervisory systems. The NBG was faced with the situation that it could be squeezed by freedom of competition if it did not change its structure and organization. While the integration of European financial markets will substantially increase the opportunities for banks from other Member States to operate in Greece; the NGB will have to cope with severe competition.

Banking in Greece

International trends towards deregulation of financial systems and the integration of European markets were the factors that gradually set in motion a similar process of change in the Greek banking system.

The dominant feature of the Greek banking system in the late 1980s was its ongoing deregulation. For example, banks were allowed to apply normal banking criteria in financing economic activities, such as trade, which used to have only a limited access to funds from the banks. Commercial banks were authorized to undertake operations that were previously the exclusive domain of specialized credit institutions. Banks were also authorized to determine interest rates on deposits, the only exception being that of the minimum rate on savings deposits.

The deregulation of the Greek banking system creates opportunities for the NBG in terms of expanding and introducing new services, but at the same time it is also increasing competition and therefore threatening the NGB's domestic market position. Some deregulation has occurred, but the powers of national authorities to intervene in this sector are still strong.

Under the Second Banking Co-ordination Directive a bank will not need to be established in the host country, nor will it need to modify its banking services to comply with the host country's financial regulations. These services are identified in the annex to the directive and include:

- deposit taking and other forms of borrowing;
- lending, including consumer credit;
- mortgage lending;
- factoring and invoice discounting and trade finance;
- financial leasing;
- transmission services;
- credit cards, traveller's cheques and banker's drafts;
- guarantees and commitments;
- foreign exchange;
- financial futures and options;
- exchange and interest rate instruments;
- securities;
- participation in share issues;
- portfolio management and advice;
- the safekeeping of securities.

While all of these services are offered by the large European banking organizations, the NBG undertakes only a limited number of them. More specifically, the NBG is not involved in financial futures and options, exchange and interest rate instruments, while factoring and leasing are undertaken only to a very limited extent.

The role of the Greek authorities

It seems most likley that after the completion of the integrated market in banking, banks from other Member States will attract a significant amount of business away from the NBG unless the latter increases the range of its services. Of even greater importance is the fact that at the present time the Greek authorities can control the amount of credit extended by the commercial banks to specific activities. The monetary authorities select their loans according to the State's interests rather than on the basis of the contribution to their own profits. The authorities require Greek banks to devote 40 per cent of their deposits for investments in treasury bills which provide low returns. This requirement permits the State to use banks' deposits to finance its deficit at below-market rates. The State is unwilling to pay market rates to finance its huge deficit. This regulatory provision imposes a heavy burden on the functioning of indigenous banking institutions and affects their ability to compete on an equal footing with other European banking organizations operating under the principle of home country control.

The Greek national authorities also require the commercial banks to devote 10 per cent of their deposits for loans to small-scale industry and another 9 per cent for long-term loans to finance productive investment at a low interest rate. Although this requirement brings market distortion, it is considered an essential element of the country's economic development policy. The authorities use this requirement to give financial support to economic sectors, or activities, that they consider to be 'productive'. Greece is still dominated by small- to medium-sized businesses which need borrowing facilities at preferential rates for growth. The Greek Government strongly believes that this credit policy promotes economic development.

The transformation of the EC from a fragmented to a pan-EC domestic market will be based on the principle of home country control. In Greece, strong restrictions are imposed on portfolio policies of the commercial banks and the latter can do very little to influence the selection of their lending. The existing regulatory regime acts as a strait-jacket on the indigenous banking organizations in the pursuit of profit and growth, and substantially restricts their ability to compete internationally. If European banking organizations were free to operate in Greece without complying with the above-mentioned regulatory regime (home country control) this would result in unfair competition against indigenous banks.

The home country control principle

The home country control principle will result in a degree of harmonization thus bringing into competition not only financial undertakings but also national regulatory regimes. The European Commission believes that the strictly-regulated Member States will reduce their regulatory constraints as their own domestic operators will be severely handicapped in the face of more flexible competitors. However, it is very difficult for Greece to abolish the controls on its banks' portfolios in the foreseeable future, as they are based on important economic factors.

National restrictions mean that the NBG cannot utilize its potential comparative advantage, for example, savers' confidence in the bank, and thereby increase profit margins. Increased profit margins are indispensable for meeting the additional cost involved in modernizing its structure, improving mechanical equipment and personnel training, all of which are essential for dealing successfully with the new competition that will emerge from the integration of European markets.

The progress of the plan to remove these controls in Greece is partly dependent on the ability of the national authorities to reduce the public sector deficit and accelerate the pace of economic development. However, in a number of respects, time is running out, as the commercial banks need time to adapt to the operating environment emerging in the Community.

The NGB's organizational response

In spite of the difficulties, the NBG is making considerable efforts to cope with the growing competition that is emerging from the partial deregulation of the Greek financial system. Emphasis is being placed on promoting dynamic operations such as consumer credit and on the provision of new services such as leasing underwriting of share and bond issues, and the establishment of enterprises to utilize new institutions in the stock market. However, in this effort the NBG faces stiff competition from foreign banks who are able to respond more quickly to opportunities provided by liberalization because they possess sophisticated financial expertise and technology not available in the Greek domestic sector. The NBG feels that its size, its extensive branch network in Greece and abroad, and the dynamism of its large group of affiliates will enable it to adapt to the emerging competitive environment. The NBG's strategy aims to:

- increase the internationalization of its operation;
- reorganize its branch network both inside Greece and externally;
- decentralize its administrative structure;
- restructure and improve its portfolio quality.

Increasing the internationalization of its operations

The developments at the European level have encouraged banks to expand their operations Community-wide and in many instances throughout the wider world. The NBG has formulated a systematic policy targeted at strengthening its international competitiveness. For example, in 1983 action was taken to improve and modernize the bank's international transactions and a new system of credit analysis for the roughly 4,000 correspondent banks abroad commenced. Furthermore, the NBG strengthened its presence abroad by establishing:

- a new branch in Boston, Massachusettes;
- a new branch of its affiliate, the Atlantic Bank of New York, in the State of New York;
- three agencies of its affiliate, the South African Bank of Athens;
- a new branch of the National Bank of Greece (Canada) in Montreal.

The NBG intends to establish branches or affiliates in other developing commercial centres abroad, for example, Singapore, Moscow and Luxemburg.

In Europe, the NBG is in the process of strengthening its existing network of branches and affiliated banks by expanding their operations and diversifying the services they offer to Greek and foreign companies. Its main aim is not only to increase trade transactions, attract investment to Greece and encourage the inflow of foreign exchange, but also to develop these branches and affiliates into powerful financial entities in the regions in which they operate. In addition, the NBG is developing co-operation agreements with a number of foreign banks. These agreements take the form of share purchase between banks from different countries, collaborations in new markets and joint services, the utilization of each bank's branch network, and the creation of economies of scale.

'We are particularly interested in penetrating new markets and using foreign banks' know-how and specialization in the supply of modern banking services in Greece and abroad.'
Mr I. Angelides, Economic Adviser, NBG

The reorganization of the branch network

The reorganization of the NBG's branch network is a top priority in the attempts to improve the bank's competitive position.

The expansion of the network in terms of number and size of branch offices, as well as their location, is determined by the economic and financial needs of the area. Two new branches were established in 1989, raising the total to 485 units. A considerable number of branches have been renovated, expanded or relocated to ensure a better working environment.

The rapid advances in electronic banking technology have resulted in a reconsideration of the bank's network expansion policy. The objective of the new policy is to ensure easy access to the retail banking market and optimal customer service at the lowest possible cost. This goal can be achieved by developing the bank's electronic infrastructure, for example, in home banking and telebanking.

Decentralizing its administration

For many years the NBG has been decentralizing its services through the creation of regional directorates, and during the 1980s it set up two additional regional centres for administration.

Regional centres were allowed greater flexibility in such areas as the setting of upper limits for new loans. Today electronic technology is capable of promoting effective co-operation between central and local units of a bank, as well as giving immediate solutions to a whole range of operational problems faced by branches established in the localities.

Restructuring and improving its portfolio quality

The need to restructure the NBG's portfolio and improve its quality is associated with the question of over-indebted 'problem' companies. The participation of NBG in these companies represents almost 70 per cent of the bank's capital. Despite ongoing deregulation, one of the existing national regulations forces the bank to support 'problem' companies. The bank has attempted to improve the financial position of many of these companies but the Government's policy of restricting redundancies has made much of this effort unsuccessful. This regulation acts as a highly-significant constraint on the NBG and has a major impact on fund recycling, profitability and growth.

The effectiveness of the bank's response to national deregulation and Single Market legislation depends decisively on the bank's ability to formulate a suitable strategy and take the necessary measures without governmental intervention. The pressure exerted on the bank's financial flexibility and profitability margins by regulatory provisions and administrative practices has considerably restricted the bank's ability to restructure its loan portfolio and the range of its operations. It would be very helpful if the bank was freed from the State's stranglehold, which has had unfavourable effects on the bank's profitability, structure and operation. It is essential to minimize the monetary authorities' intervention and to speed up the process of deregulation.

'The bank has already submitted to the authorities proposals that could serve as a basis for a revision of the existing regulations. We have much expertise and knowledge about the whole issue.'
G. Nickolaides, Corporate Stratergist, NGB

Human resources issues

Success in the single banking market will require high skill levels. At the end of 1983, the NBG's payroll included a total of 15,896 employees as against 12,044 at the end of 1980. The gradual expansion of the branch network and continually-growing demand for banking services made it necessary to increase the number of employees. In recent years, the bank has been burdened with official recruitment policies which have forced it to recruit people with inadequate skills. The Greek State has adopted recruitment criteria inappropriate for a modern banking sector. This decision could count heavily against NBG over the next few years when EC financial markets and capital movements are freed.

The absence of State-funded training programmes in banking has forced the NBG to meet the high cost of general and specialized training courses for its employees. Since 1980 a total of 1,715 bank employees have taken part in special training programmes. At the same time, the bank has continued to offer two types of training course. The first covers preliminary training of new recruits, foreign languages and general studies, and has been attended by 1,263 employees. The second covers topics relating to business administration, bank credit, marketing, banking techniques and the operation of electronic equipment. This course has been attended by 3,473 executives.

Senior management feels that the upskilling of the bank's personnel at all levels will significantly contribute to the successful efforts to restructure its portfolio, establish new methods and practices of operation and internationalize its activities.

'Unless the quality of the personnel improves, the bank's attempts to improve the quality and quantity of its services will fail.'
A senior manager, NBG

In terms of providing training, the NBG faces additional problems, for example, its employees are spread across the whole country and this makes the running of training programmes difficult. In addition, in recent years the NBG has found it increasingly difficult to support the operation of these programmes due to poor profits.

Production

In order to provide a faster service to borrowers, the bank accelerated the procedures involved in approving and supplying credit; this has greatly helped smaller companies. The bank is trying to improve its electronic facilities (for example, by introducing cash dispensers). At present the NBG has an inadequate technological base; sometimes customers have to wait an hour in a queue to draw small amounts of money from their accounts. This situation is very different from what is happening elsewhere in Europe.

In spite of these problems, special projects included in the bank's modernization programme were carried out in 1989 in order to improve and expand customer services, reduce operational costs and upgrade the exchange of information between various units of the bank. The main changes are :

- **Improvement in procedures and organizational support of the domestic branch network.** For example, the branch reorganization study was applied at a pilot branch in Athens and the 'special cash counter' concept was extended to 118 branches representing 25 per cent of the total and serving 54 per cent of on-line business.
- **Reorganization and modernization of the international transactions division.** For example, a new electronic data processing system was applied on a trial basis for the reconciliation of foreign correspondents' accounts and the management of foreign correspondents' accounts was further rationalized.

The provision of banking services to companies and the public in general requires an advanced electronic infrastructure. The internationalization of transactions, the supply of new bank products and the modern technology employed by most companies make it necessary for the bank to adapt its own facilities accordingly.

National restrictions mean that the NBG lacks adequate resources to purchase additional high-technology equipment. While a private bank is in a position after a few days' discussion to purchase computerized equipment, the NBG as a public sector organization needs at best a few months, and at worst over two years, to obtain a decision, as approval to purchasing this type of equipment has to be obtained from a number of committees. For example, purchase of electronic or other equipment requires the approval of both the Ministry of Commerce and the Ministry of State, and this bureaucratic procedure has often frustrated plans to buy essential high-technology equipment.

Appendix A: Glossary of terms

Banker's draft.   Cheques for settlements of large amounts.

Commitment.   A bank commits itself to a future transaction that will normally result in the bank acquiring a credit exposure (either an asset or possibly a guarantee) at some future date.

Exchange and interest rate instruments.   Exchange of funds in different currencies (i.e. contracts to pay and receive specified amounts of one currency for another at a future date at a predetermined exchange rate) and exchange of interest rate payments which are undertaken in order to minimize risks and make profits.

Factoring.   A continuing arrangement by which the bank purchases all the trade debts due to the business as they arise. The business will be paid up to 80 per cent of the value of invoices as they are raised.

Financial futures and options.   These items are essentially foreign exchange or interest rate agreements in most cases binding on both parties but in some cases exercisable at one party's discretion (e.g. options).

Foreign exchange futures are exchanged traded contracts for the delivery of standardized amounts of foreign currency at some future date. The price for the foreign currency is agreed on the day the contract is bought or sold.

Interest rate futures are similar to foreign exchange futures except the contracts are for delivery of a standardized amount of a specified security, normally Treasury bills or Government bonds.

Foreign exchange options are option contracts that allow the holders to exchange a specific amount of one currency for another at a predetermined rate during some period in the future.

Interest rate options are similar to foreign exchange options. The buyers of the options have the right to lock into a predetermined interest rate at some time in the future.

Financial leasing.   The financing by a bank of the purchase of assets.

Guarantee.   An undertaking by a bank to stand behind the current obligations of a third party and to carry out these obligations should the third party fail to do so, e.g. a *loan guarantee* under which A makes a loan to B against a guarantee of repayment provided by a bank C.

Invoice discounting.   An agreement similar to factoring but involving particular selection of invoices.

Money transmission services.   Electronic fund transmission services.

Portfolio management and advice.   Assets legally the property of customers and other parties but managed by a bank sometimes on the basis of discretion in the choice of investments.

Appendix B: Affiliated and subsidiary companies of the NBG

National Credit Bank

This is a credit institution specializing in financial support investment. Its main task is to finance the investment programmes of manufacturing and other firms, and supply credit and consulting services to its customers.

Traders' Credit Bank (TCB)

Its main task is to extend loans to medium-sized firms.

National Housing Bank

Its main concern is to extend mortgage credit and grant loans for the purchase, construction, repair, completion and renovation of buildings through the NBG's network.

Arab-Hellenic Bank (AHB)

It specializes in serving the country's foreign trade.

National Management and Organization Company (NMOC)

It is engaged in organizing and developing operations relating to personal loans, payment systems and credit cards.

National Investment Company (NIC)

A financial company with an impressive performance because of the favourable conditions in the stock market.

National Securities Company (NSC)

Founded by the NBG to engage in stock market operations. Initially, the company intends to engage in the trade of securities but gradually its operations will expand to cover all brokerage services.

Atlantic Bank of New York (ABNY)

Its main aim is to provide the NBG with a strong link with one of the world's foremost financial and banking centres.

National Bank of Greece (Canada)

It specializes mainly in business transactions between Greece and Canada.

The South African Bank of Athens (SABA)

It provides the usual range of banking services to the local Greek community in South Africa.

Banque Nationale de Grece (France)

It connects the Greek market with Paris, one of the major financial and commercial centres of Europe.

The Ethnic Hellenic General Insurance Company (EHGIC)

This the largest insurance company in the Greek market.

'Astir' Insurance Company (AIC)

This is one of the largest insurance companies in Greece.

Questions/discussion topics

1. Identify the main threats and opportunities facing the NBG as the integration of the European banking sector comes into view.

2. How, and to what extent, does public intervention restrict the profitability and the ability of the NBG to compete internationally?

3. Evaluate the NBG's strategic response to national and European developments.

4. Advise the NBG on how it could improve its competitive position.

Case 5
Gates Hydraulics Ltd – Total Quality Management and the Single Market[*]

John Pike

Advice to readers

It is generally recognized that one of the greatest challenges facing businesses in Europe during the 1990s is competition from the Single European Market. This presents enormous opportunities as well as threats. Already, in 1990, some 50 per cent of the European Community's trade in goods, services and capital is amongst Member States, and this is before many barriers and restrictions are finally removed. Survival and growth in these new and immensely competitive conditions will depend very much on how companies perceive these opportunities and threats, and how effectively they respond in strategic terms to this new environment.

This case is a study of how one organization, Gates Hydraulics Ltd, has looked at the impact of the Single European Market, its ability to compete and how it has adopted a Total Quality Management Strategy as a response.

Introduction

Gates Hydraulics Ltd is part of the Gates Rubber Company's international operations. The Gates Rubber Company in turn is part of a multinational corporation. The Gates Corporation, whose world headquarters are in Denver, Colorado, USA, was founded in 1911 by Charles Gates Senior when he bought the Colorado Tire & Leather Company for $3,500.

[*] The author would like to thank Ron Scouse, Quality Director at Gates Hydraulics Ltd for his assistance in the development of this study.

The Gates Corporation – profile of its major operations

The Gates Corporation is now one of the largest privately-owned corporations in the USA with 1989 sales of $1.33 billion. Gates is focused on four major lines of business: automotive and industrial rubber products, batteries, formed fibre products and automotive accessory drive systems.

Other subsidiary companies are Gates Energy Products Inc., Gates Formed Fibre Products Inc. and Gates Power Drive Products Inc. Worldwide the Gates Corporation employs 18,000 people. Of these, approximately 10,000 are located in the USA, including 2,500 at its head-quarters in Denver. Overall the company operates 47 plants, 15 distribution and service centres, 17 marketing offices and three joint ventures in 18 states and 16 other countries. Gates' products are marketed by a network of 150,000 distributors, dealers and sales specialists in more than 100 countries.

The Gates Rubber Company

The Gates Rubber Company is the largest of the subsidiary companies. Its reported sales in 1989 of more than one billion dollars represent 78 per cent of the Corporation's total revenue. It is the world's largest non-tyre rubber company, employing 13,000 people worldwide – 7,000 in the USA and 6,000 in other countries. In the USA the Gates Rubber Company operates 17 manufacturing plants, six full product line distribution centres, two material product service centres and one technical/sales centre. International operations include 20 manufacturing plants, seven distribution centres, eleven marketing offices and three joint ventures in 15 countries.

Gates Hydraulics Ltd

Gates Hydraulics Ltd is one of these 20 manufacturing plants, based at St Neots, Huntingdon, Cambridgeshire, in the United Kingdom. It manufac-tures and markets hydraulic hose assemblies and coupling products, and has done so since the 1960s. However, it was not until 1982 that the Gates Rubber Company acquired the plant when it bought Imperial Eastman

Hydraulic Coupling Operations in England and France, and renamed them Gates Hydraulics Ltd.

The company now employs approximately 400 people across its three operations in St Neots (UK), Lyon (France) and Düsseldorf (Germany). The latter two are assembly and warehousing operations only. Of the 400 employees, 320 are based at St Neots.

From April 1990 the company reports to its European Corporate Office in Brussels instead of to Denver, USA.

The nature of the company's products and services

Gates Hydraulics produces hydraulic hose made from a range of synthetic rubber and thermo-plastic compounds combined with a variety of reinforcements designed to suit most applications. The Gates Rubber Company is the largest manufacturer of wire-braid hose in the world.

The company produces an extensive range of hose couplings designed to be coupled with the appropriate hose to produce a consistently high performer assembly. There are more than 1,000 types and sizes of couplings. The assembly of hose and hose couplings to produce hose assemblies is completed by crimping presses which are also designed and made by the company to ensure that the assembly process meets with their precision requirements. Hose assemblies are produced for use with working pressures up to 7,000 psi and temperatures ranging from –40 to +170.

Product development

The company recognizes the need for constant improvement in its range of products and services, and invests heavily in research on a global basis as part of its mission to be a global supplier with global products. Evidence of its commitment to product development is the appointment of an Advance Process and Development Director who, at the time of writing, had been in this job for three months. One of his objectives is to bring together all the people concerned with new product development to ensure they work effectively as a team.

Sales and Marketing within Europe

Gates regards itself as a global company with a presence in most major manufacturing countries. Its objective is to produce standard products that can be manufactured at any site worldwide to the same specification. European distributors operate under the label of the Gates QED Distributor

Network. QED stands for 'quality-ensured distribution' and quality standards are already in place governing this distribution network. Within the UK alone there are 32 accredited distributors who are extensively trained and retrained in order to share the same standards and attention to detail as the Gates employees themselves. Within the UK market the company enjoys a 16 per cent market share. Its major competitors are BTR-Dunlop, Aeroquip and Europower.

With the advent of the Single European Market the company has considered whether changes need to be made to its Sales and Marketing policies. It feels that with its assembly operations in France and Germany and with its network of distributors in each country it already has a good European infrastructure. This is not to say, however, that it is not exploring each major area for possible assembly and new distribution opportunities.

One major factor to be taken into consideration and which will influence future strategic decisions regarding the structure and location of production and distribution operations is the costs and ease of transportation. Transportation and distribution will become much easier within the Single Market as customs and other barriers are removed but customer expectations for a faster service and JIT philosophies must be considered.

The company is working with major customers to become a sole supplier on a global basis who will satisfy the requirements of all customer manufacturing locations – working together as a partnership from design to manufacture. Another factor influencing strategic decisions regarding its structure and location of production operations is the belief that smaller European companies will fall out of the market if they cannot provide a European service.

Apart from developments with the European Community, the company is also considering the impact of developments in Eastern Europe. As far as the former East Germany is concerned, its current position is that it will establish and strengthen its distribution structures through its German operation, and expects considerable growth in these areas.

If any reorganization within the company has to take place, it will almost certainly be towards a more integrated European Hydraulics Division which will be product, rather than geographically, orientated.

Advertising and promotion within Europe

Gates' policy is to promote quality and reliability rather than low price. With new legislation regarding product liability, quality and reliability are seen as increasingly vital marketing tools. Gates aims to be an integrated supplier of hose couplings and assembly equipment, and advertises to emphasize the technical advantages of its designs, the high standard of its sales and after sales service, and the quality of its products. Competitors do not always appear to see the advantages of selling such a package or to be capable of providing it.

Finance

Statements of the company's financial position are confidential. However, the company is willing to disclose its overall financial objectives in the following terms:

- to ensure the successful growth of Gates Hydraulics and its ability to achieve increased sales, profits and return on assets;
- to ensure that salaries, suppliers' accounts and other cash payments are made in an orderly and controlled manner;
- to control credit in order to maximize cash flow consistent with the growth of the business;
- to produce monthly information in an orderly and timely manner.

Pricing policy

It would be unreasonable to expect the company to disclose publicly its pricing policies. Nevertheless, they are willing to reveal that they feel a weakness in that there has been a lack of a structured approach to pricing in different markets. Their pricing policy is currently more nationally based, not simply a European-wide one. There is a move towards trying to unify pricing policy throughout Europe, recognizing that distribution costs will always vary between countries. Currently, pricing policy is also affected by the range of different currencies in use, and the financial advantages of trading in many of these have to be reaped. They do not see the ECU being used extensively in the near future and believe that any single monetary market will take a long time to evolve.

Purchasing

In recent years, the company has paid considerable attention to the development of formal systems and procedures governing the purchasing process, and these are now in place. They are mandatory for all managers. Previously, each person was able to exercise his or her own discretion based upon their own industrial job knowledge and this led to a great deal of inconsistency where the rules were changed to suit the individual circumstances. Despite the introduction of a formal system, however, there is still a perceived weakness in that in emergency situations there is still a tendency for people to revert to the old system. Since registration to BS5750/ISO9000 Part 1, this system has played a major part in making the adoption of these formal systems a reality. The auditing of the system and the need for compliance to the procedures is eliminating these weaknesses.

Purchasing as a function used to work in isolation from the rest of the company but it is now working with the other departments as a result of the introduction of the Total Quality Management approach which is dealt with in the following section.

Competing in Europe – accepting the challenge

As part of its normal process of forward planning, the Gates Corporation looked ahead and foresaw that the future of the organization lay in Europe, hence the establishment of a European Corporate Office in Brussels. Some key issues arising from its commitment to Europe are:

- exploring the opportunities for increased growth in sales in the German market;
- exploiting the full potential of the French market;
- improving the levels of customer service throughout the Single European Market.

In preparing itself to operate within this rapidly-developing market place, the senior management team have recognized that there is a need for all managers to have knowledge of employment law and industrial legislation. With this end in mind, the company lawyer presented a seminar on EC legislation and product liability to all managers on 22 November 1990. In support of their commitment, the Managing Director has also issued an instruction that, despite the current economic climate, training and management development must be given high priority at all levels. Top of the priority list, however, is the company's commitment to Total Quality Management, as endorsed by the Gates European Operations Director in Brussels.

Total Quality Management (TQM) in Gates

Although its parent company, the Gates Rubber Company, has for many years promoted, documented and maintained a Total Quality Control approach, it was not until April 1988 that Mr A.J. Roberts, the Managing Director of the Gates Hydraulics Ltd plant at St Neots, made a public declaration that in response to the need to become more competitive the company was going to adopt TQM as its goal. The policy pronouncement is set out below.

TOTAL QUALITY MANAGEMENT

'QUALITY' is the key operating priority in Gates Hydraulics. Our goal is to give Quality Top Priority, Top Status and Top Dedication in every action and decision we take. We all think that we understand the subject and are convinced that our ways are right. However, few of us would like to explain it and discussions on the subject of Quality are usually short and superficial.

WHY CHANGE?
The pursuit of Quality must be recognized as the most important objective within the company. Quality is a prime determinant of competitiveness in contract awards, retention and overall profitability. I have, therefore, decided to adopt a policy of 'Total Quality' within our company under my direction.

The factors affecting product quality are so numerous that it is difficult to identify an area of management that is not involved in some way. Quality influences are to be found not only in the technical area of design and production, but also in marketing, purchasing, personnel, finance and indeed every sector of the company's activities.

Quality planning must not be considered in isolation, but must be approached in the context of overall management planning, which is concerned with the corporate long-range plan for profitable growth.

It follows that all this demands clear quality objectives being set, of which the prime objective must be to achieve a high degree of customer satisfaction with due regard to quality costs. Here 'quality' must include any aspect of the product or service for the customer.

'Get it right first time' must be the golden rule for each and every department of the company if the aim is to operate cost-effective Quality Management. Basic changes of attitude will be required affecting all departments and levels within the company, including myself and fellow Directors. This may be like putting new wine into old caskets and is likely to necessitate an extensive review and possibly revision of our existing management systems.

This announcement is to inform you of my immediate objectives. You will shortly receive more information about the plans and objectives relative to individual department from your functional Directors and Managers.

Through Total Quality Management, our goal will be a target of 90 per cent reduction in defects in products and service in three years, with a 25 per cent reduction in the first 18 months.'

A.J. Roberts
26 April 1988

This announcement followed on from discussions between the Managing Director and Ron Scouse, the Quality Director, who was one of the first to recognize the need for change. As he put it: 'We were always firefighting – we were professional firefighters and very good at it – but we did not have the right objectives'.

After consultation with the Managing Director it was realized that the change required was best formalized in the shape of a TQM strategy. The need for senior management commitment to the overall objective of 'setting out to do the right things right' emphasized the importance of discussions at Board level. It was also recognized that all departments needed to develop a quality policy and that Ron Scouse's job as Quality Director would be to monitor the whole project.

Within Gates Hydraulics each senior manager reports to the Managing Director and all managers and departments are involved in planning the TQM strategy. One of the aims of this approach is to break down compartmentalization so that each department knows and understands what the others do and they work together as a team.

Two days after the initial policy announcement, the following statement of company objectives for the TQM process was issued by the Managing Director.

TOTAL QUALITY MANAGEMENT

Company objective

- Customer serviceability
- Zero defects
- Waste elimination
- 100 per cent achievement of customer S.Q.A.'s (Supply Quality Assurances)
- Inventory accuracy
- Forward quality planning
- Improved process controls

A.J. Roberts
28 April 1988

Implementing the plan

Not long after the Managing Director's policy announcement an Implementation Programme was published. This is reproduced below.

TOTAL QUALITY MANAGEMENT

Implementation programme

The programme	The method
1. Company policy statement by Managing Director	Display board in strategic position
2. Company's key objectives by managers	As above
3. Departmental objectives by managers	Display in department
4. Section objectives by supervisors	As above
5. Manager/supervisor group objectives	As above

5. Content to include:
   - (i) Clear objectives
   - (ii) Activity to achieve objectives + timing
6. Monitor and publish:
   - (i) Scrap costs
   - (ii) Customer returns
   - (iii) Number of suggestions
   - (iv) Quality circle achievements
   - (v) Safety record   Team brief
   - (vi) Achievement of production volumes
   - (vii) Departmental achievements
   - (viii) Others
7. Morning Market
   Product rejects should be brought together each morning for review by Production & Quality Supervision to discuss corrective action

8. Quality Performance (monthly) Monitor quality performance in manufacturing departments for quality defects and meeting target dates	Layout drawing of department Sections & processes displayed in each department Pins on layout against each section or process Nil rejects 'blue' Rejects 'red' Meeting targets 'green' Continuous over 12-month period

For this programme to be effective each department should develop its own method of monitoring and must have clear objectives.

Remember – to manage is to plan, to implement, to delegate, to review and redirect as required.

Preparation of departmental objectives

As part of the implementation programme, Ron Scouse arranged a series of meetings with individual managers to discuss the need for individual departmental objectives which related to the Managing Director's statement of overall company objectives. Consideration was also given to the effect these would have on other departments. Individual departmental managers then met as a group to discuss these objectives collectively with the aim of breaking down the isolation of these departments. Ron Scouse acted as the co-ordinator of these and prepared a synthesis of the individual contributions. This was then put back to Function Directors who discussed these objectives with their individual managers and prepared action plans and timing commitments.

Preparation of the Quality Manual

It was recognized at an early stage in creating a Quality Culture in Gates Hydraulics that here was an opportunity to establish systems and procedures essential to the effective development of a Total Quality process. It was also recognized that the Quality System BS5750/ISO9000 was a good foundation stone upon which to build the TQM strategy. Hence a decision was taken to combine the two processes and pursue their implementation simultaneously. The lack of departmental systems and procedures meant that the first task was to revise the existing Quality Manual. This was followed by a request to each department to prepare its own quality procedures, taking into account the relationships that existed with internal as well as external customers. These included Accounting, Materials, Safety, Statistical Process Control, Purchasing and Personnel Procedures.

The role of Quality Managers

Faced with the nature of the challenge to implement a Total Quality Management philosophy throughout the whole organization, the Quality Director soon began to question the previous role of the Department Managers with responsibility for quality and began to challenge line managers' perceptions of their role and function in relation to meeting quality standards. In his view, the Department Managers should have been functioning as facilitators of **conviction, commitment** and **conversion** (the three Cs). With this aim in mind, a series of internal seminars was arranged by the Quality Director to develop these Department Managers as facilitators of Total Quality Management. The Managing Director demonstrated his own total commitment to the process through his involvement in these facilitator seminars, setting out the guidelines and the overall objective of reducing rejects in production by 90 per cent in three years and 25 per cent in the first 18 months. Serviceability was to be the major aim.

Barriers/problems encountered

The introduction of any significant change into an organization is almost certain to encounter resistance from some affected quarters or to encounter problems which may or may not have been anticipated. Although considerable efforts were made to convince employees of the benefits and need for adopting a Total Quality Management approach, it appeared that there was not always true commitment from everybody in the business. Some Department Managers saw it as an extra job to be done and did not feel they had the extra time required to do it. The message did not get through.

At the same time, there were some obstructive attitudes from some of the managers which stifled enhanced production, keenness and motivation. These attitudes were caused by feelings of insecurity and uncertainty. It became clear that there was a need for these managers to work more closely with their subordinates and cross structural or departmental boundaries in order to build bridges and trust, and to strengthen the level of teamwork rather than continue the practice of working in isolation from each other. One of the major difficulties was trying to overcome the entrenched attitudes, especially such views as 'It's the excitement of trouble-shooting that makes the job worthwhile' or 'It's nothing to do with me, it's somebody else's problem'. However, despite these difficulties, progress was made.

Monitoring or review

A monthly reporting system with each department was established in order to monitor and review progress. These reports were a two-way process examining both expectations and criticisms. At the same time monthly team briefings were introduced together with a monthly magazine publicizing successes. Whilst no monetary rewards were offered, achievements were noted and given recognition, and these accolades contributed towards individual promotion within the company. Offering congratulations to staff on performance was considered to be extremely important.

To illustrate the process of reporting, the following is an example of a monthly progress report prepared five months after the Managing Director's initial policy announcement.

GATES HYDRAULICS LTD

MEMO

To:　Mr A.J. Roberts　　　　　　　　　　Date: 30 September 1988
From:　J.J. Shaw

Total Quality Management

The Administration Dept's TQM projects are under three different sections, Finance, Personnel and Data Processing. The Finance section has been a little slow in implementing its monitoring systems partially because, I believe, it felt it was 'washing its dirty linen in public', but as can be seen from the 'Total Quality' section report they have now been implemented.

Personnel conducted its first survey and implemented recommendations which again can be seen in the section 'Total Quality'.

Total Quality

In the 1980s only the successful companies have survived. The Japanese have shown that the most successful companies are those that have achieved high customer satisfaction by serviceability, quality of product and low cost.

We in Administration are responsible for three areas without which the company would cease to exist:

- people
- cash
- computer systems

Essentially we are a service department; other departments are our customers, and customer serviceability must be the keynote of everything we do. The quality of these services determines, to a large degree, the success of Gates Hydraulics. Therefore, only the best can be good enough. Our aim must be to get everything right, first time, on time, every time. Everything we do should have the hallmark of quality.

Too much time is spent correcting errors that could usefully be spent on other more productive tasks. We must spend more time correcting our systems so as to eliminate the chance of error. This cannot be done overnight – it is better to make steady, consistent progress than to work with great enthusiasm to start with, but fail to keep up the progress. Quality improvement never stops – there will always be new ways of doing things better.

It has been said that quality is never your problem, it is the solution to your problem.

So far you will notice no mention has been made of the cost of obtaining quality. This is because experience has shown that if the quality is right the cost is lower.

We need some overall objectives as a guideline for producing quality goals. As an administrative function, these fall into three areas: Finance, Data Processing (DP) and Personnel. The objectives could be defined as follows:

Finance

- assist in achieving the cash flow necessary to grow the business profitably;
- provide a monitoring system to measure Company progress in a timely and accurate fashion.

Data processing

- provide an accurate and timely information system to all users.

Personnel

- manage the human resource function so that we have adequately trained people for all functions.

We must always remember that customer serviceability is our goal and, in our case, customers are other departments as well as our external customers.

As an overall motto we could adopt a slogan. How about '**only the best**' with the idea of adding '**because we are the best**' at a later stage?

DP not only implemented its programme extremely quickly, but has also had its TQM board working on a daily basis for the last three months. I point this out because your memo on TQM said that there were no boards operating in the Company.

1.   Finance

Finance identified immediately three areas to look for improvement.
(a)   Reduce the number of working days required to produce the accounts package.
(b)   Reduce the number of errors in the bookkeeping area.
(c)   Reduce the number of daily sales outstanding with customers.

The target for the production of the monthly accounts is set at ten days. The July accounts and the August accounts took 14 and 15 days respectively. Contributory factors to this are the number of corrections of errors that need to be made and a separate monitoring system for this has been set up. This is a high number, but it must be borne in mind that it was an inexperienced staff that was producing it. A further factor that is not helping the target is that invoices are not being cleared fast enough. Consequently, we are now monitoring the number of items that we have to account for because an invoice was not cleared by month end. The balance on a sales ledger that represents money due to us has usually resulted in some other paperwork being incorrectly processed. This item is also being monitored. Copies of the charts are attached. The one chart that we are not putting up is the DSO (Daily Sales Outstanding) as it is possible this item could be seen by customers. However, the figures do appear in the monthly accounts package.

2.   Personnel

I   Team Brief Project
It was agreed that the Team Brief needed to be reviewed and changes made in order that its impact be improved.

Timing plan
Produce Team Brief in normal format   1st week May
Audit quality of Team Brief through

questionnaire at operator level	12–13 May
Publish primary findings	16 May
Act upon findings in preparation of June Team Brief	1–8 May
Second audit of Team Brief	13–18 Oct

The findings are contained in the memos dated 16 May, 24 May and 30 September, which are attached.

    II Company Communications Systems
    Problems
    The amount of 'traffic' passing through the switchboard appears to be increasing and at times causes delays in the answering of calls. This obviously impairs the quality of service we aim to provide.

Measures to be taken

1. Retrieve switchboard traffic information collated 18 months ago — Immediate
2. Repeat monitoring tests over the next 4–6 weeks — 19.9.88 – 28.10.88
3. Compare results and suggest corrective measures — Ongoing

Programme of monitoring tests

1. Tannoy calls — 19.9.88 – 23.9.88
2. Switchboard traffic — 26.9.88 – 30.9.88
3. Paging via switchboard — 3.10.88 – 7.10.88
4. Incoming switchboard traffic via M.M.U. — 3.10.88 – 7.10.88
5. Telephone recalls to discover any individual or departmental hold-ups — 10.10.88 – 14.10.88
6. Any further monitoring needs highlighted by above measurements — 17.10.88 – 21.10.88

Results of the survey of tannoy usage is attached.

3. D.P. Progress Report

The introduction of TQM coincided with a need to tighten up the procedures within the D. P. Department to ensure that daily, weekly and monthly schedules were met.

It had been recognized that the completion of the overnight processing run and the subsequent distribution of reports was often not within the accepted time scale. In order to address this problem, it was decided to concentrate our efforts on reducing the number of variables which might have an impact on overnight processing and to investigate thoroughly and rectify any faults which occurred. We had previously fallen into the trap of devoting virtually all software development resources to new or updated applications whilst there were recurring problems with the day-to-day operations which had not been rectified.

Our investigations showed that whilst there were deficiencies in certain areas of the software, a high percentage of the problems which prevented the 'Job Queue' from completing were caused by screens being used later in the evening than expected or jobs left running when the user had gone home.

The software problems were fixed by rewriting many of the procedures involved, taking into account errors that had previously been identified. Training people to ensure that they correctly sign off their terminals at the end of each day is not easy, particularly when the latest screens automatically dim after not being used for a specified period of time. It was obvious that however many times we reminded users of the correct procedures there would inevitably be occasions when screens were left on. We decided to develop a 'fault tolerance' routine which took account of any device left on and shared the computer resources with programs still running without affecting the overnight run sequence.

This has proved very successful and it is now only on rare occasions that overnight processing is interrupted. An overnight checklist is produced daily to keep users in key areas informed of the status of the previous night's processing.

Other factors delaying the distribution of daily reports were the additional calculations and reduced photocopying required for the GH06. A new program was developed which was directed to print output to a laser printer and also calculated the necessity for the 'balance to ship per day' figure.

These changes have not only produced a clearer image on the document but also saved the computer operator 15 minutes a day.

In order to monitor the effect of these changes a TQM board was set up at the end of May to record the timing, accuracy and distribution of all reports generated overnight. The original target time for completing the processing and distributions was 10 am but as this time was being achieved 100 per cent in most weeks, the target was changed to 9.45 am. The level of results recorded on the

TQM board with the new target is still encouragingly high and the target will again be reduced within the next two weeks. The cumulative percentage total since May is currently at 97.3 per cent.

We have now incorporated reports generated weekly and monthly and will be taking steps to ensure that similar results are achieved.

The next TQM project will be to apply the same principles to software development and updates. A form has been designed which will be used for specifying precisely what the requirements for software changes are with a written specification from the user. It itemizes the various functions which have to be completed and also requires the originator to sign off the changes as having been tested and conforming to the original specification. It ensures that all aspects of the change are completed, such as cross-referencing and documentation, and also includes a TQM check which requires another programmer to verify that the software coding is correct. All software development projects will be entered onto the 'Milestone' project planner which details each step of the development cycle. Reports showing the current status of scheduled projects will be circulated each week to ensure that progress can be monitored. The implementation of this TQM project is scheduled to commence at the end of October.

In order to ensure that the computer hardware is functioning correctly, TQM charts will be set up to monitor the availability of the system. The first chart will measure the accessibility of the computer within the core time of 7 am to 7 pm. Our initial target is 98 per cent availability and measurements will be taken at specified daily intervals and plotted on the chart to check that the objectives have been met. The same style of chart will be used to monitor screens and printers to ensure that they are connected and functioning correctly. This will also be measured daily and the target is to have 98.5 per cent availability of all peripherals. Both of these projects will be implemented from 10 October.

It will be noted that these reports are dated September 1988, thus illustrating that the Company has now had several years of experience installing the processes of Total Quality Management. Some other factors of these early years of developing the process included the encouragement of operators to be videoed whilst working so that they could study and monitor their own performance; quality familiarization discussions were held for each department; a quality market was introduced to encourage and promote open discussion of key issues and to create an opportunity for problems to be identified and corrected; monthly enquiry meetings are held during which the Managing Director can sit in on any meeting but does not take over the meeting – he can contribute if he makes a request through the Chair.

Training for quality

About 18 months after starting the implementation phase, whilst a considerable amount had been done to get the process working, Ron Scouse had some reservations about the extent to which the opportunities of the approach were being exploited. A feeling that still more effort was required to gain the conviction, commitment and conversion referred to previously prompted the following memorandum.

GATES HYDRAULICS LTD

MEMO

To: See Distribution List   Date: 23 October 1989
From: R.A. Scouse
Copies: A.J. Roberts
             I. Gardiner

TQM – Training for Quality

TQM has been recognized since May 1988 as the way forward to improving quality of product and service, together with improved efficiency. It is fair to say improvements have happened in many areas, but we are only on the fringe of the many opportunities open to the company.

We have not reviewed our progress with current objectives, neither have we prepared TQM objectives for 1990. In November 1988 I suggested we should form a Quality Council, which would be the steering group for the TQM programme and should comprise members of the Operations Committee who should address themselves only to TQM issues. If this were successful it should reduce the need for other committees and meetings.

I do not believe we have real **conviction**, **commitment** or **conversion**.

- **Conviction** comes when the Management Team recognize that 'quality' is really important and decide to bring about quality improvement.
- **Commitment** comes when members of the Management Team decide they want to take actions necessary to bring about quality improvement.
- **Conversion** comes when members of the Management Team are willing to make the pursuit of quality a routine part of the company's operation.

The three C's must be accepted and I suggest we should step back and consider them so far as our operation is concerned. Once they are accepted, we should embark upon a planned programme of training and work experience.

Effective training is particularly important for any TQM programme. The key element is that we cannot produce quality products or services unless we have well-trained and competent staff. Without quality products we can fall into a descending spiral, where we compete only on price, losing inevitably to our competitors. More serious, it creates a poor image, making consumers reluctant to buy and workers reluctant to join.

Nowhere in our business should we tolerate poor quality; and we cannot have quality without trained people to produce and maintain it.

This is where the Operations Committee should come in as a 'ginger' group, looking at the overall scene from a position of experience, identifying any blank areas, 'gingering' all concerned to make good the deficiency and monitoring the results.

Trying to promote plain good sense is inevitably an up-hill struggle. It should not deter any of us. It should be part of our training – of ourselves and our colleagues.

Ron Scouse

Review of progress and the formulation of new objectives for Total Quality Management

Arising from the above memorandum, each of the departments were stimulated into preparing a statement of objectives completed for the period 1988/89, and also a set of improvement objectives for 1990. Some examples of these are outlined below.

Automotive/tube manipulation
Objectives completed 1988/89
Total Quality Management objectives

Tube

(a)   Reorganize Llanelli radiator into cell. Completed by November 1988.
(b)   Regenerate Quality Circles with support from both shifts. Completed March 1989.
(c)   Improve quality and efficiency and elimination of scrap. Ongoing, with the help of Quality Circles and production engineering.

Automotive

(a)   Revise layout of automotive line for Nissan pressure pipes and cooler loops. Completed May 1989.
(b)   Investigate automotive stores area. Completed and in place May 1988.
(c)   Paint floors in working areas with automotive. Completed March 1989.

Automotive/tube manipulation
Total Quality Management objectives – 1990

(a) Move automotive and tube manipulation into one department and look at flowline production for this one area.
(b) Look at the feasibility of moving the CNC tube-bending machines into a cell unit with its own tool stores.
(c) Look at the feasibility of moving the end-forming machines into a cell unit, again with its own tool stores.
(d) The set-up of a controlled area for production fixtures and gauges.
(e) The modernization of CNC tube-bending equipment (Ref: project of S. Corke/D. Hillyard).
(f) The set-up of a cellular unit for the production of Ford Genk parts.
(g) Continuity of crimp date (move to metric only).

Data Processing
Tangible results – 1988/89

(a) The number of calls to the DPM and computer room has reduced considerably.
(b) Response times improved from 4.5 secs to 3–3.5 secs.
(c) Programmers are able to make faster progress with new developments without having to de-bug live applications.
(d) Reduction in movement of peripheries caused by failing units.

Data Processing Departments
TQM targets 1990

Section A
(a) Ensure that daily, weekly and monthly reports are processed, printed and distributed within specified time-scale.
(b) All major files to be purged of redundant records on a regular basis according to monthly schedule.
(c) Software development conforms to TQM principles 'right first time' and any faults are monitored to prevent problems recurring.
(d) All hardware is checked on a regular basis to ensure that it is functioning correctly and that users are fully conversant with its operation.
(e) New developments are only introduced when the users are competent in the operation and control of the new functions.

Section B
(a) Develop and update software that adheres to the principle of 'right first time'.
(b) Ensure that procedures are thoroughly checked before implementation.
(c) Regularly check with users that software meets their requirements and that any faults are reported and rectified.

(d)   Monitor level of reported software faults to ensure 90 per cent of software implemented is 'bug free'.

Section C
All items as above

Section D
(a)   Monitor all daily, weekly and monthly reports and ensure that level of service as depicted on TQM board does not drop below 95 per cent.
(b)   Monitor hardware to ensure that level of 98 per cent availability is maintained and record on TQM board.
(c)   Maintain level of computer consumables to provide 100 per cent availability.
(d)   Maintain record of monthly procedures on TQM board to indicate purge/back-up routines completed on time.

Machine Shop
TQM objectives 1990

(a)   Target for zero defects with the aid of SPC (Statistical Process Control).
(b)   To investigate pre-set tooling with possible implementation.
(c)   Communication with production engineering to assist in new methods of manufacture.
(d)   Maintain and improve housekeeping standards.
(e)   Maintain and improve training standards through ongoing assessment and appraisal.
(f)   Ensure production of piece parts to agreed due dates.
(g)   Productivity to be maintained to pre-determined targets.

Second Operations
TQM objectives 1990

(a)   Training in process quality and safety.
(b)   Minimize waste, aim for zero defects.
(c)   Chart input–output production targets.
(d)   Introduce control charts.
(e)   Housekeeping improvements.

Personnel Department
TQM objectives 1990

(a)   Implementation of a supervisory and management training plan.
(b)   Continue to ensure that all personnel procedures are up to date and in line with company policy.
(c)   Improve links with outside agencies with reference to the expected decline in labour availability in the 1990s.

(d)   Investigate alternative methods of supplying our recruitment needs.
(e)   Total implementation of COSHH Regulations and revision of all company safety procedures.

Plant Services
TQM objectives 1990

(a)   Rationalize maintenance stores and establish records of spare parts. Complete May 1990.
(b)   Extend planned maintenance programme to encompass Hose Assembly Department. Fully operational August 1990.
(c)   Planned maintenance programme on CNC benders. Fully operational January 1990.
(d)   Update asset register and fit identity plates to each asset. Complete December 1989.

Brazing Department
TQM objectives 1990

(a)   Introduce quality monitoring and production target graphs.
(b)   Liaise with planning department to improve customer service through weekly set programme.
(c)   Apply Quality Circle problem-solving techniques to key-in process problems.
(d)   Introduce line process manufacture to high-volume runs to reduce lead times and further improve furnace loading.
(e)   Liaise with Engineering Departments to improve brazing techniques.
(f)   Provide training in quality techniques for all Department personnel.

It would seem from this outline of Total Quality Management objectives for each of the departments that considerable efforts are being made to improve the competitiveness of the organization and to make it more efficient and effective in the European market place. It is too early, however, to demonstrate the extent to which each of these objectives has been met.

Areas of responsibility for Quality Management

The current structure is outlined in Fig. 2.5.1. Underpinning this structure, the company philosophy regarding quality is that each person is responsible for the quality and service of the job which he/she operates or undertakes – each being a manager of his/her own process and accountable for the results. This philosophy is seen to service the main objective of customer serviceability, whether the customers are internal or external to the organization.

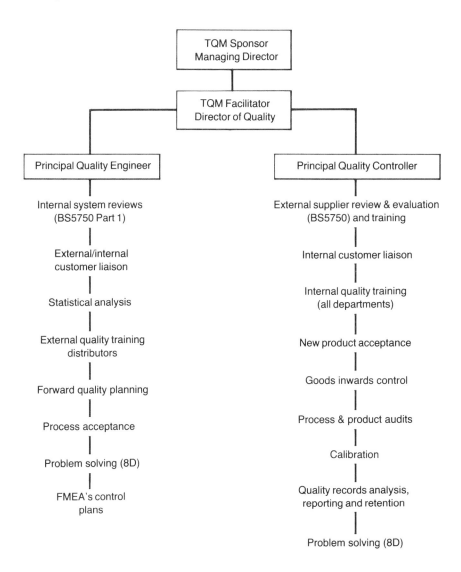

Fig. 2.5.1   Organization chart – quality management

Meetings to support the TQM strategy

Another element of the implementation strategy for Total Quality Management is the series of meetings which support the process. Operations Staff (Board of Directors) meet three times a month to review what has been achieved and what actions are needed to generate further requirements. The plans are then discussed with the remainder of the staff. Once a month there is an Operations Committee Meeting to discuss issues related to either France, the United Kingdom or Germany on a rotating basis. Management are then briefed on the outcome of these meetings and these briefing sessions provide opportunities for the attendees to speak about their successes and failures.

Other meetings include a monthly meeting of managers to discuss requirements and performance of internal customers and internal suppliers, customer relationships, and investigating new business. In acting as a co-ordinator between customer and supplier, Gates has offered consultancy on Statistical Process Control techniques to its suppliers to improve their ability to supply Gates with quality products. In addition a link-up has been established between the Production Manager and Sales personnel on the one hand and the customer on the other to follow through the customer's order to its ultimate distribution. Again, as part of the strategy to foster closer customer relationships, arrangements are made for groups of staff to meet the customers. Sales managers meet regularly and have full sales meetings two to three times a year. There are also international marketing meetings once a year, focusing on production requirements, quality levels and service levels. These annual meetings have a worldwide input embracing the USA, Canada and Europe.

Results of the strategy

At the time of writing, it is approximately two-and-a-half years since the three-year Total Quality Management Strategy was initiated within the Gates Hydraulic company at St Neots. Many of the initial problems have now been overcome and the general consensus amongst the management team is that the primary objective of increasing the company's competitiveness in advance of the creation of the Single European Market is going to be achieved. Already there are indications of this improved competitiveness in the form of more on-time deliveries and acceptable prices leading to increased business potential. Customers have recognized the importance of the strategy and now Gates have been invited to act as consultants to some of their customers. Ron Scouse describes customer reaction as 'Good – purring with approval'.

In the production area, process improvement has become an ongoing activity – it is never static and Gates is moving more towards automated methods of production. One outcome of the Total Quality Management approach is a change in the policy of storing parts. Now they have reorganized this sector so that parts are delivered direct to the processor, thus saving on storage space, energy and staffing. This has brought about a reduction in inventory. For the future, the company is moving towards a 'making it to order' policy with a view of achieving a 'Just-in-Time' (JIT) system.

The European Corporation Division maintains that Total Quality Management will be mandatory throughout the European organization and emphasis will be placed on measuring and improving performance by individual plants on a corporate basis. Ron Scouse, the Quality Director, recognizes that measuring performance has been, until recently, one of the weaknesses in the implementation of the process. However, each and every department within the Gates plant is now measuring its own performance and these measurements are being reviewed by the Board of Directors on a continuous basis. An example of this, within the Product Development area, is that the Department practise 'competitive bench- marking' as part of their process in order to assess their own product performance against their competitors'.

Future developments

Gates Hydraulics, as we have seen, is part of the Gates Corporation in the USA. It is not surprising, therefore, that developments in one part of the Corporation influence developments in another. In a recent edition (September 1990) of the Corporation's newspaper *Spectrum*, which provides worldwide news for Gates employees, an article entitled 'Shareholders discuss TQM plans criteria' outlined an update to shareholders by the Administration Vice President of the Gates Rubber Company, on the Rubber Company's Total Quality Management effort. An extract from the article is summarized below.

'Quality no longer focuses just on product manufacturing. In the world-class business arena the focus must broaden to include the total business environment. Quality must permeate the services as well as the products that Gates provides and it must encompass both internal and external customers. The process is called Total Quality Management, or TQM.'

To accompany this, Gates Rubber Operations has decided to base its TQM strategies on the criteria for the Malcolm Baldridge Quality Award. This award was created by US public law in 1987. It is named after Malcolm Baldridge who served as Secretary for Commerce from 1981 to his death in 1987. Past winners include Globe Metallurgical, Motorola, Commercial Nuclear Fuel of Westinghouse Electric, Xerox Business Products & Systems and Milliken. Many of these companies have experienced dramatic turnarounds after subscribing to TQM.

The seven Baldridge criteria are:

- leadership;
- information and analysis;
- strategic quality planning;
- human resource utilization;
- quality assurance of products and services;
- quality results;
- customer satisfaction.

The article in *Spectrum* spells out in more detail the requirements under each of these headings and goes on to describe the implications for the Gates Rubber Company. It concludes:

'This is a major undertaking. Full TQM implementation will be a three to five year process – a new Gates Rubber Company should emerge. We will be more responsive to customers' needs and we will supply higher quality products. Our operations will be more cost effective and our employees will be more productive and challenged with greater responsibility. More importantly, our customers will be satisfied. We are pursuing this quest because the Gates Rubber Company is committed to excellence.'

Operating with this cultural framework and with the other strategies and policy decisions which have been outlined above, Gates Hydraulics is proving that it is making a positive response to the challenge of competing in the Single European Market.

Questions/discussion topics

1. To what extent do you think the adoption of a TQM strategy by Gates Hydraulics Ltd is an effective response to the impact of the Single European Market?

2. In what way is the response of Gates Hydraulics Ltd to the Single European Market any different from its response to other global markets?

3. In what other ways could Gates Hydraulics have responded to the pressures of the Single European Market?

4. From your reading of this case how do you think Total Quality Management would be defined by Gates Hydraulics Ltd?

5. What do you consider to be the main elements in the Total Quality Management strategy that Gates Hydraulics have adopted?

6. Identify what you believe are the main strengths and weaknesses of Gates' approach to Total Quality Management.

7. What would you have done differently if you were:
   (a) the Managing Director?
   (b) the Director of Quality?

8. What should the company do next?

Case 6
Greater Peterborough Training and Enterprise Council (GPtec) – A study of a training response to the Single Market[*]

Jill Preston

Advice to readers

In Part 1 it was noted that the EC has identified vocational training as a major factor in the successful completion of the Single Market. In 1989 the EC Commission's Report *Employment in Europe* identified a number of training needs, for example, skills resulting from technological change and multiple competences required in management training. It is generally accepted that the UK is lagging behind many countries of the EC in terms of both education standards being achieved and the training provided for people in work. British companies spend about 0.15 per cent of earnings on training compared to six times that amount in France, Germany and Japan. Lack of competences ties too many British factories to outdated technology.

In France and Germany education and training have been identified as the cornerstones of an effective response to 1992. By contrast, the UK has been slow to wake up to the training implications of the Single Market. Figure 2.6.1 shows the participation rates of 16–18-year olds in education and training in the UK, France, Germany, Italy, Japan and the USA.

In the UK the extent and quality of training will become increasingly important if companies are going to compete successfully with European organizations in an increasingly competitive home market, or if they are going to expand their operations into other Member States. Of equal concern is the fact that the UK is facing increased competition from the wider world, most notably the Pacific Basin. A country such as India is

* I should like to express my thanks to Lynda Purser, Chief Executive of Greater Peterborough Training and Enterprise Council (GPtec), and her staff for the help given during the writing of this case study.

viewed as having an educational system as good as most European countries but its average wage rates are about 25 per cent lower, hence industrial costs are lower.

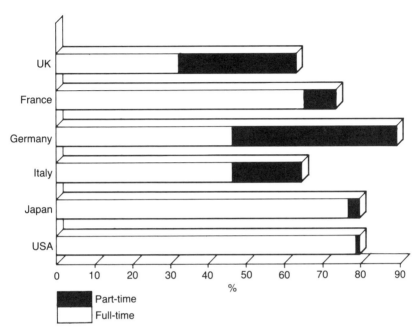

Fig. 2.6.1   Comparison of 16–18-year olds in education and training 1986

The Training and Enterprise Councils (TECs) are the latest attempt by the UK Government to reform the training system. A key function of the TECs is that they are to act as catalysts to encourage local employers to invest more in training as part of their overall business strategy. Part of the remit of the TECs is to develop training for the Single Market.

This case study describes how, in the general context of UK training policy, GPtec is developing a response to the training requirements of the 1990s, including training for the Single Market.

Readers should consider some of the general issues identified in the study, for example, the advantages and disadvantages of an employer-led training response; the possible tensions existing between an enterprise and a Civil Service culture within a TEC, and an evaluation of GPtec's developing European strategy.

Introduction

The UK's response to the training implications of the Single Market

Across Europe traditional employment and career patterns are changing and this will have a number of consequences for the skills needed to enter and to stay in work. The EC displays high levels of unemployment, especially amongst the young, and yet, at the same time, there are severe skill shortages in certain sectors.

For UK companies the Single Market raises three separate but related issues. Firstly, the increased training requirements resulting from greater competition from other Member States. Secondly, the training needs relating more specifically to Single Market legislation. Thirdly, knowledge about business practices in other Member States.

By the end of the 1980s there was much evidence to suggest that many areas of British business, especially the small- and medium-sized companies, were failing to respond to the needs of the Single Market. One factor in this failure has been the varied and uncoordinated responses by UK government departments. For example, in 1990 the Department of Trade and Industry (DTI) launched its new training support programme on '1992' for intermediaries such as trade associations and chambers of commerce. The Employment Department established European units for further education, which were followed in 1990 by the Department of Education and Science's 'PICKUP Europe' scheme to improve the effectiveness of further and higher education in Single Market training. An issue behind the low-key response of the Department of Education and Science to Single Market issues was the use of the sovereignty argument to keep issues of education reform separate from EC policy. For example, the British Government was obstructionist towards the LINGUA Programme, the EC's languages initiative. Yet, education measures are central to creating a demand for training.

Training and Enterprise Councils (TECs)

The proposal to establish TECs was originally put forward in the Government's White Paper *Employment for the 1990s* (Department of Employment, 1988). The need to overcome Britain's skills shortages in the light of the impending shortage of school leavers and heightened competition associated with the deregulation of the European market are major themes. The basic prescription of the Government was to create an employer-dominated framework for training at national, industry and local levels. The Government has opted for a decentralist approach to training in an attempt to get the support of industry as well as to obtain targeted high-quality training for specific sectors as opposed to training which, in the 1970s, was more concerned with unemployment than specific skills issues.

Nationally the Government established the National Training Task Force, largely consisting of leading figures from business, to advise the Secretary of State for Employment on training matters, including the establishment of a network of TECs. In April 1991 its role was expanded to include the assessment of TEC performances against local and national objectives.

The White Paper of 1986 left the training needs of industrial sectors to employers but recommended that they adhered to the work of the National Council for Vocational Qualifications (NCVQ). The NCVQ is in the process of establishing national standards for vocational training. The aim is that all training will be categorized into one of five categories, from Level One which covers pre-vocational training to Level Five which includes post-graduate and professional qualifications.

At the local level the White Paper proposed the establishment of about 100 TECs, with the responsibility to plan and deliver training and to promote and support the development of small businesses. This activity was to entail the adaptation of national programmes to meet local needs. National training programmes include: Enterprise Training (ET) for unemployed adults; Youth Training (YT) for young people; and the administration of business support schemes such as the Enterprise Allowance Scheme (EAS), the Small Firms Service (SFS) and the Business Growth through Training Scheme (BGTS).

In 1989 Michael Howard, Secretary of State for Employment, stated that the TECs were to be based on four key principles:

- having a local focus;
- being employer-led;
- having real power to make decisions;
- striving to encourage excellence with reward linked to performance.

Interested parties in the regions were invited to discuss the formation of a TEC with the appropriate Regional Director of the Training Agency

(TA). Once a proposal was finalized, it went forward for development funding. Development work involved preparing a three-year corporate plan.

In 1990 the TA was abolished and some of its functions were taken over by the newly-created Training Enterprise and Education Division (TEED) of the Employment Department. Later in 1990, the Government set out its thinking on the role the TECs (Department of Employment *1990s The Skill Decade*):

- to encourage employers to invest more effectively in training;
- to raise the levels of skills and qualifications of young people;
- to encourage individuals to take more responsibility for their own development;
- to improve the opportunities for the unemployed and disadvantaged;
- to work with the providers of education and training;
- to foster self-employment and small-business growth.

A major theme of *1990s The Skill Decade* is that the manner in which each TEC responds to these ideas must depend on its assessment of local needs and priorities.

The White Paper *Education and Training in the 21st Century*, published in May 1991, stated that at the heart of the reforms of post-16 education and training, is the recognition that vocational training should be given equal status to academic education. In addition, the Government aims to establish national standards for vocational training through National Vocational Qualifications (NVQs). It is expected that the TECs will play a major role in these developments.

By May 1991, 76 TECs were in operation in England and Wales, and by the end of 1991 it is estimated that all 82 TECs should be in operation. The TECs operate under contract to TEED and as part of their contract they are required to produce an annual business plan. In Scotland there are 22 Local Enterprise Companies (LECs), with a similar group of functions.

Organization of the TECs

The TECs are companies limited by guarantee. They are managed by Boards of which two-thirds, including the chair, are senior local employers and the remaining members are senior figures from local education, voluntary bodies and trade unions. The Board's function is strategic rather than representative and directors are appointed as individuals, not as representatives of their employing organizations – the only direct financial reward is out of pocket expenses. Most TECs have set up some system of advisory groups or panels.

Each year the Employment Department identifies certain strategic priorities to be addressed by the TECs. For example, for 1992/3, these priorities are likely to include:

- the setting of targets for the number of local businesses making a commitment to become investors in people, this is a national standard to raise employer commitment to training;
- adult credit vouchers or individual training account arrangements for appropriate services provided by TECs;
- plans for promoting NVQs to employers.

Functions of the TECs

(a) Analyse local labour market trends to establish where additional skills are required.
(b) To develop a business plan defining the TEC's role and vision, training and enterprise priorities and measurable performance objectives.
(c) Managing training and enterprise programmes, with the scope to adapt these to local needs and develop new projects and activities.
(d) Encourage local employers to invest more in training, as part of their business strategy.
(e) Liaise with schools and colleges to raise skill levels.
(f) Act as a forum for business.

The Corporate Plan produced by each TEC describes how these functions will be carried out. The Plan also forms the basis of the annually-renewed three-year management contract between the TECs and TEED. Studies would suggest that the place of European issues in most Corporate Plans is not very prominent or secure.

Staffing

Staff from the former Training Agency area offices were made available to the new TECs on a secondment basis. TECs may recruit outside the former TA if there are no suitable secondees, otherwise they have to pay for staff from their own resources. In the first instance, TEC staff are contracted for three years, it seems likely that some could be tempted away from the profession. The TECs had to appoint a full-time Chief Executive and they were strongly encouraged to consider the former local TA manager for the post. However, a number of TECs have appointed external candidates, the argument being that this makes the TEC more market-orientated. Performance bonuses can be paid to staff.

Funding

The precise budget of each TEC depends on its size and economic conditions. At the outset the Government made it clear that no new money would be made available to TECs. Since then it has considerably reduced public funding for training in the hope that additional private sector funding will be forthcoming. The budget for 1990/1 is £300m less than in 1989/90, and by 1992/3 public investment will amount to £2.8bn.

Government financial support for the TECs is divided into five blocks:

(a) **Employment Training** – to help unemployed people gain skills for the job market.
(b) **Youth Training** – directed at young people to enable them to obtain vocational qualifications and a job; emphasis is being put on enabling young people to obtain a Level Two NVQ qualification. Youth Training (YT) is the largest programme in this area.
(c) **Growth and enterprise** – to assist small company start-ups and expanding businesses. The Enterprise Allowance Scheme (EAS) helps unemployed people to set up their own businesses. The Business Growth Training Scheme (BGT) supports training in new or established companies, for example, business skills for owner-managers.
(d) **Management budget** – to assist with the administration costs of a TEC.
(e) **The Local Initiative Fund** – this funding is available for innovatory activities. For example, it can be used to stimulate further business education partnerships in a locality as well as providing advice and information centres. In the first year of operation, £250,000 was available for each TEC.

From April 1991 full Government funding has been dependent on training outcomes. For example, a TEC receives only 75 per cent of its funds for delivery, the rest of Youth Training or Employment Training funding depends on outcomes such as obtaining a job or an occupational qualification such as an NVQ Level Two. Output-related funding is applied to payments made by TECs to the training providers. The TECs are being encouraged to institute quality measures and a number are examining the relevance of BS5750 and Total Quality Management approaches.

As a company, a TEC can generate its own income, for example, by sponsorship and membership schemes. For the first year of operation the Government has indicated that it is prepared to match finance from other sources up to a ceiling of £125,000. To a limited degree, the TECs can transfer resources from one block to another and carry over expenditure between financial years.

There is a need for the TECs to represent their interests to the Secretary of State for Employment, individual chairs can contact the Minister but this does not have the force of a united approach. The Group of Ten was formed by the TECs in 1991 to act as a sounding board; each of the ten regions in England and Wales is represented in the Group.

Greater Peterborough

The Greater Peterborough area covers north Cambridgeshire and south Lincolnshire; it has four main centres of population, Peterborough, Stamford, Wisbech and March (see Fig. 2.6.2).

The area is one of the fastest growing regions in the UK, although economic growth has been reduced by the recession of 1990/1. The population of Greater Peterborough was approximately 342,000 in 1990 and is expected to rise to about 358,000 by 1995. In line with the rest of the country, fewer young people will be entering the job market in the mid-1990s. This means that the majority of those who will make up the labour force in the year 2000 are already at work.

During the development phase of GPtec in 1990, a number of local economic surveys were carried out. At that time unemployment was 3 per cent in Stamford, 5 per cent in Peterborough and 8 per cent in Wisbech, the latter being above the national average. By June 1991 these figures had risen to 5.5 per cent in Stamford, 8 per cent in Peterborough and 9 per cent in Wisbech. It should be noted that the method of calculation had changed during this period and it is generally felt that these figures understate the true level of unemployment.

Seventeen per cent of the population of Greater Peterborough is from an ethnic minority background. Ninety per cent of companies in the area employ less than 25 people. Traditionally, engineering has been an important sector but the 1980s saw the development of a highly significant service-orientated sector concentrating on finance and insurance. A number of major organizations, such as Pearl Assurance and the Royal Insurance Group, relocated to Peterborough from London. It is estimated

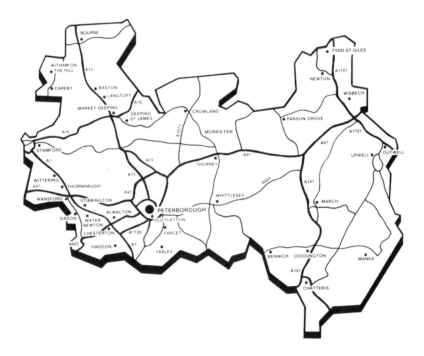

Fig. 2.6.2   GPtec area

that the financial sector will continue to grow during the 1990s and for this to happen a skilled work force is vital.

Greater Peterborough contains the prosperous agricultural areas of the Fens, but this could be greatly affected by the proposed changes in the EC's Common Agricultural Policy, including the reduction in financial support. Employment in agriculture is declining but there is an increase in demand for labour in food processing. Therefore, there is an urgent need to diversify and to bring an enterprise culture to Fenland. These developments have important implications for new skills training.

Skills shortages in the area

In the GPtec area over 45 per cent of the 16-year olds continue their education into sixth forms or further education colleges as opposed to approximately 38 per cent nationally. Colleges are located at Peterborough, Stamford and Wisbech but there is no provision for higher education above HND level in the area, although first-year degree programmes are being franchised by Peterborough Regional College.

By the end of the 1980s the area was beginning to be affected by skills shortages, especially in managerial, professional, technical and craft areas. In spite of the recession of 1990/1, it is estimated that demand for these skills is likely to increase during the 1990s and training is one way of easing the skills shortage problem.

Skill shortages identified by GPtec include: office administration, especially computing and keyboard skills; hotel and catering cooks and chefs; hairdressing; and engineering and motor trades skills up to NVQ Level Two.

Evidence would suggest that there is only limited knowledge of Single Market issues within the business community in the region.

Establishing GPtec

Originally, the Employment Department expected that the whole of the County of Cambridgeshire would be covered by one TEC. The Department researched within the business communities of the county and a county-wide steering group was formed. This group met on a number of occasions to put together a bid for development funding. However, there was a split in this group; strong feelings had been expressed by business people especially from the Peterborough and March areas that if a county-wide TEC was established, 'Peterborough as always would be the poor relative, in comparison to Cambridge'. The Peterborough Development Agency along with David Burrell of Wisbech, David Clayton and Ian Williamson of Stamford, were prime movers in developing a separate proposal for the Greater Peterborough area. Although hoping for a county-wide bid, the Employment Department agreed to give development funding of £100,000 for one year, for a TEC to be developed in the Greater Peterborough area.

A Development Team was established to put together a bid for the establishment of a TEC. This included a Corporate Plan as well as a Business Plan and the identification of suitable premises. Two members of this group were in effect seconded by the local office of the Training Agency to assist in this work, Jim Burns and Nigel Clemson.

The Secretary of State approved that GPtec should be established. The Board appointed Lynda Purser as Chief Executive in January 1991. She joined the TEC from KPMG Peat Marwick McLintock, where she led the higher education consultancy. Formerly, she had been Deputy Director of a polytechnic as well as having close connections with both the private and public sectors, having worked on projects for British Aerospace and Thorn EMI. GPtec was launched in February 1991

GPtec – strategy and organization

'To evolve partnerships within the Greater Peterborough area which will bring about economic growth and prosperity through investment in people.'
The GPtec Mission statement

'GPtec's role is essentially an enabling one – in partnership with the local community, using locally-inspired initiatives to help local people reach their potential.'
Lynda Purser

The strategic objectives of GPtec are as follows:

One – to assist employers to take action to invest in the skills and potential of their work force.
Two – to increase the pool of suitably trained and motivated labour available to take advantage of local employment opportunities.
Three – to increase the success rate of new businesses and to improve the growth potential of existing ones.
Four – to improve the links between business and education.

Action

GPtec delivers programmes through a network of training providers, including local colleges as well as private sector organizations. It develops initiatives to achieve strategic objectives, these include using national programmes to respond to local needs. These policies are implemented in the following ways for each strategic objective.

Strategic Objective One

GPtec aims to increase the number of medium-sized companies (those employing 25–200 people) having formal company training plans from 35 to 45 per cent over a three-year period. It aims to enlist 75 medium-sized companies in the 'Investors in People' campaign by 1993.

Strategic Objective Two

To improve the effectiveness of the Employment Training (ET) and Youth Training (YT) programmes in the area is a major feature of Objective Two. Less than 2 per cent of local companies use ET. GPtec is also considering developing a scheme which will link a training-credits scheme with ET. In the area of youth training the TEC aims to increase the number of trainees gaining NVQ qualifications.

Marketing activities are directed at increasing the number of employers taking part in the scheme, and customized training is being promoted to help employers address their recruitment problems. To increase the size of the labour force, GPtec is also encouraging employers to recruit from current sources of under-utilized labour such as the disabled, women returners, and those from ethnic minorities. Within the YT programme, 20 per cent of available provision is set aside for trainees with special needs.

GPtec only contracts training providers who have achieved a minimum Approved Training Organization standard. To assist them to provide training related more directly to local market needs, the TEC organizes quarterly meetings to brief them on labour market trends.

In 1991 GPtec commissioned a report which identified the existing guidance and counselling services within the GPtec area and recognized gaps in provision.

Strategic Objective Three

Estimates suggest that about a quarter of all new businesses fail within the first two years. GPtec is using the Enterprise Allowance Scheme (EAS) and the Business Growth Training Scheme (BGT) to assist both start-up and developing businesses. The assistance available ranges from open-learning workbooks designed for someone starting a new business, to a range of services offered by experienced business counsellors through GPtec's Business Counselling and Enquiry Service; it keeps a registry of business consultants. In addition, companies wanting to improve their management development structures will be eligible for financial assistance on a matching basis, to agreed limits.

GPtec intends to provide an information service on opportunities arising from changing markets. GPtec's Enterprise and Small Business Advisory Group plays an important role in implementing this objective.

Strategic Objective Four

A Business/Education Advisory Group has been established to look at the best way that GPtec can become involved in facilitating links. For example, it disseminates good practice in business–education links to groups of local employers. In 1992 the TEC will establish a database of local labour market information for use by schools and colleges in curriculum design and planning. GPtec is responsible for the Work-Related Further Education (WRFE) initiation in the area. A major aim of many vocational courses in further education is to prepare students for the world of work, the WRFE scheme provides funding for courses with a strong job-related element. In addition, this scheme encourages colleges to keep a close eye on local labour market needs. For example, if there is an under-supply of people with word processing skills and an over-supply of plumbers, funding would be used to encourage the development of word-processing courses and to reduce the training provision for plumbers.

Aims

In volume terms the TEC expects to have about 1,850 YTS trainees and 550 ET trainees. Over a one-year period they would expect to assist 135 business start-ups, and provide business development grants to a further 15 to 25 companies.

Single Market issues are not addressed in the Corporate Plan.

The Board

By composition the Board aims to provide geographical coverage, sector representation and representation of the wider community. Chaired by Philip Salisbury, the Managing Director of a local engineering company, the Board is composed of nine businessmen; two educationalists, including the warden of the Centre for Multi-cultural Education; the manager of the local office of the Citizens' Advice Bureau; a trade unionist and the Chief Executive. According to the Chief Executive, GPtec has had some difficulty in identifying 'an appropriate trade union representative'.

The following is a list of the Board members of GPtec as of February 1991:

Roger Ali Warden, Peterborough Centre for Multi-cultural Education.

A local magistrate, he is an Associate of Homerton College, Cambridge and a Fellow of the Royal Anthropological Institute. Mr Ali was a member of the MSC Area Manpower Board for Cambridgeshire and Bedfordshire.

David Burall Chairman and Managing Director of Burall Brothers Ltd, Wisbech.

A past president of the East Anglian Alliance of the British Printing Industry's Federation, he serves on the Information and Technology Committee of the Printing Industry's Research Association.

Mr Burall is Chairman of FenBET – the Fenland Business and Enterprise Trust.

David Clayton Chairman and Managing Director of Whitworth's Prepared Produce and Bravi BV Holland.

He is Managing Director of Whitworth's Produce Ltd – a subsidiary of Booker PLC.

Mr Clayton is also a director of Booker Belmont Wholesale Ltd, Slade End Farms Ltd, and Curf Farms Chatteris Ltd.

John Durance Equity partner in Ruddle Wilkinson Partnership.

He is a non-executive director of Peterborough Health Authority and a member of the governing council of the Steering Committee of the Centre for Urban Studies in Peterborough.

Mr Durance is a past president of Peterborough Rotary Club and a past chairman of Peterborough and District Local Employer Network.

Tony Gilroy Managing Director, Perkins Engines Group Ltd, Peterborough.

He is a member of the CBI Eastern Region Council and is a director of Varity Holdings Ltd, Perkins Engines Ltd, Perkins Engines Ltd, Perkins Engines (Shrewsbury) Ltd, L Gardner and Sons Ltd, Moteurs Perkins SA, France, Motori Perkins SA, Italy and Perkins Engines Inc. USA.

Tony Harding Represents the small-business sector.

He is Managing Director and co-founder of Advanced Handling Ltd, materials handling equipment manufacturers based in Market Deeping.

Geoffrey Morris Chief Education Officer, Cambridgeshire County Council.

He took his degree at Cambridge and started his career in teaching in Bordeaux, later entering the administrative side of education.

Mr Morris became Chief Education Officer for Cambridgeshire in 1976.

John Peake Chairman of Nene Park Trust.

He is a former Chairman of Baker Perkins PLC and the CBI Education and Training Committee, and was a commissioner for the MSC and Training Commission.

Mr Peake is currently chairman of the RSA Examinations Board, BTEC Advisory Board for Engineering and the Design Council Education Committee.

Lynda Purser Chief Executive GPtec.

She joined the TEC in December 1990 from KPMG Peat Marwick McLintock, where she led the higher education consultancy.

Born in Sheffield, Ms Purser obtained a first-class degree in biochemistry at Leeds University. She taught in a comprehensive school before moving into higher education as Humberside Polytechnic's deputy director.

Lynda Rowbotham Manager, Citizens' Advice Bureau, Peterborough.

Trained as a solicitor, she was Head of Business Studies at Peterborough Regional College and is now a part-time lecturer on the subject at the college.

Ms Rowbotham is a director of the National Association of Citizens' Advice Bureaux, honorary national legal adviser to the Alzheimer's Disease Society, and a Women's Legal Defence Fund member.

Philip Salisbury Chairman of GPtec.

He is Managing Director of Peter Brotherhood Ltd, and an executive committee member of the Mid-Anglian branch of the Engineering Employers Federation.

A Peterborough city councillor, Mr Salisbury is involved in the Science and Engineering Research Council teaching company scheme at Cambridge University.

Ron Seddon Regional officer for the Inland Revenue Staff Federation.

He is the full-time official representing about 4,000 Inland Revenue Staff Federation members in the region and is a member of East Anglia TUC.

Ian Williamson Managing Director of Newage International (Stamford) Ltd.

An engineer and technologist by training, he is Governor of Stamford College and active in encouraging school–industry links in the Stamford and Bourne areas.

Ian Worner Director and Chief General Manager (corporate services) of Pearl Assurance PLC, Peterborough.

He is a certified public accountant and holds a Bachelor of Commerce degree.

Mr Worner is a member of the Australian Associated Society of Accountants, the Australian Insurance Institute and the Chartered Institute of Managers.

The main aim of the Board is to develop policy at the strategic level but at times there are difficulties. According to the Chief Executive, each member of the Board is dynamic and powerful in his/her own environment, but '. . . the difficulties relate to developing an appreciation of their roles within this new situation. Genuine debate on most issues is limited, I have to see each one of them individually.'

Communication and consultation with the region is viewed as vital for the success of the GPtec. To develop partnerships with the local community, three business forums have been established across the

Greater Peterborough area. At least two GPtec Directors are active in each. The main function of the forums is to inform the TEC of industry's needs at a grass-roots level; it also gives the Board feedback about progress. The forums, which are centred on Peterborough, Stamford and March, are composed of business people and those directly involved in training; there are few representatives from the wider community.

Management structure

GPtec has approximately 27 staff, the majority of whom are secondees from the former Training Agency. In mid-1991 the Chief Executive negotiated with the Employment Department and the Board to bring in several people who were not Civil Service employees. In terms of management structure, the Chief Executive has limited autonomy, for example, she is faced with the problem of not having a senior management tier in the organizational hierarchy (see Fig. 2.6.3). The Employment Department has a control over the establishment of the TECs. As most of the staff at GPtec are civil servants on secondment, it is not surprising that their enterprise expertise and experience is limited.

The TECs are limited in terms of changing their establishments, but they are less restricted when it comes to consultants and secondees from outside the Civil Service, although funding can be an issue. At GPtec the Chief Executive is using 'long-term' consultants and external secondees to supplement in-house expertise and experience. One consultant who has extensive industrial experience, as well as a background in higher education, has been contracted to develop business–education relationships, especially the Accreditation of Prior Learning (APL) and the development of a training-credits scheme. He is also concerned with developing a Total Quality Management system for GPtec.

In the area of European developments, two consultants have been appointed to develop and implement a European strategy. In addition, Lynda Purser has appointed a consultant, with business experience at senior level, to carry out research projects. For example, one project is to identify facilities in the region to enable people with domestic responsibilities to return to the labour market. GPtec also uses the services of a public relations consultant.

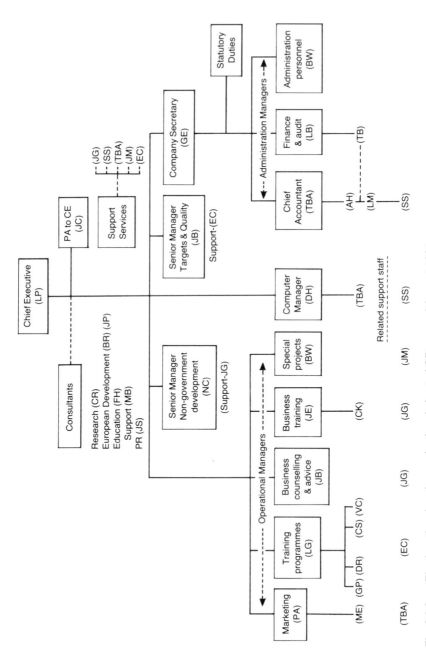

Fig. 2.6.3   The functional and organizational chart of GPtec as of August 1991

Communications with the local community

Effective channels of communication are regarded as essential for the success of GPtec. The three business forums play an important role in this respect. A number of advisory groups have been established, for example, the enterprise advisory group, the ethnic minority advisory group, the GPtec market intelligence group and the industry/education group. The economic development officers at Cambridgeshire County Council, Peterborough District Council and Fenland District Council have formed a market intelligence group, and GPtec has established good contacts with them. In addition, a wide range of informal networks are being established.

GPtec circulates a quarterly newsletter and it has a 15-minute slot on BBC Radio Peterborough once every three weeks. The staff from the TEC have given presentations to a wide range of organizations in the area to explain the aims and function of the organization.

Funding issues and the pricing of products

In line with other TECs, GPtec is faced with the major problem of funding constraints imposed by the Employment Department. In the area of pricing of courses GPtec is facing the problem that prices negotiated by the former Training Agency were too low. To make a European comparison, an alternative way of funding training is to levy on the payroll of companies, a system which is used in French and Germany. GPtec's funding for two four-week accounting periods in 1990/1 are shown in Table 2.6.1.

Table 2.6.1   GPtec's budgets (£)

		1990/1	*1991/2*
Block 1	Youth Training	0.457m	4.12m
Block 2	Employment Training (adults)	0.137m	1.456m
Block 3	Business start-up & development	0.042m	0.576m
Block 4	Admininistration/ running costs	nil	0.308m
Block 5	Local Initiative Fund	0.076m	0.676m
Total		**0.712m**	**7.918m**

The figures for 1990/1 are for two four-week accounting periods only at the end of the financial year March 1991.

Competitors

In the Peterborough area there are other providers of training and business support, for example, the local authorities, the Chamber of Commerce and the Peterborough Development Agency. A number of these organizations see GPtec as a threat because of the size of its budget. However, GPtec's Chief Executive views these organizations as partners, not competitors.

During 1991 each of these organizations offered some type of Single Market seminar and/or workshop. Good working relationships have been established with three further education colleges in the area.

New products and new customers

A major objective of GPtec is to identify and respond to local needs. The Board has stated that the development of new courses and projects in the area requires good marketing expertise based on the concept of consumer-orientated products – the training voucher scheme is an expression of this approach. But the cultural background of the majority of its staff does not help GPtec to become consumer-orientated in terms of new product development. Marketing expertise is required to identify new markets as well as the marketing of courses.

The evolving European strategy

There is little reference to Single Market issues in either GPtec's Corporate Plan or its Business Plan, for 1991/2. In April 1991 the Chief Executive initiated the development of a European strategy to assist companies and training providers in the region to prepare for the Single Market. Lynda Purser saw that 'Europe should be integrated into many of the activities of companies in the region'. Of equal importance to GPtec, the Chief Executive viewed the EC as a source of funding for businesses in the region as well as for the TEC itself.

To overcome the lack of European knowledge amongst the permanent staff, the Chief Executive appointed two consultants to develop and implement the European strategy. The first, Bruce Reed, head of European Economic Development Services Ltd, drew up a report 'to consider the applicability of EC policies, programmes and funds, to identify areas of activity and projects for EC funding and to recommend ways to take advantage of EC funds, to further the activities of GPtec.'

The report identifies a range of EC programmes which could assist GPtec to implement its overall strategy. A number of EC objectives in the area of training and enterprise are very similar to the TEC's strategic objectives. A major theme of the report is that funding applications must be 'strategy-led not funding-led'.

A major training priority of the EC is to assist certain groups to acquire skills and join or rejoin the labour market. These groups include: the long-term unemployed; young people disadvantaged in the labour market; women; disabled people; ethnic minorities and people in small- and medium-sized companies affected by economic and technological change. The EC has a number of programmes which give financial support to participants. These programmes include:

- COMETT, which encourages partnerships between higher education and industry in the area of high technology;
- FORCE, which is concerned with continuing vocational training;
- HORIZON, which focuses on the needs of the disabled;
- LINGUA, which is the Community's languages initiative;
- PETRA, which is aimed at enabling young people to receive at least one year's vocational training on leaving school;
- the European Social Fund which supports training for particular groups of workers and potential workers, such as women returners and the long-term unemployed.

EC enterprise policies are concerned with encouraging industrial competitiveness, supporting the development of small- and medium-sized enterprises and helping companies of all sizes to adapt to the changing needs of the Single Market. The EC also supports a range of R&D programmes in which companies and institutes can participate.

EC funding is highly competitive and many of the programmes require partners in other Member States. For this reason Bruce Reed's report suggested that GPtec should give some priority to the development of European networks, by, for example, building on the networks already established by town-twinning arrangements.

The report recommended that GPtec should concentrate on a number of areas, including:

- training for enterprise, to give people starting their own companies the skills needed to survive and develop;
- management training on how to thrive in an increasingly competitive environment;
- training for 1992, to deal with the threats of increased competition and the acquisition of skills to seize opportunities;
- increasing the pool of trained labour, by training women and people with a disadvantage or a handicap.

The report also recommended that GPtec should concentrate on four locally important sectors which are likely to be affected by various EC policies including the Single Market programme:

- agriculture, food processing and food marketing;
- engineering;
- financial services;
- tourism.

In addition, the report suggested that companies in the Greater Peterborough area should look at the opportunities provided by the Community's R&D programmes. The EC puts out to tender a range of R&D schemes and companies, research institutes and institutions of higher education can participate on a cost-sharing basis.

GPtec is beginning to act as an *animateur*, encouraging companies and training providers to apply to participate in these EC programmes. It gives practical advice and support on EC funding, and applications under the FORCE programme had been submitted at the time of writing, it is also intended that applications for other EC programmes will be submitted.

Furthermore, the report also proposed that GPtec should try to influence the content of appropriate EC programmes, possibly in conjunction with other TECs or other organizations in the region, for example, the Peterborough Development Agency.

The Board accepted the report on 7 August 1991. This has encouraged GPtec to look at the feasibility of providing other European services, for example, a Single Market advice service, but there are important resource implications in developing a comprehensive service. The Local Initiative Fund could be used to develop this type of activity. However, it appears that Peterborough District Council 'is working towards the establishment of a European Information Office'. In addition, both the Chamber of Commerce and the Peterborough Development Agency provide a number of Single Market services, such as exporting assistance and seminars on 1992.

Accountability

The relationship between GPtec and the regional office of the Employment Department has been described as 'going through an interesting evolution'. GPtec sees the regional office of the Employment Department as a 'controller' especially in the area of funding decisions.

By general agreement the relationship between the Chief Executive and the Board would appear to be good.

'I view the Board as crucially important, they are the strength of the TEC – I want them to know what is happening and be able to influence development. They are very supportive and they are learning a lot about the Employment Department's approach.'
Lynda Purser

Notes

1. For a discussion of this point see Dyson K. 'Preparing for the Single Market: a new agenda for Government industry relations'. *Political Quarterly* 1991 pp. 338–50.
2. For a discussion of this point see Incomes Data Services Ltd (IDS) Study, 'TECs training & Enterprise Councils'. Study 485, July 1991, London.

References

Department of Employment *Employment for the 1990s* Cmnd 540 (London, HMSO, 1988).

Department of Employment *Training and enterprise councils: a prospectus for the 1990s* (London, DoE, 1989).

European Economic Development Services report for GPtec 'The applicability of EC policies and programmes' June 1991.

Evans, R., 'Training and Enterprise Councils – an initial assessment'. *Regional Studies* Vol 25.2 i, 1991.

Finegold, D. and Cosmic, D. 'The failure of training in Britain: analysis and prescription', *Oxford Review of Economic Policy* Vol 4 1988, 21–53.

GPtec *Corporate Plan, 1990.*

Parson, R., Andruetti, F. and Holly, S., *The European labour market review: key indicators.* (Brighton, Institute of Manpower Studies, 1990).

Preston, J. *EC Education, Training and Research Programmes: An Action Guide.* (London, Kogan Page, 1991).

Questions/discussion topics

1. 'The narrow short-term interests of industrialists are likely to prevail over strategic, sectorial and community interests'. Discuss this view of the TECs.

2. 'Sustained levels of public investment in skills training are essential, especially if employers are having to compensate increasingly highlighted deficiencies in the education system'. Discuss this view in the light of the experience of GPtec.

3. 'The effective management of policy depends, to a significant degree, on achieving a match between the strategy being pursued and a structure that can ensure the implementation of that strategy – structure should follow strategy'. Evaluate the match between the strategy being pursued by GPtec and its structure.

4. Striking a balance between the Civil Service culture, with its emphasis on public accountability, and an enterprise approach is not easy. What does the development of GPtec tell you about this relationship and its difficulties?

5. TECs, local authorities, and Chambers of Commerce would appear to have a number of overlapping functions. What does the case of GPtec suggest about the difficulties of balancing competition and co-operation?

6. What is your response to the view that the private sector will have to display a much more positive interest in training than in the past to justify its prominence on TEC boards, and that public-sector organizations often have a much better record of training of staff?

7. An Employment Department Review document of July 1991 stated that the relationship existing between the Department and the TECs is at breaking point. What type of relationship do you think ought to exist between the Department and the TECs?

8. Discuss the view that 'a decentralized training system militates against national strategies being drawn up, there is a need for a wider industrial strategy, training policies cannot be pursued in a vacuum'.

9. Evaluate GPtec's use of consultants. In general terms, what are the advantages and disadvantages of an organization such as GPtec using consultants.

10. Read the third chapter of Part 1. How would you evaluate GPtec's response to the Single Market?

11. Carry out a SWOT analysis of GPtec.

Case 7
Pan-European motoring assistance – A suitable case for National Breakdown?*

Alan Marchant and Ian Cox

Advice to readers

In terms of the development of strategic business initiatives in response to the implications of the Single European Market programme, you should use this case to explore those issues likely to prove critical for the future of each of the organizations discussed.

Although National Breakdown provides the focus of the case, discussion of its potential development must address the nature and extent of the competitive interaction developing throughout the motoring assistance sector.

It is recommended that you examine the discussion questions prior to reading the case as the issues they raise can be used to structure your analysis. A critical issue for both National Breakdown and its rivals is whether the very favourable business environment can remain as they make substance of their aspirations to operate increasingly in the pan-European market.

If your analysis generates as many questions as it does possible solutions, the case will have succeeded in illustrating the complexity and uncertainty of the European environment within which the sector will have to operate.

The origins of National Breakdown

It all began back in late 1970 when Bradford estate agent Colin Wilkinson and his brother-in-law, John Blyth, were enjoying a relaxing drink one

*   The authors would like to thank the following for their comments on the draft of this case study: Bob Slicer, Managing Director, National Breakdown, 1971-82; Ian Barnes and Campbell McPherson of Humberside Business School.

evening. Wilkinson recounted his recent bitter experience with a big and expensive car which kept breaking down and repeatedly had to be towed to a garage.

> 'I'd bought this new vehicle in about 1970 and in the eleven months that I had it, it was off the road umpteen times, it must have been a 'tea-break' model.'
> *Bradford Telegraph and Argus*, 7.9.84

They bemoaned the poor state of service provision for motorists when stranded at the roadside by either mechanical failure or accident damage to their vehicles and were convinced they could do better than the existing motoring organizations. Assistance for the motorist in the UK had always been synonymous with the traditional and long-established motoring organizations, the Automobile Association (AA) and the Royal Automobile Club (RAC). Although both were dominant in the provision of roadside mechanical assistance for their members, neither offered a breakdown recovery service. For this the motorist had to rely on a fragmented system of local garages, whose standard of service provision was of variable quality and often priced extortionately. This was particularly the case for those motorists unfortunate enough to be stranded on motorways who were a source of rich pickings for what had become known as 'tow-truck pirates'.

As early as the 1930s various 'car marque clubs' had operated schemes through which, in return for payment of a 'bob' a week, any member experiencing serious mechanical problems during a trip could be towed home by a fellow member, the latter being reimbursed out of the 'breakdown kitty'. Invention of the concept of a commercial recovery club is, however, credited to Dennis Thrustle of Anlaby Road, Hull, with the formation of the Car Recovery Club in 1969 which he operated as a family business with his son. Although little capital and the absence of garage agents confined recruitment to a parochial area around Hull, it was soon followed by other entrants to the field, including:

- Red Rovers;
- Autohome;
- UK Recoveries;
- Parishes of Hull Mayday Service;
- Knights of the Road;
- Car Recovery Club, London;

- The Good Samaritans;
- Autospeed of Hessle;
- Glew's of Goole.

On a recent visit to Hull, Wilkinson had observed the local operators and soon persuaded his two colleagues of the potential of the business idea. Within a few months each subscribed £1,000 of the equity to fund the creation of the National Breakdown Recovery Club Limited, with Wilkinson as managing director. The untimely coincidence with a national postal strike resulted in minimal recruitment during the first few months and threatened the early demise of the fledgeling company.

In early 1971 Wilkinson invited local entrepreneur and councillor Bob Slicer to have a look at the ailing business.

'I spent about three months going in on a daily basis having been appointed Sales Director by Wilkinson. At the time of my arrival the business was trading insolvent with only 146 members and large debts. Around July 1971 I called a meeting of the directors and informed them that things were in a terrible state and that if I were to invest time and money in the operation I would have to be in charge. I forecast that it would take five years to achieve our first profit and it would be ten years before we became nationally known – how true that was to be. I left the meeting saying, 'If you want me on those terms, give me a ring at home, I'm playing golf in the afternoon'. Within five minutes of my returning home they phoned their agreement to my conditions. From that day on I not only ran but financed National Breakdown as Managing Director. Six weeks later I had to ask Wilkinson to depart and we bought his shares back later.'

'After paying for my quarter share in the business, my next step was to guarantee a bank overdraft and over the next five years I loaned it some £20,000 in cash. We were always short of cash in the early days and I often had to pay the wages out of my back pocket. I must have had the strongest fingernails in the business from hanging on like grim death ... the wife never knew that I put up our home as security for one of our overdrafts ... National Breakdown was like my baby. Although I was not an accountant and could hardly tell one end of a car from another, I was damn good at communicating with people and knew the importance of providing the punters with the best value for money service.'
Interview with Bob Slicer, 10.9.91

The nerve centre of the operation, with its staff of one, was an office of 200 square feet above the Claremont Garage, Morley Street, close to the centre of Bradford. At night and at weekends Slicer and his wife Sheila had emergency calls routed to one of their two fish and chip shops, from which they would often have to organize long-distance recoveries.

For an annual charge of either £1.50 or £2.00, motorists were offered a 24-hour-a-day breakdown service, providing free recovery of both car and passengers from anywhere in mainland England, Scotland or Wales. Members who opted for the lower charge, although insured for recovery after accident, had to get qualified confirmation of major breakdown, either from a local garage or the AA or RAC, for recovery by National Breakdown. In contrast with other service providers, it was the vehicle which was the club member, irrespective of driver. A telephone call to 'headquarters' from a stranded motorist, quoting membership number and explaining the nature of the breakdown and vehicle location, was all that was required for recovery to be organized via one of 40 local agents which, being established garages, only turned out for National Breakdown as and when required, payment being on a pro-rata basis per contracted call-out. The rescued driver had the option of recovery with his vehicle and up to five passengers to either an agreed garage or preferred destination. Insurance cover initially excluded assistance with simple problems such as: running out of petrol, punctures, plugs, points, that could either be cured on the spot by the motorist himself, or by a local mechanic.

Growth of the company

During the first six months progress was mediocre with only a few hundred members recruited. The cofounders put this down to the public thinking that, with membership fees so low in comparison with the AA (£3.30) and RAC (£3.15), the service offered could not be any good. Their identification of what proved to be a substantial gap in the UK market is illustrated in Table 2.7.1.

A combination of Slicer's avuncular personality and his 'hands on' approach to the business was highly effective during the first decade in its growth, as its chief salesman's deals with clients were struck on a personal level, often verbal and sealed with a nod and a handshake. Members of Yorkshire County Cricket Club remember the early days of National Breakdown when Slicer, an avid supporter of the Club, issued honorary life memberships to many of them. His management style enabled a healthy membership base to be established and, within the first 18 months, links had been formed with several commercial and fleet operators, including a national security firm. Several local garages also agreed to offer free membership with new car purchases, a marketing device which was to assume increasing importance throughout the motoring assistance sector in the UK as from the mid-1980s. A number of high-volume optional membership deals were made with organizations, including: the Civil Services Motoring Association (CSMA) (65,000 members), the Institute of Advanced Motorists (100,000 members), and the local government officers union NALGO, which gave its approval to the National Breakdown Club scheme.

Table 2.7.1 Enrolled membership of National Breakdown

Year	Members
1971(mid)	300
1971(end)	3,000
1972	15,000
1973	27,000
1977	100,000
1981	250,000
1982	283,000
1986	600,000
1987	750,000
1989	1,000,000
1990	1,500,000

Source: Company and authors' estimates; Yorkshire Post; Bradford Telegraph and Argus

Reputation

During the 1970s the company built a strong reputation of efficiency and economic subscription charges amongst the cautious northern motoring public. The scheme developed for the CSMA proved a highly-effective source of new members for National Breakdown, contributing 27,000 in 1975, 40,000 in 1976 and over 100,000 by 1980.

The individualistic approach Slicer adopted for managing what soon became a rapid-growth business was graphically illustrated by the *Bradford Telegraph and Argus* (20.12.73).

'Bob Slicer (48) regards his Managing Directorship of National Breakdown as a spare-time appointment. He has many other interests including a garage, the building trade, and he owns a fish and chip shop in Buttershaw. He regularly works a 17-hour day and one day recently left for Hull at 7.45 a.m.

for a meeting and arrived back home at 8.30 p.m. and then fried fish and chips at the shop until midnight.'

'He began in a building office, moved into the works, was apprenticed as a joiner and gained his City and Guilds. At 22 he had his own business as a joiner and builder at Low Moor (Bradford). He didn't believe in allowing the grass to grow under his feet. Even when he went on his honeymoon to London he found his way to London airport to take measurements for the doors to the fire station, then went back to Low Moor to make them.'

In 1972 Ernest Smith, who had established his own specialist company in 1969 for transporting veteran and vintage vehicles around the country for their owners, was working with another vehicle-recovery club. He summarized the origins of his link with National Breakdown in the *Yorkshire Post* (July 1989).

'I was not part of that company, but when it ran into difficulties and was taken over by National Breakdown, they asked me to join them to help organize their work . . . I got closely involved, bought stock in the company and became one of the four owners of the business.'

Smith's extensive operational and mechanical skills proved the perfect complement to the marketing flair of Slicer who was soon to recognize his new technical director as his 'right-hand man'.

Expansion by takeover

Autospeed's recruiting system was very effective at generating membership volume and by 1973 it was the largest in the field. Unfortunately, its sales staff seemed to specialize in recruiting cars which were already broken down and, with a membership breakdown rate estimated at near 70 per cent, the company was soon heavily in debt. After an approach from its owners, National Breakdown agreed to take over Autospeed by assuming the running-out costs of its membership, and paying-off its vehicle hire purchase commitments. Although a costly operation, estimated at £30,000, if National Breakdown had not intervened, the failure of a rival with 27,000 members would have aborted the development of the 'recovery industry'.

The integration of Autospeed also extended National Breakdown's agency base from 80 to 130 and was soon followed by the introduction of a scheme referred to at the time by Bob Slicer as an 'Assist List' comprising a nationwide database of 200 approved garages which would undertake minor repairs to members' cars at reasonable prices.

Competition to the AA and RAC

Although at the time National Breakdown had a very low profile amongst the general public, that a mere three-year-old entrant to the sector prompted the 68-year-old AA to move into the recovery field with their 'Relay' service in 1974, followed by the RAC's recovery scheme in 1975, confirmed the threat it posed to what appeared to have been a long-standing and cosy duopoly relationship between the AA and RAC. Their response was, however, limited to offering a car and passenger recovery service as optional extras to basic repair facilities which remained the core of their road service. By extending the scope of its service portfolio in 1974 to include roadside assistance National Breakdown was, in effect, in direct competition with the industry majors.

When the AA set up its 'Relay' service, the Insurance Division of the Department of Trade and Industry by coincidence decided that recovery organizations were supplying commercial insurance services and, as such, their operations must be underwritten. National Breakdown subsequently acquired five more of its rivals who were unable to comply and by 1980 only Autohome of the early entrants remained in business. In about 1978 when National Breakdown was incurring annual underwriting costs at Lloyds of £90,000, Slicer resolved to avoid them and adopted the simple expedient of purchasing a small established pecuniary loss insurance business. This was then capitalized and used exclusively as a subsidiary by National Breakdown for writing its own insurance. Within a few years Ultra-Keen Insurance was itself reporting pre-tax profits approaching £200,000.

Six years after its formation National Breakdown had become the largest independent vehicle recovery operator in the UK and laid claim to being the fastest growing company in Britain. In 1977 it introduced its first computer system to handle its burgeoning membership and administration, and became first in the UK to offer a national breakdown/recovery service to the commercial vehicle sector, including heavy goods vehicles. Subsequent development of its links with commercial vehicle manufacturers, distributors and operators, meant that by 1989 seven out of ten new HGV trucks registered in Britain were covered by National Breakdown insurance.

New premises

By 1979, 50 staff were needed to control more than 600 agents and depots and rapid expansion led to transfer of the company's headquarters to the former offices of Ciba Geigy at Low Moor, Bradford which, at a purchase price of £215,000, provided 29,000 square feet of office space to accommodate any foreseeable expansion.

'Work to convert the Low Moor premises, including installation of 83 telephone lines and a new control room is under way. In addition to its computerised membership control systems, the group is installing the latest postal handling equipment able to deal with nearly one million envelopes a year. It is hoped that Yorkshire and England cricketer, Geoff Boycott, a close friend of Councillor Slicer, will attend the ceremony.'
Bradford Telegraph and Argus, 30.1.79

Service provision

One of the key issues for National Breakdown lay in the nature of the service it offered. Until 1971 services available to the stranded motorist concentrated upon provision of basic roadside repair. If the member's vehicle could not be repaired at the roadside, the only option was for it to be towed to a local garage for repair. The only alternative was reliance upon local garages to provide 'situation recovery', a relatively poor alternative because of its restricted geographical coverage and operating hours and the requirement for 'on the spot' roadside payment for a service of very variable quality.

The opportunity this presented was summarized by Steve Kitson, press officer for National Breakdown, in *Marketing Week* (16.2.90).

'Initially we took over where the others left off – if they couldn't fix a vehicle then we recovered it. We grew from there and virtually invented the garage recovery business – before we set up, the best most of them could offer was a Land Rover and a tow-rope.'

National Parking Corporation (NPC)

By the early 1980s it had become clear to most of the board of National Breakdown that it had reached the point where, although profitable, its potential for further development would level off without a significant increase in its public profile. Reliance upon franchised agents and the centralization of its operations on a single site meant that, in contrast with the AA and RAC, it had no high street, and only minimal 'on the road', presence. This was confirmed by internal market research which suggested a level of public awareness of its name and activity as low as 3 per cent.

In January 1982 Bob Slicer resigned after a period of 'boardroom differences', with a financial settlement subject to his agreement not to work for any competitor for a period of three years.

National Car Parks link with National Breakdown

Later that year, during an initial approach by National Breakdown to National Car Parks Ltd (NCP) to discuss the possibility of sales leaflets being distributed through their car parks, a close affinity between the business philosophies of their senior managements became apparent. Both provided the motorist with readily available services, were highly profit-orientated, and emphasized the financial audit and control of their operations. In September 1984 National Breakdown was acquired by National Parking Corporation (the parent of NCP) for a sum believed to be in excess of £5 million. Although considered by many as a low-profile acquisition, Ernest Smith, who was appointed Managing Director after the acquisition, summarized its rationale as:

> 'National Car Parks issue over 100 million tickets a year, so with this potential market at our disposal the future growth is assured. NCP have over 600 sites and deal with 300,000 motorists a day. We have also the means of improving contact with the motoring public and, at the same time, NCP has carefully followed our progress. It considers the acquisition of National Breakdown an ideal opportunity to broaden its services to motorists.'
> *Bradford Telegraph and Argus*, 6.9.84

Whilst National Breakdown has been profitable in its own right since 1976, when its pre-tax profits were estimated at £5,000, and it is now the second largest profit centre within the NCP group, the secure financial stature of NCP should not be ignored. Since the acquisition, National Breakdown appears to have been autonomous in its decision-making processes where these relate to sales, marketing, administration and operational services. In September 1984, Colin Wilkinson retired and, although retained as a consultant, was replaced as Chairman of National Breakdown by G. Layton who also joined Ernest Smith as Managing Director. By 1989 six of NPC's directors also served on National Breakdown's board of ten. Other than NPC, Smith is now its only remaining shareholder.

NPC background

NPC is one of the largest private companies in the UK and was ranked fourth by pre-tax profits (£54 million) by a Jordan's Survey in 1989, with an estimated total company valuation of £464 million. A summary of the range of NCP's activities, together with extracts from its consolidated accounts, is given in Appendix 1.

Although the holding company NPC is relatively unknown to the public, its principal trading face is its subsidiary, National Car Parks (NCP) which has a very high profile as Europe's largest car parking organization. In its survey of car parking facilities in the UK, *Which?* (June 1990) concluded:

'By far the largest company dominating the private sector is NCP, which owns, leases or manages 650 city, town and airport car parks throughout the UK. NCP has 250,000 customers a day and last year had pre-tax profits of around £29 million. A few companies, such as Apcoa Parking (UK) Ltd (with 60 car parks) and Euro Parks (around 90) are providing some competition but NCP remains very much in the driving seat. Nearly three out of four NCP car parks are leased from landlords such as local authorities. Many are long term, e.g. all Gloucester City Council's car parks are leased to NCP for up to 99 years.'

The origins of NPC were even more humble than National Breakdown's. In 1949 its founders, Donald Gosling (knighted in 1976) and Ronald Hobson, started out by charging six pence a day for drivers to park on a London bomb site. In 1959 they acquired National Car Parks, which was followed by diversification into related areas, such as petrol stations and hotels – subsequently disposed of to provide scope for expansion into vehicle breakdown and property trading activities. NPC's current trading portfolio also includes property letting, income from coach activity and property sales. As indicated in Appendix 1, breakdown and recovery activities are now second largest to car parking in terms of both group turnover and pre-tax profit.

Future prospects

The Independent (15.1.90) commented that the group looked set to continue growing strongly whether or not it took the unlikely step of obtaining a future stock market listing. In their report to shareholders in 1989, the co-founders, who are joint Chairmen, expressed confidence that

'. . . the story of the last ten years will continue well into the turn of the century'. Their assessment of the implications of the new phase in National Breakdown's development represented by its move to its new purpose-built £5 million headquarters at Pudsey, outside Leeds, was that '. . . the technology available in the new control centre to process calls for assistance represents a considerable improvement on already very efficient systems, and provides excellent facilities for future expansion.'

This was the third time that rapid expansion had forced National Breakdown to move premises. By 1989 it had outgrown its headquarters at Low Moor and staff were having to work under cramped conditions in portable buildings. Ninety additional staff were subsequently recruited when the new headquarters became operational in April 1989, by which time its control room was manned by 90 controllers employed on a 24-hour-a-day duty rota to process up to 4,000 daily calls for assistance.

When interviewed by the *Yorkshire Post* in July 1989, Ernest Smith was unequivocal in his assessment of future prospects for the company.

'. . . our growth over the next 3 to 5 years will take us to 2.5 million members, and maybe the 3 million mark, at which stage I believe we will have overtaken the RAC and become number two in the UK.'

Unlike its larger competitors, pursuit of market share is not in itself a strategic objective for the company and any proposals regarding either membership schemes or service developments must fulfil a rigorous requirement to be both cost-effective and profit generating.

Computerized communications network

This, together with its 1,500 franchised agents, has been critical to the successful delivery of National Breakdown's service to the motorist. The network was set up to handle incoming calls, the objectives being to:

- assist the correct diagnosis of the nature of the problem with the motorist's vehicle;
- identify the service required;
- identify and mobilize the nearest agent able and suitable to deal with the problem.

From the outset, speed of response to the stranded motorist has been the core of operational strategy. When members call in, the operations room controllers have immediate access to the central computer to validate their membership by name, address, car registration, or membership number, within a few seconds. At this point clients need only give their location and a sophisticated computerized laser mapping system pinpoints the nearest, and most suitable, agent. Although the maximum targeted time of the operation from receiving a telephone call for assistance to its being answered is ten seconds, the achieved average is two seconds. Single digit differences in telephone numbers enable controllers to identify a caller's membership group before the call is answered. This has made an important contribution to the development of dedicated services for corporate clients using whatever 'brand name' they require.

National Breakdown's software systems were designed in-house with close liaison with Hewlett Packard to develop the required hardware. Management at National Breakdown claim they had once considered the system on which the RAC's Computer-Aided Rescue System was later to be based, but rejected it as being unsuitable.

By 1989 two Hewlett Packard 3400 mainframe computers were being used to handle both the operational and administrative aspects of the business, the system operating at approximately 25 per cent of its available capacity. Staffing of the control room has sufficient built-in capacity to cope with the peaks and troughs of demand so that typically during a year there will be less than ten days when their target maximum response time of ten seconds is not met. All control room operators are taught mechanical engineering and how to communicate effectively and sympathetically with members who phone in for help.

Agents

The 1,500 agents used to provide the service are paid promptly at above average rates, but are subject to strict quality control procedures. Since the early 1970s, any member of National Breakdown in receipt of assistance is sent a questionnaire for completion and return via a freepost envelope. Detailed comments are invited as to the quality of service provision experienced and the system has a response rate in excess of 67 per cent. Agents are also subject to comprehensive and random on-site inspections. An estimated pool of 4,000 potential agents further encourages compliance with required service quality as does the prospect of payment within ten days for franchise work. Although now rectified by their introduction of direct debiting systems, it was not uncommon in the past for agents to await payment for work sub-contracted by the AA and RAC for up to four months.

Target markets

Car manufacturers

As with other players, increasing emphasis is being given to establishing marketing links with car manufacturers and lease organizations, for example, as provider of a rescue service for Lada, Mazda, Vauxhall, and Alfa Romeo. In August 1989 Citroën introduced their *Citroën Assist* accident management and breakdown recovery scheme, through which all new cars sold in Britain carry assistance cover with National Breakdown as part of their warranty with the option of renewal on discount terms.

An assessment by *Marketing Week* (16.2.90) of the links with car manufacturers by motoring organizations concluded that:

> 'the biggest potential for growth, and for a pitched marketing battle, lies with the motor manufacturers. It is uncertain who will win the battle for motor manufacturers business, but what is certain is that as more and more manufacturers offer breakdown recovery packages, the breakdown organizations will have to market themselves more aggressively to win these business allies.'

Private and corporate customers

The private individual motorist is, however, still regarded as the most important market segment in terms of profit contribution and accounts for over 50 per cent of National Breakdown's total membership. Although they are numerous, private motorists are a diffuse group, with limited individual sales volumes, and tend to base purchase decisions on information of the likely incidence and extent of their need for breakdown/recovery assistance which is both limited and inherently subjective. They are, therefore, likely to have a low sensitivity to price in selecting which organization to join and the most appropriate level of cover to adopt. In pursuit of a product which promises both peace of mind and convenience, subscription rates have traditionally been regarded as less important than perceptions of quality and brand image in the purchase decision. In contrast, corporate customers with large vehicle fleets to manage have access to more accurate quantitative information on which to base their decisions. Although similarly motivated by risk reduction, their purchases are much more financially orientated. Price sensitivity for the corporate sector is, therefore, likely to be high with low brand commitment unless it clearly reflects superior value for money.

European cover

Since the mid-1970s National Breakdown has, like most other UK service providers, offered short-term European cover primarily for the tourist market but until 1982 this was done via the agency of a general insurer or, in the case of recovery assistance, by one of the large continental operators such as Europ Assistance. Unlike the AA and RAC who have relied on arrangements with other traditional motoring clubs in Europe to act on their behalf – from which it has always been excluded – National Breakdown has had to establish an independent network of direct agency links with European garages which now provide a base for continental operations.

Its aspirations to exploit the wider European market became clear in April 1989 when, in anticipation of its capacity expansion, the company became the first organization to provide free annual breakdown/recovery assistance throughout Europe for those members opting for its Total Protection and Comprehensive policies. Adoption of a more aggressive marketing profile is also apparent from its move into prime-time television advertising and sponsorship of weather forecasts in the YTV area.

The significance of just how far it has come as an organization is apparent when its operational staff, many of whom have been with National Breakdown for more than six years, talk fondly of the old days when they only had 100 agents and struggled to cope on a bad day. It is also illustrated by NPC's 1990 accounts which make reference to National Breakdown of the USA Inc., in which NPC has a 41 per cent interest.

The competition

UK-based organizations

The Royal Automobile Club

Since its formation in 1897 as 'a society for the encouragement for the motoring movement and the motor and allied industries in the British Empire', the RAC has been regarded as the national motoring authority in the UK. Motoring organizations throughout the Commonwealth are associated with the RAC, as are nearly 100 motor clubs in the UK.

Like the AA, as an unincorporated non-profit making association, any financial surplus has to be ploughed back to fulfil 'the general good of its members'. The internal organizational structure reflects its range of membership services. The Committee of the RAC, the ultimate governing body, comprises the board of directors of the parent company, RAC Limited (limited by guarantee), and is elected by the 13,500 full members of the club.

The RAC serves its 13,500 full members through the exclusive Gentleman's Club House in Pall Mall, London, and the Country Club at Woodcote Park, near Epsom in Surrey, each of which has a separate operating company accountable to the Committee. The interests of associate members (the general public) are met by RAC Motoring Services Limited, also limited by guarantee, whose work is monitored through the Associate Committee by the General Council of the RAC. This body exists to represent the interests of associate members, both individually and through affiliated motor clubs. Its activity as the governing body for motor sport in the UK is directed by the RAC Motor Sports Council and administered by the RAC Motor Sports Association Limited. The latter represents a wide range of motor sporting interests, both as members of the company and as members of the Board of Directors. In 1990 a total staff of 4,100 were employed by the RAC.

Services available to members include: patrol rescue, vehicle recovery, and an at-home service. In recent years a strategy of related diversification has resulted in an increasingly important contribution to the RAC's business portfolio coming from: motor insurance, home and foreign touring assistance, publication of maps and guide books, legal, technical and information services. A major activity in its wider role is the representation and protection of the general interests of the British motorist through negotiation with Government departments, local authorities and representative organizations.

The company has a substantial personal lines insurance broking business, specializing in motor insurance, and a significant motoring travel business for motorists taking their cars abroad. Subsidiary insurance underwriting and broking companies together generate £100 million annual turnover, whilst its insurance broking division is the fourth largest motor broker in the UK. Although its insurance companies sell their services beyond RAC members, in-house policyholders account for around 20 per cent of all their insurance customers.

Unlike National Breakdown, the RAC use their own in-house patrol fleets for delivery of most of the rescue/recovery services to the motorist. A policy of 'one man, one van' is operated to encourage patrolmen to take personal pride in their standard of service provision. The RAC estimates that its skilled mechanics, who operate its fleet of 1,500 rescue vehicles, are able to mobilize broken-down vehicles at the roadside in over 80 per cent of cases. It also has access to 900 independent rescue agents to whom the RAC sub-contracts nearly all recovery work and 10 per cent of its repair/rescue activity.

A further contrast with National Breakdown is that both the RAC and AA schemes use the motorist, irrespective of the number of cars driven, as their membership base. During 1989, however, the RAC introduced a car-based scheme which is now the only form of membership offered to new clients.

During 1988, Phase I of the CARS system – the RAC's Computer-Aided Rescue Service – was implemented. This is a command and control system developed by the RAC to provide a nationwide communication system to link the member requiring assistance to its service patrols. Five new centralized control and co-ordination centres replaced 17 control rooms scattered around the UK. Using this new system, the stranded motorist dials a freephone number, calls being answered at any one of the rescue controls by staff using a computer-based nationwide gazetteer to locate the stranded motorist. Control centres are computer-linked to rescue command centres in each of the 17 area offices from where staff use their discretion in deploying the most appropriate resource to each call for assistance. Implementation of this project has involved a major deployment of resources over a very short time span with over 500 management and operational staff being trained in the use of the new system and building work at 19 locations. CARS Phase II will link the rescue command centres through a new advanced trunk network radio system to a terminal in every service vehicle. There, details of the patrol's next breakdown appear on a liquid crystal display, exactly as entered at the moment of the member's call.

By late 1988, use of the CARS system had identified a significant problem whereby a very small proportion of members were making excessive use of services. As a result, all members who use the service ten or more times in any one year are now required to pay a substantial surcharge on renewal of their subscription.

Product extensions in recent years include: RAC Mastercard – a credit card developed in conjunction with Barclays Bank, Octagon Recovery Limited – the commercial heavy goods vehicle arm of the RAC's rescue and recovery service. The latter is the first European-wide roadside rescue service for all makes of commercial vehicle and makes use of the RAC Calais control centre. Other services include: full vehicle inspections, legal services, insurance broking and leisure products, the latter encompassing first-aid kits, car accessories, ferry bookings and various publications such as maps, car-care handbooks and motoring guides. The development of the RAC is indicated in Table 2.7.2.

Table 2.7.2   RAC Membership (UK)

1909	5,170
1920	18,500
1985	2,500,000
1986	3,000,000
1987	3,400,000
1989	4,200,000
1990	5,040,000

Source: RAC

As from September 1989 all buyers of Ford cars, vans and pick-up trucks have had a year's free membership of the RAC, worth, at the time, £89.50, included in their manufacturer's warranty. Also included are services such as car recovery from the Continent and free accommodation and travel in the event of breakdown. The general assessment of this development was reflected by *The Times* (8.9.89),

'The package is the first shot in what promises to be a fierce marketing war between the major car manufacturers. High interest rates are expected to put an end to the boom in the last four months, forcing the manufacturers to look for new ways to maintain sales. The Ford announcement could give the RAC as many as 500,000 new members on top of its present four million.'

In February 1990, John Spillane, the RAC's commercial marketing manager, confidently claimed

'75 per cent of all new cars are now automatically with the RAC and that's something we are going to build on. Free membership to a motoring organization has proven a big selling point for manufacturers and so the majority are now doing it as an aggressive piece of marketing.'

With an estimated increase in its share of the company fleet to 36 per cent by the end of March 1990, the RAC were forced to create a separate division, RAC Business Services, launched at the Fleet Motor Show in May 1990. As with the other major players the RAC recognizes the potential for membership growth in signing deals with motor manufacturers as they attempt to give added value to the new car purchaser by inclusion of breakdown/recovery services in new car warranties.

Similar deals have been entered into with Volvo, Lotus, Jaguar in the UK (Mondial has the contract for the European Jaguar market), and Renault, but with Ford accounting for 26.5 per cent of all new car registrations in 1989 this contract contributed a major advance in membership volume. Membership of motoring organizations by this method are shown in Table 2.7.3.

Table 2.7.3   UK membership of motoring organizations via new car warranties

Year	AA	% market share Mondial	Others	RAC
1988	58	22	3	17
1989	49	21	6	24
1990	29	9	7	55

Source: based on figures supplied by the RAC to *Marketing Week*, February 1990

The RAC also runs an emergency assistance scheme through insurers, under which the services provided to policyholders are linked to the premium paid and, in the case of fleet operations, the insurers pay a regular fee to the RAC for fleet control. This reflects a general trend towards the development of tie-ups with insurance companies for both the private and corporate segments of the motoring assistance market.

The change towards a more overtly commercial philosophy in recent years reflects, in no small part, the appointment of Arthur Large from British Leyland as new Chief Executive to RAC Motoring Services in 1985. As well as being responsible for implementing its investment in computer technology to replace the antiquated paper-based call system, on which RAC operations were reliant up to 1986, he initiated a policy of strategic acquisitions of motor insurance companies.

His view of the competitive implications of new entrants to the sector was summarized in *Motor Industry Management*, April 1987.

'The dozen or so recovery clubs which are nibbling away at this business are in the "tow" business rather than the "go" business, whereas our trained mechanics fix 80 per cent of the troubles which cause our members to break down. The recovery clubs don't have skilled task forces and the garages they use have a good commercial reason for towing the car away for leisurely repairs.'

The RAC has recognized that it has suffered over the years from a rather old-fashioned image and that the AA has historically had the highest profile and membership base. In *Marketing Week*, (16.2.90), Andy Brown, RAC General Marketing Manager, contended that it is the membership base of the AA which is now being being eroded.

'It's true that in the 70s and early 80s the AA was dominant but we have put on two million members in the past three years and have been taking the competition apart . . . The organisation has changed radically in the past five years and been brought up to date. We are the fastest-growing motoring organisation in Europe and intend to continue in the 1990s.'

In March 1990 the RAC made clear its aspirations to develop its business strategy in mainland Europe by announcing its intention to sell roadside assistance to European drivers by establishing a pan-European rescue service comparable to that operating in the UK. Its plans are that this will be available to UK and continental drivers wherever they may be driving in Western Europe and will be accessed via freephone telephone systems. The new rescue service is to be made available through a new subsidiary company, RAC France, located at the RAC's main European control centre at Calais and through which drivers will be able to obtain rescue and recovery in the event of breakdown, accident, or vehicle immobilization. The RAC network, consisting of patrols with associated motoring clubs in Europe and agents, has been increased by a third bringing the total network to almost 10,000.

'A call to a freephone number from wherever a driver may be in Western Europe will connect with a control centre and will be answered by a manager speaking the caller's language. The driver will usually be helped within the hour.'

Arthur Large, *Personal Finance*, Winter, 1990

The Automobile Association

The Automobile Association was founded in 1905 to protect the interests of motorists during a period of national hostility to cars and their owners. It now claims to be the world's largest motoring organization, with the objective to 'be an innovative membership-based service organization' (Simon Dyer, Director General, AA, 1988). (See Table 2.7.4 for figures of growth.)

AA Developments Ltd is the holding company for the principal service subsidiaries of insurance and travel overseas and the growing businesses of AA Financial Services and AA Mobile Communications. Roadside breakdown assistance is carried out using the AA's in-house fleet, with a total work force of over 3,500 people. Calls for assistance are received at three operation centres at Stanmore, London, Thatcham, near Newbury in Berkshire, and Maidstone, Kent.

Table 2.7.4   AA Membership

1909	10,000
1920	100,000
1933	500,000
1950	1,000,000
1957	2,000,000
1963	3,000,000
1969	4,000,000
1973	5,000,000
1986	6,000,000
1987	6,480,000
1988	7,011,000
1989	7,357,000
1990	7,574,000

Note: Membership of spouse accounts for approximately 17 per cent of total.
Source: The Automobile Association

A distinctive feature of AA membership is that it is based on the individual who has access to the level of assistance to which he has subscribed, whether travelling as driver or passenger in any vehicle.

Commencing in the early 1970s, a policy of related diversification into overtly commercial activities has been pursued for longer than any of the other UK motoring organizations. Its diverse portfolio of activities is now organized into three business groupings: Member Services, Insurance and Financial Services, Commercial Services.

The AA wholly own the following two companies: Automobile Association Developments Limited, which is a holding company for new commercial developments, and AA Reinsurance Company Limited, whose principal business activity is reinsurance. By 1988 the following were wholly owned either directly or indirectly via AA Developments Ltd:

- AA Insurance Services Ltd – the largest private motor insurance broker in the UK, its policies covering everything from household contents to leisure activities;
- AA Insurance Brokers Ltd;
- AA Travel Services Ltd – travel agent and tour operator;
- AA Underwriting Services Ltd – insurance underwriters;
- AA Protection and Investment Planning Ltd – life insurance and investment advice;
- AA Commercial Insurance Brokers Ltd;
- AA SARL – continental breakdown assistance;
- AA Distribution Services Ltd – book distribution.

Given its commercial orientation, AA Developments has a clear objective of paying a dividend to the club. Although a dividend of £4.5 million was paid in 1987, a 43 per cent rise in administration costs, from £91 million to £130 million transformed a £5 million profit in 1987 to a post-tax loss of £50,000, which prevented a dividend from being paid in 1988. A key area of recent difficulty has been in the cut-throat travel business market with AA Travel losses increasing from £2.5 million in 1987 to £5.4 million in 1988. All eight subsidiaries of AA Developments were hit by spiralling administrative costs, the most significant rise being in its car insurance business. Two areas subject to subsequent extensive rationalization were its mobile telephone business where losses forced the sale of its subscriber base to GEC, and the AA's aviation business.

Public recognition of its strategic difficulties was apparent in the AA's annual report for 1988.

'In order to improve efficiency in all the activities of the AA, a management reorganisation began in mid-1988. The object is to improve the contribution of each business division and there will also be a programme for reducing central costs. It is confidently expected that the result will be improved service to members in future years.'

Whilst recognizing that service providers will have to attach increasing importance to competing in a European context, by 1990 provision by the AA was still limited to its traditional 5-Star European policy package option which provided short-term, single-trip cover for UK motorists visiting the continent.

Britannia Rescue/Recovery

In terms of its origins, membership volume, method of service delivery and focus of operations, Britannia Rescue is, of the other UK-based operators, the most closely competitive with National Breakdown.

The Civil Service Motoring Association (CSMA) originally relied on a contract with National Breakdown to provide optional breakdown/recovery assistance for its members on discount terms. In 1983, however, CSMA management considered that its membership base, which at the time represented more than half of National Breakdown's clients, was sufficiently large for it to organize the same service more cost-effectively in-house.

Britannia Rescue commenced trading as a wholly-owned subsidiary of CSMA in January 1983 and was joined by a number of operational staff who had previously worked for National Breakdown. Since 1984 Britannia's policy options have been marketed to the general public. It operates from Huddersfield and relies on the same agency pool as National Breakdown to deliver a service which is very similar. Like National Breakdown, Britannia Rescue covers the vehicle rather than the driver and uses a freephone telephone service. Although its membership database is computerized, it relies on the knowledge of its total staff of 40, in conjunction with its agents, to locate the stranded motorist. Although its service is based on a focused, low-cost operation, it has proven successful, with membership having grown to 270,000 and with 95,000 breakdowns handled in 1990. Unlike other players, its strategy for growth concentrates on market (rather than service) development, the financial consequences of which are summarized in Table 2.7.5.

Table 2.7.5   Financial performance of Britannia Rescue/Recovery in £000s

	1986	1987	1988	1989	1990
Turnover	763	1,112	1,121	1,314	1,604
Pre-tax profit	283	792	663	927	1,090
Business ratios					
Return on sales (%)	37.1	71.2	59.1	70.6	68.0
Return on capital (%)	49.2	69.0	58.4	57.4	53.7
Return on total assets (%)	14.7	23.9	18.2	23.2	20.2
Employees	30	32	36	39	45

Source: Company accounts

It is perhaps no coincidence that since 1987 Bob Slicer (often referred to in the trade as 'the Freddie Laker of the Highways') has combined globe-trotting between his homes in Andorra and Australia with his role as consultant to Britannia.

Frizzell Insurance and Financial Services Ltd

This service is targeted at the Civil Service and Local Authority type car owner. It is essentially a low-cost breakdown insurance service which, when a stranded motorist rings the Frizzell control room, dispatches one of 1,500 agents to assist the driver. Having paid the agent on the spot, the motorist reclaims the cost from Frizzell. By this method it is claimed that, if credit cards are used, the agent is paid immediately and the motorist can be reimbursed before the credit card invoice has to be paid.

Hambro Rescue

This package of roadside help and recovery was launched in the autumn of 1988 by Hambro Legal Protection, an insurance company that provides cover for expenses in litigation. The basic package is for 24-hour assistance delivered via a network of 1,500 independent garages.

Stranded motorists telephone the control room at Hambro House, Colchester, where experienced car recovery personnel can call out local operators to effect a roadside repair or recovery of the vehicle to a garage.

This system is computerized using a series of networked personal computers.

Whilst not prepared to reveal the size of its client base, Hambro confirmed in May 1990 that what was originally a trial extension of its product range had proved very successful and would be a permanent feature of its portfolio.

Other services offered by Hambro include: uninsured loss recovery, legal protection 24 hours a day and a 24-hour helpline for households, through which subscribers can have access to plumbers, electricians, glaziers and roofing experts as required.

Swinton Insurance

In February 1990, the news that the second largest motor insurance broker, and previously a very large customer of National Breakdown, was to enter the breakdown service market, was reported by *Marketing Week* (16.2.90) as

'. . . confirming that the market was becoming increasingly competitive with the AA and RAC having to fight each other for membership while fending off the newer organisations such as National Breakdown and Britannia Rescue . . . It is believed that the breakdown service will form a completely new division of the company and offer services similar to those of the AA and RAC.'

Contrasting views on the impact of this potential entrant on the market came from the AA and National Breakdown.

'. . . the AA is not unduly concerned about newcomers because we have a membership of 7.3 million and have had a record three years in recruiting new members.'
John Douglas, Marketing Director, AA

'Swinton has been a long-standing customer of ours in the past but although we wish them well, they will find it difficult. Avis, the car-hire people, tried it and it hasn't been a great success because the market is so competitive and tightly carved up.'
Steve Kitson, spokesman, National Breakdown

By September 1990 Swinton's rival service had not appeared in the market, which suggests that it had abandoned its diversification plans which, if realized, might have been regarded by the sector as signalling overt competition with the AA.

European players operating in the UK

In addition to competition indigenous to the UK, National Breakdown has also to address rivalry from major continental insurance operators who have made significant, if somewhat low profile, progress in the UK during the past decade. A critical issue for the future of the sector is likely to be the strategies adopted by these continental rivals both in developing their interests in the Single Market and in response to UK players extending their competitive scope throughout the European Community.

GESA

GESA (Group European SA) was one of the pioneers in the provision of international emergency assistance services, having opened its first office in Barcelona in 1959. As with the other established pan-European players, GESA is owned by a general insurance company but, to date, is the only one operating in its own right as an insurance company in each national market served. Its international activity has become widespread and is now managed via a worldwide network of 18 national emergency centres, each manned by multi-lingual staff responsible both for providing assistance locally and co-ordinating assistance for clients whilst in another country. Each centre manages its own local network of experts including doctors, lawyers, and vehicle specialists.

GESA's global operations extend to over 135 countries via a wide range of partnership links established with: insurance and assurance companies, international banks and credit card organizations, tour operators, European automobile clubs, and motor manufacturers. It estimates its customers throughout the world at 20 million individuals.

Although GESA Assistance has operated in the UK ever since its parent company commenced trading, a significant increase in its UK profile came in 1976 with the establishment of its London Emergency Centre providing direct access to its worldwide network. In addition to motor vehicle assistance similar to that of the other providers, its tailored assistance packages can include any, or all, of the following:

For individuals
- emergency medical treatment - arranging hospitals/ambulances;
- organizing emergency repatriation, including air ambulance.

For homes

- emergency household assistance and co-ordination of salvage work;
- emergency assistance during household removal.

For insurers

- recovery of accident-damaged vehicles;
- repatriation of vehicles from overseas or disposal abroad;
- pursuit of recoveries abroad against foreign motorists damaging vehicles insured in the UK.

For corporations

- any combination of the above.

By 1990 its UK operation provided assistance for over one million UK residents travelling overseas and short-term holiday cover for 50,000 vehicles visiting the continent. Within the UK it estimates that 300,000 vehicles are currently eligible for its assistance services and that, in total, 2.5 million people are currently entitled to some form of assistance service from GESA. However, if restricted solely to breakdown/recovery, this reduces to 100,000.

In contrast with others in the industry, GESA has no retail products and is generally regarded as the major European 'wholesaler' of breakdown/ recovery services. It supplies these to a growing number of large motor insurers, including Avon (since 1985 GESA has provided Avon Road Rescue) and Churchill Insurance Direct. The recent policy extensions by 'retail' operators to provide more comprehensive assistance packages, particularly coverage for consequential costs such as hotel accommodation, have always been GESA's stock in trade. The problem of insurance companies not wishing to release client details does not arise as GESA is only provided with a code number indicating that an individual is entitled to assistance. Although the absence of end-user details carries the potential for abuse by non-subscribers, this is not considered by GESA to be significant. The company also acts on a referral basis for many other organizations.

Their operational HQ for the UK at Leatherhead in Surrey utilizes a system of interconnected personal computers to manage its client/agent database. The software used, which is based on a video-disk mapping system with around 5,000 scrolling maps covering the whole of the UK with controllers using touch-sensitive VDU screens to manipulate the system, is considered by GESA to be 'state of the art'.

'Front-end' breakdown/recovery is exclusively agency-based and is reliant, in large part, on the same agency pool as other operators. Its current UK agency network comprises 850 independent recovery/repair operators with more than 4,500 vehicles at their disposal.

On 22 February 1990, *Insurance Weekly* announced that GESA had been acquired by a French consortium comprising UAP (the state-owned insurers), and the diversified French water company, Générale des Eaux, who contributed 80 per cent and 20 per cent respectively to the purchase price of f. 850 million. GESA's recent performance was illustrated by the following:

Year	Profits (f. million)
1989	46.8
1988	38.1
1987	23.5

Although additional equity holders were anticipated, UAP was expected to ensure it retained future management control of GESA. In 1989 GESA's turnover of f. 529 million was more than treble that of UAP's subsidiary, UAP Assistance, which was more dependent upon the French domestic market.

When interviewed in early February 1990, Trevor Wilkinson, Managing Director of GESA UK, expressed confidence that, for the foreseeable future, there would continue to be plenty of room in the UK for all operators in the motorist assistance business. This view was based not only on the very low (in European terms) penetration of the general UK market but also on the fact that the major players were neither currently involved in, nor seemed keen to provoke, overt 'head to head' competition.

The Europ Assistance Group

Created in Paris in 1963 by its parent, Assicurazioni Generali SpA, an Italian private company, Europ Assistance defines its business as the provision of 'assistance' in a global context. Its core activity is the provision of medical and technical emergency services in 180 countries through a network of 19 national co-ordination centres, through which 300 agencies are accessible on a 24-hour basis for service delivery.

By 1989 over 70 million people and 7.5 million vehicles were covered worldwide and in the UK market, over 1.5 million motoring covers were divided amongst three ranges of products:

Total covers – 1989

Motoring Assistance	1,100,000
Personal Motoring Service	450,000
Fleet Motor	40,000

Having first entered the UK market in 1973, the majority of its policies are now sold via financial and travel-related intermediaries. Their network of retailing links includes: Eagle Star Insurance, Commercial Union Assurance, the Royal Bank of Scotland, the National Westminster Bank, building societies, credit card companies, tour and ferry operators, and travel agency chains. Policies are retailed by such outlets as their own-branded products to supplement their own service packages. Although both motoring assistance and personal motoring service are also available as direct sale products to the general public, retail accounts contribute only 50 per cent of Europ Assistance's total sales.

Within the UK, their Motoring Assistance service is delivered via a network of 1,500 approved garages and the franchised dealerships for all makes of car, the range of product options being very similar to that of the other agency-based providers.

Whilst its UK operations, which are Croydon-based, cover 1.5 million UK vehicles, Europ Assistance promotes itself as the largest European motoring service, with branches in eight EC countries through which it has direct access to 11,000 affiliated garage agents, all of whom are subject to close monitoring and are equipped to invoice Europ Assistance direct. Its advertising also emphasizes both its worldwide branch network and the tailoring of assistance packages to meet the particular needs of corporate customers.

Mondial

The Mondial Assistance Group was formed in 1974 as a joint venture comprising the Automobile Club de France and two large French insurance companies, AGF and GAN, and is now the largest motor assistance company in France.

Motoring assistance is only part of its global operations which include medical repatriation insurance for corporate and personal sectors and payment for medical treatment outside the insured's country. Its foreign motoring and repatriation contracts are essentially short term, averaging three weeks in duration.

During the past decade its parent company in Paris has been joined by others in Croydon (1980), Madrid, Casablanca and Brussels (1981), and Rome (1982). Operational centres are also located in Spain and Germany. Each company operates worldwide through the Mondial Network in over 150 other countries. Each centre is manned 24 hours a day by multi-lingual staff. Assistance to clients in other countries is supplied via franchised agents. Since its inception, Mondial's total client base has increased from 40,000 to 12 million. Its repatriation capability. which is based on aero-medical equipment and an aircraft fleet owned by Mondial, together with its own doctors, enables treatment equivalent to a hospital intensive care unit to be given to repatriation clients in flight. Mondial estimates that it has the global capacity to resource 50 simultaneous repatriation flights.

Each operating company has the autonomy to tailor its assistance contracts to best suit local market conditions, a feature which Mondial regards as a major factor in explaining its rapid growth. Although the general public in the UK perceive Mondial in terms of provision of motoring assistance, on the continent it provides a wide variety of emergency assistance programmes including, in France, the organization of child-minders for families in difficult situations.

In its first year of operation, policies by Mondial UK covered only 12,000 people and 4,500 vehicles, but by 1990 these had grown to over 1.25 million and 400,000 respectively. Motoring breakdown/recovery assistance packages are similar to those of other operators and are provided in the UK by a network of 1,500 recovery agents supported by authorized car dealerships, both for the personal and corporate markets. Incorporation of such packages in motor manufacturer new-car warranties is a relatively recent development for other service providers but is nothing new to Mondial who pioneered such links over ten years ago. In contrast with its competitors, however, Mondial has tended to concentrate on supplying bespoke schemes for up-market manufacturers such as BMW, Audi/VW, Lamborghini, Maserati and Jaguar (Europe) as well as Porsche. Mondial argues that such manufacturers would not appreciate what they regard as the somewhat unsophisticated approach adopted by motoring organizations for getting the motorist suffering difficulties back on the road. Thus, when a Mondial-insured vehicle breaks down the owner is given a replacement vehicle whilst their's is transferred to the nearest authorized specialist dealer for repair. Their scheme is unashamedly exclusive and targeted at the fastidious owner of vehicles of highly service-orientated manufacturers.

'We wouldn't turn down Skoda out of hand but it's highly unlikely that they would want our sort of service. Some manufacturers are offering membership of one of the motoring organisations to lend credibility to their cars but Audi and BMW don't need to prove their credibility.'
Alex Minajew, Market Development Manager, Mondial Assistance, *Marketing Week* (16.2.90)

Although comprehensive, individual membership is also available at a price comparable to that of its rivals; to date, this has not been generally advertised in the UK.

Mondial has a comprehensive network of 4,000 agents working for it on mainland Europe with which it has close day-to-day working relationships. In contrast, although both the AA and RAC are dominant in their domestic market, they are dependent on the reciprocal goodwill of foreign motoring clubs through which they operate on mainland Europe and whose standard of service provision is not consistent in either range or quality.

An indication of Mondial's possible future strategy in the UK appeared in *Marketing Week* (16.3.90)

'Mondial Assistance, the specialist breakdown recovery organisation, are developing an emergency assistance package for general drivers and will provide emergency help in non-motoring situations. Details are still under wraps, but in France it runs a number of schemes including providing child-minders if parents are in hospital. Mondial are also to relaunch its Road Service scheme and are supporting the new developments by a £500,000 advertising campaign. They will be targeting a variety of UK business sectors.'

The vehicle breakdown/recovery market

The common experience of all countries in the European Community is that higher economic activity has led to a dramatic increase in demand for transport and travel. This is most evident in the UK where, in the period 1950 to 1990, passenger transport volume trebled and that for freight doubled. Within the vast increase in traffic volume over the period, the share of passenger transport going by road increased from 80 to 93 per cent, and goods moved (ton miles) by road increased fourfold (Department of Transport, 1990). Nearly two-thirds of households now have regular use of a car, compared with only 14 per cent in 1951 (see Appendix 3). The UK motor-car ownership increased from 17.8 million vehicles in 1981 to over 21 million in 1989, of which cars accounted for 86 per cent and 90 per cent respectively and, as illustrated in Appendix 4, a similar trend pervades mainland Europe.

It is therefore not surprising that the derived demand for motoring assistance services, as indicated by membership of motoring organizations in the UK, has increased dramatically since the early 1980s (see Tables 2.7.6 and 2.7.7). Indeed, the domestic breakdown assistance market in the UK is now estimated to be worth in excess of £700 million annual premium income.

Table 2.7.6   Estimated UK membership of motoring organizations (000s)

Year	Membership
1982	5,538
1983	6,457
1984	8,303
1985	9,217
1986	10,138
1987	11,700
1988	13,200
1989	13,957

Source: Derived from motoring organizations; Consumers' Association; authors' estimates.

Market buoyancy, together with long time lags between changes in market behaviour by any of the organizations and recognition of their impact on annual membership volumes by rivals has enabled both established players in the UK and new entrants to enjoy significant growth without resort to aggressive competition for market share. Although the past decade has witnessed a significant increase in penetration of the UK market by service providers, most consider that there remains potential for its further exploitation.

The latest National Road Traffic Forecasts published in 1989 suggest that, in comparison with 1988, road traffic demand within Great Britain could increase by between 83 and 142 per cent by the year 2025, with car ownership growing by between 60 and 84 per cent over the same period. Such forecasts are, however, based upon the following core assumptions.

(a) Economic growth will generate sufficient commercial activity and opportunities for people to travel more frequently and over longer distances.
(b) Major constraints on ownership and use of road vehicles are not imposed by either national or Community governments in pursuit of, for example, integrated transport management policies to limit consequential costs to the environment.

Even if favourable underlying conditions of demand continue into the foreseeable future, the indications are, based on the UK experience, that a more overtly competitive market structure is likely to develop in the supply of motoring assistance services. Although, in terms of absolute size, the AA and RAC retain their traditional dominance of the domestic market in the UK, at least four other significant entrants have emerged since the early 1970s. As illustrated in Table 2.7.7, all appear to have gained at the expense of both the AA and RAC. Excluding the achievement of National Breakdown, the most dramatic growth during the 1980s was by the French-owned Mondial which only recruited 4,500 members during its first year in the UK market in 1980, but by 1989 had achieved a membership of 500,000.

Table 2.7.7 UK membership of major motoring organizations (000s)

	1985	1987	1989	1990
AA	5,700	6,480	7,357	7,574
RAC	2,500	3,400	4,200	5,040
National Breakdown	450	750	1,000	1,500
Europ Assistance	352	500	700	na
Mondial	242	400	500	na
Britannia	140	170	200	270
Total	9,384	11,700	13,957	

Sources: Derived from estimates by motoring organizations and the authors, Which?, Consumers' Association, May 1987; Marketing Week, February, 1990.

The service packages on offer are becoming more varied with most providers viewing continuous investment in market and product development as critical for maintenance of their growth record. In the past, the main alternative to provision of a breakdown/recovery service via membership of a motoring organization was for the motorist to rely on a highly fragmented and variable quality service from local garages. Only a small number of insurance schemes, such as those offered by the Guild of Experienced Motorists (GEM) or Frizzell Financial Services Ltd, enabled the motorist to recoup the costs of breakdown repair/recovery on a 'pay and reclaim' basis.

In 1989 only six insurance companies including Avon, Folgate and Hambro offered rescue packages in the UK as an option within their motor insurance policies. By 1990, however, 20 general insurance companies, including major companies such as Legal and General, Commercial Union, Pearl and Provincial, were including optional cover in their policy portfolios. To them the business they are in is the provision of 'assistance', of which emergency motoring services are but one segment.

Strong interest in extending their activity into the breakdown/recovery sector is now apparent amongst organizations such as GESA, Hambro and Sun Alliance, who have significant interests in the general insurance business throughout continental Europe. Another emerging trend with potentially dramatic implications for competitive behaviour in the sector is the provision of pan-European cover, originally introduced by Mondial in 1980 but ignored by UK players, other than for short-term optional cover for holidays abroad such as the AA's 5-Star package. Entry into this field since 1989 by the three main UK motoring organizations confirms their expectation of its future importance.

Single Market issues

The Cecchini report (1988) suggested that the potential impact on the motoring assistance sector by the Single European Market could mean an average gain of 4.5 per cent in the EC's GDP, together with a fall in total unemployment equating to 1.5 percentage points. Although authors such as Cutler, T. *et al.*, (1990) regard such projections as both exaggerated and speculative, it is likely that the pattern of demand for motor travel and transport by the personal and business sectors implicit in Appendices 3 and 4 is likely to be accentuated by completion of the Single Market.

Such developments will continue as long as travel aspirations are not frustrated by barriers to transport movement by road. The EC has confirmed its commitment to easing such barriers by a number of important initiatives, including the introduction of the standard style of European passport and driving licences, both of which originated well before the formal adoption of the Single Market campaign. The harmonization of access to health care may also have some impact in this context in so far as it builds confidence in travel, although it is recognized that variation in the standard of provision amongst Member States is still considerable. Such policies are clearly in line with the philosophy of the Single European Act and the 1990 Schengen Agreement between France, Germany and the Benelux countries. The potential impact of the latter has been emphasized by Portugal, Italy and Spain having signalled their intention to join. If its provisions for the abolition of all significant customs and passport controls are fully realized, it offers the prospect of open land borders and un-hindered movement amongst all major EC states.

The breakdown of ferry usage by type of passenger between the UK and continental Europe, as illustrated by the experience of Dover over the past decade, confirms the general pattern of dramatic increase in traffic by road vehicles (see Table 2.7.8).

Table 2.7.8   Cross-Channel ferry traffic by user type – Port of Dover

	1980	1990	Estimated % of all such ferry traffic between UK and Europe 1990
Foot passengers	11,032,082	15,600,000	35
Tourist cars	1,387,742	2,218,160	50
Coaches	62,473	124,832	70
Road haulage vehicles	508,348	1,088,878	40
*Cargo (tons)	6,759,817	13,016,557	na

Note: *Cargo includes bulk plus that carried by road haulage vehicles in transit.
Source: Dover Harbour Board.

In the longer term, completion of the Channel Tunnel should further encourage movement to and from the UK by creating, in effect, a land border with the continent for the first time in modern history. As part of the on-going study of the cross-Channel market, Eurotunnel Ltd receive regular information updates from independent traffic and revenue consultants about the total cross-Channel market. The first definitive study in 1987 forecast that 64.3 million passengers would cross the Channel in 1993. These forecasts were virtually achieved in 1989, when passenger flow equalled 64.2 million (*Eurotunnel Briefing*). By 2013 the OECD expect that half of all cross-Channel passengers will be road users (OECD, 1990).

When combined with existing trends in tourist activity, and the changes in the size and composition of European motor car ownership summarized in Appendices 3 and 4, such projections of future developments would appear, prima facie, to confirm the prospect of buoyant European demand for motoring-related services in the future. By the late 1980s the volume of tourist arrivals into continental European states was increasing by 5 per cent per year (OECD, ibid. 1990 p. 35), and the number of tourists leaving the UK for the nearer continental destinations increased even more rapidly with 28 per cent of all holidays by UK residents being taken abroad. Over the period 1984 to 1989 the two most popular destinations were Spain and France, with the number of arrivals from the UK increasing by 20 and 25 per cent respectively. Table 2.7.9 summarizes the breakdown by mode of transport for tourist arrivals in selected European countries.

Table 2.7.9   Foreign tourism by mode of transport, 1989

| | Breakdown of arrivals (%) | | | | Total volume |
	Air	Sea	Rail	Road	(000s)
Eire	57.6	35.0	3.3	4.1	2,950.0
Italy	11.2	2.4	8.7	77.7	55,131.1
Portugal	16.2	1.5	0.9	81.4	16,475.8
Spain	31.3	3.3	4.9	60.5	54,256.4
Turkey	52.6	16.7	1.7	29.0	4,459.2
UK	67.8	32.2	–	–	17,292.0

Source: OECD, 1990, p.94

The greater burden of international mobility carried by Europe's roads is likely to compound the need for motorist support services to operate beyond their traditional national markets. In cases where the model of vehicle is standard and distribution widespread, the availability of parts and servicing expertise is less difficult, but for less common models there can be significant problems. In all cases, however, there is likely to be increased motivation for the personal and corporate sectors to reduce the degree of risk associated with motoring abroad. Just as a very high percentage of travellers leaving the UK feel a need to insure against the cost of medical care, and in extreme cases repatriation, it seems reasonable to suggest that there will be a growing need for a similar service for the motorist presented with the possibility of vehicle breakdowns. In the past, insurance services of this type have typically been bought in the country of departure, not only because of the consumer's need to feel that the organization offering the service is familiar to him and can be trusted, but also because the domestic market is likely to offer the best points of direct and indirect sales.

In this context, movement by UK motoring organizations to extend their service coverage across Europe for domestic clients would appear to be a natural extension of current activity in their national market. However, predicting its likely implications for organizations in a sector not previously subject to aggressive competitive rivalry is couched in uncertainty, particularly if players pursue their intentions to market their services to the corporate and retail sectors throughout the European Community. The aggression with which companies pursue their pan-European aspirations and the methods employed to operate beyond their traditional markets may prove to be of critical importance.

Appendix 1   Company data

Exhibit 1a   Nationwide Breakdown Recovery Services Limited

	1977 (£000)	1983 (£000)	1985 (£000)	1987 (£000)	1988 (£000)	1989 (£000)	1990 (£000)
Turnover	683	4,330	6,836	13,106	16,880	22,113	33,692
Trading profit	n a	215	487	876	931	2,036	2,654
Depreciation	12	(115)	(149)	(208)	(205)	(232)	(391)
Operating profit	n a	100	338	668	726	1,804	2,263
Non-trading income	5	95	81	154	216	337	(140)
Interest payable	n a	(9)	(1)	(0)	(0)	(5)	(41)
Pre-tax profit	38.6	186	418	822	942	2,136	2,082
Retained profit for year	30	72	217	566	602	1,467	n a
Retained profits b/f	(14)	483	555	882	1,448	2,050	n a
Retained profits c/f	(14)	555	772	1,448	2,050	3,517	n a
Business ratios (%)							
	1977	1983	1985	1987	1988	1989	1990
Return on sales	5.7	4.3	6.1	6.3	5.6	9.7	6.4
Return on capital	55.7	18.4	24.6	33.9	29.1	42.4	33.4
Return on total assets	23	11.3	13.1	17.2	12.7	17.5	13.9
Employees							
Total	n a	102	115	190	213	243	315

Source: Company accounts

Exhibit 1b National Parking Corporation

Turnover (£m)

	1986	1987	1988	1989	1990
Parking & motor trade revenue	75	86	101	117	122
Property trading & income	4	5	7	5	5
Vehicle breakdown & recovery	8	13	17	22	33
Coach activity	5	5	7	8	9
Dealing in securities	–	–	–	–	0.6
Total	**92**	**109**	**132**	**152**	**169.6**

Profit (Loss) before tax (£m)

	1986	1987	1988	1989	1990
Profit & motor trade revenue	14.3	17.2	22.2	29	31.9
Property trading & income	3.8	4.3	4.7	3.6	4.2
Vehicle breakdown & recovery*	0.9	1.8	2.2	3.9	5.8
Coach activity	0.4	0.5	0.9	0.8	1.1
Dealing in securities	–	–	–	–	0.6
Sale of property	1.7	12.2	2.1	9.8	5.6
Interest receivable					
Unallocated	–	4.8	5.8	6.9	10.9
Total	**21.0**	**40.8**	**37.9**	**54.0**	**60.1**

*Figures differ from Exhibit 1(a) as they reflect the accounting conventions and definitions of the parent company and also appear to include income from all related activities such as insurance.

Business ratios (%)

	1986	1987	1988	1989	1990
Return on sales	22.8	37.4	28.8	35.6	35.5
Return on capital	43.6	48.0	36.0	37.5	34.9
Return on total assets	20.1	26.9	21.2	23.2	21.9

Employees					
Total	3,375	3,478	3,177	3,253	3,370

Source: Group Consolidated Accounts

Appendix 2   Comparative performance of motoring organizations

Exhibit 2a   Percentage of motorists reached

Organization	within 1 hour of call-out	more than 3 hours of call-out	Sample size
Local garage	70	8.6	3,151
AA	63	2.1	4,193
Britannia Rescue	85	1.2	168
National Breakdown	75	0.5	213
RAC	69	1.6	1,949
Others	63	4.5	201

Note: Average response times reported by subscribers to Which? magazine who were members of motoring organizations and had been assisted by them during the previous three years.
Source: Adapted from Which?, The Consumers' Association, July 1987.

Exhibit 2b   Degree of satisfaction with assistance received

Organization	Percentage of motorists assisted who were Very satisfied	Very dissatisfied
Local garage	66	3
AA	67	3
Britannia Rescue	76	3
National Breakdown	75	3
RAC	66	3
Others	62	6

Source: as for Exhibit 2a

Exhibit 2c   Service response time experienced by simulated vehicle breakdown requiring recovery of the vehicle and driver

Organization	Response time	Vehicle recovery time
AA	1 hour 45 minutes	2 hours 45 minutes
Britannia Rescue	50 minutes	2 hours 15 minutes
National Breakdown	30 minutes	2 hours 25 minutes
RAC	4 hours 15 minutes	3 hours 45 minutes

Note: Results relate to experience of a woman journalist left in the same deliberately immobilized car at four locations equi-distant from Sheffield.
Source: Adapted from Auto Express, 28 November, 1989.

Appendix 3   The demand for personal transport

Exhibit 3a   Personal travel: passenger distance: 1965 to 1985 billion passenger kilometres

Mode of travel	1965	1975	1985
Motoring	199	294	401
Bus and coach	59	55	42
Rail	35	35	36
Other	12	8	11
All surface passenger transport	305	392	490

Source: *Transport Statistics Great Britain 1976-86*, tables 1.1 and 7.1

Exhibit 3b   Household expenditure on travel 1965 to 1985 £ per household per week at 1985 prices*

	Motoring	Other	All	As percentage of total household expenditure
1965	12.5	4.3	16.8	10
1975	16.7	4.2	20.9	14
1985	20.7	3.8	24.6	15

* Adjusted for general inflation by the retail price index (all items)
Source: *Family Expenditure Survey*, Department of Employment, 1988

Exhibit 3c   Car ownership 1965 to 1985

	Percentage of all households with		Households in GB (m)	Stock of household cars (m)	Cars per household
	one car	two or more cars			
1965	36	5	17.2	8	0.46
1975	46	10	19.1	13	0.69
1985	45	17	20.7	17	0.84

Source: *Transport Statistics Great Britain 1976-86*, tables 2.11, 2.19, 7.2 and 7.5

Appendix 4 International road vehicle stock

Exhibit 4a Road vehicle stock (000s) by type 1978 and 1988

Country	Cars & taxis 1978	1988	Goods vehicles 1978	1988	All vehicles 1978	1988
UK	14,700	19,900	1,650	2,110	17,600	23,200
Belgium	2,970	3,610	199	270	3,750	4,030
Denmark	1,410	1,650	260	290	1,710	1,990
GDR	21,200	28,900	1,180	1,320	25,100	32,700
France	17,700	22,500	2,330	3,230	26,200	29,300
Greece	745	1,450	265	650	1,127	2,309
Eire	643	749	60	118	736	895
Italy	16,200	25,000	1,410	1,910	22,100	33,500
Luxembourg	153	168	10	10	167	181
Netherlands	4,100	5,250	290	468	5,490	6,380
Portugal	1,110	2,070	145	370	1,350	2,564
Spain	6,530	10,790	1,190	1,980	8,930	13,700
Total	**87,461**	**122,037**	**8,989**	**12,726**	**114,260**	**150,749**
Austria	2,040	2,790	162	235	2,840	3,630
Czechoslovakia	1,840	2,800	n.a.	n.a.	n.a.	n.a.
Finland	1,120	1,800	136	214	1,480	2,200
DDR	2,390	3,740	230	230	3,980	5,350
Hungary	839	1,790	129	179	1,710	2,410
Norway	1,150	1,620	146	287	1,450	2,130
Sweden	2,860	3,480	169	267	3,060	3,790
Switzerland	2,060	2,760	153	228	3,020	3,820
Yugoslavia	1,860	3,090	151	261	2,170	3,470
Other Europe	16,159	23,870	1,276	1,901	19,710	26,800
Japan	19,800	30,800	12,620	21,400	44,200	70,900
USA	114,000	155,000	30,410	41,200	152,100	202,200

Note: Vehicle stock refers to road vehicles registered by the reporting country for use on its road network.

Source: *International comparisons of transport statistics*, 1970-1987, HMSO, June, 1990, Tables A, C. *Transport Statistics Great Britain*, Department of Transport, HMSO, Sept., 1990, Table 6.5

Exhibit 4b   Characteristics of the road and rail transport systems (EC12) 1950-1985

	1950	1960	1970	1980	1985
Road					
Motorways (000 km)	2	4	13	26	30
Cars owned (million)	6	20	58	96	114
Cars per 1000 population	22	72	194	300	354
Commercial vehicles (million)	3	5	8	10	12
Railway					
Coaches (000)	113	102	79	76	70
Goods wagons (million)	1.5	1.3	1.1	0.9	0.7
Total track (000 km)	163	148	136	129	127
Multitrack, electrified (000 km)	10	18	27	34	36

Source: Molle, W.,1990, *The Economics of European Integration*, Dartmouth Publishing Co, Table 15.2

Exhibit 4c   New vehicle registrations and total vehicle stock (000) in the UK 1975 to 1989

	Cars	Goods vehicles	New registrations Buses	Commercial vehicles	All vehicles	Total vehicles currently licensed
1975	1,194	220	5	225	1,419	
1976	1,286	209	6	215	1,501	
1977	1,324	225	6	231	1,555	
1978	1,592	256	6	262	1,854	
1979	1,716	301	5	306	2,022	18,616
1980	1,514	266	6	272	1,786	19,200
1981	1,485	213	5	218	1,703	19,347
1982	1,555	227	4	231	1,786	19,762
1983	1,792	264	4	268	2,060	20,209
1984	1,740	266	3	269	2,009	20,765
1985	1,832	284	3	287	2,119	21,157
1986	1,883	289	2	291	2,174	21,699
1987	2,014	311	2	313	2,327	22,152
1988	2,216	354	3	357	2,573	23,302
1989	2,301	368	3	371	2,672	24,196

Source: *Motor Industry of Great Britain 1990 World Automotive Statistics*, Society of Motor Manufacturers and Traders, London, 1990, Table 27; *Transport Statistics of Great Britain*, Department of Transport, HMSO, Sept.1990, Table 2.22

Appendix 5

New car warranties with inclusive recovery service: by manufacturer and motoring organization – as at December 1989

AA
Fiat - free membership for 1st year
Nissan
Peugeot
Rolls-Royce
Rover – AA Relay service

RAC
Ford
Jaguar – scheme operated in conjunction with Group European (GESA) to
    provide coverage both in UK and Europe
Lada – two years' free membership
Renault
Volvo – includes reimbursement for car hire
Mercedes

National Breakdown
Vauxhall – includes reimbursement for car hire
Citroën
Lada
Mazda

Mondial Assistance (pan-European breakdown cover as from November 1988)
Audi & VW – cover for 6 years for cars regularly serviced by agents
BMW – first year cover and then option of discount renewal premium with
    Mondial
Mitsubishi – commenced August 1988
Porsche
Saab

Manufacturers with no motoring organization linked recovery service in their
warranties:
Honda
Skoda

References

Cecchini, P. *The European Challenge*, (Aldershot, Wildwood House, 1988).
Cutler, T. *et al*, *1992 – The struggle for Europe*, (Berg, 1990).
Eurotunnel Briefing, Issue 3, July 1990.
Department of Transport, *Trunk Roads, England into the 1990s* (London, HMSO, 1990).
OECD, *Tourism Policy and International Tourism*, (Paris, 1990).

Questions/discussion topics

1. Why has National Breakdown proven so successful since its formation in 1971?

2. (a) How has the competitive environment facing National Breakdown changed since 1971?
    (b) What do you consider will be the most important future changes which it will have to address?

3. 'The key to growth, even survival, is to stake out a position that is less vulnerable to attack from head-to-head opponents, whether established or new, and less vulnerable to erosion from the direction of buyers, suppliers, and substitute goods.' M.E. Porter, 'How Competitive Forces Shape Strategy', *Harvard Business Review,* Vol.57, No.2, 1979.
    In the light of Porter's comments appraise the past strategies adopted by the organizations referred to in the case and recommend those that would be most appropriate for them to adopt in the future.

4. In 1990 National Breakdown became the first organization to include free annual pan-European cover as part of its policy package.
    Examine the arguments for and against its adoption of such a strategy for expansion.

5. Compare and contrast the alternative methods that might be used by UK service providers to exploit the continental European market.

6. Assess the proposition that the completion of the Single European Market will result in the demise of those organizations which focus solely on the provision of breakdown/recovery services.

7. Present the case for and against the assessment that European competitors pose no threat to UK service providers.

8. On what grounds may it be said that the European market in the provision of motoring assistance services is 'heading for a breakdown'?

9. Compare the influence of organizational objectives on the behaviour of the AA, RAC and National Breakdown.

10. Contrast three alternative scenarios of how you think the European market in motoring assistance services may develop during the next decade and illustrate their implications for each of the organizations discussed in the case.

Case 8
Essex Water PLC – A study in market extension[*]

Tony Bennett

Advice to readers

Essex Water PLC provides a unique set of marketing development issues to ponder. By merging with Lyonnaise des Eaux in the spirit of the Single Market, the company has been able to develop from a small parochial organization to one having a truly global orientation.

An underlying assumption of many contemporary management theories is that growth and development are always aggressive; this study questions this view. The case gives the reader an opportunity to examine the issues involved in the synergy that has developed between Essex Water and Lyonnaise des Eaux.

Readers should refer to contemporary management theorists, for example, Michael Porter, H. Igor Ansoff, Charles Handy, and Rosabeth Moss-Kantor, in order to obtain maximum benefit from the case. A major issue addressed in the study is whether planned and sustainable growth can legitimately be achieved through collaboration.

The organizational response to events leading up to the purchase of Essex Water by Lyonnaise des Eaux in July 1988

Essex Water PLC is a private water company with its own set of statutes and its own board of directors. It is important to note that in the UK there is a distinction between the ten statutory water companies and the private water companies such as Essex Water. The latter enjoy a high degree of commercial independence although they are subject to fairly tight

[*] The author would like to thank David Parr, Managing Director of Essex Water and David Knight, Business Manager, Essex Water Management Services for the help and support that they have provided during the development of this case study.

regulation. The regulation of the water industry in the UK is the responsibility of the following four bodies:

- the Office of Water Services, which is concerned with looking after the customers' interests, including the level of charges;
- the National Rivers Authority which has the power to regulate the resources of the water industry, including water quality;
- the Drinking Water Inspectorate, which ensures that drinking water quality is monitored and maintained;
- HM Inspectorate of Pollution, which checks pollution controls.

The partnership with Lyonnaise has helped Essex to take full advantage of the opportunities provided by privatization. For example, the company has been able to develop new business areas complementary to its core business of supplying water; these areas are Essex Water Projects, Water Analytical, and AQUIT 2000 and Eurecart.

Privatization of the UK water industry

Many overseas companies, especially from France, became interested in the British water industry once the issue of privatization had been placed on the political agenda in the 1980s. The water privatization legislation was passed in 1989. At that time France was the only other member of the EC that had a privatized water industry. French organizations, such as Lyonnaise des Eaux, wished to diversify and the UK market provided them with major opportunities.

At the same time the management at Essex Water was feeling vulnerable; a major fear being the possible takeover by one of the larger water organizations, for example, the Thames or Anglia Authorities. To quote David Parr, Managing Director of Essex Water, 'our customers would not have got a better deal by becoming some far outpost of Thames Water'.

In the early months of 1988, immediately prior to the water flotation, there was much share activity and Essex Water began to investigate the possibility of a joint venture. At the same time Lyonnaise was looking for partners in the UK.

The takeover

In general terms if either a British or a US company wishes to be associated with another company, the usual approach is that of a takeover, 'to go for 100 per cent'. The approach of Lyonnaise des Eaux to acquisition is quite different, it approaches other companies and says, 'We'd like to become involved. Do you mind?' If, as a consequence of this initiative, the company obtains a large enough holding, it follows this up by saying, 'We'd quite like a seat on the board. We're not rushing to take you over.'

David Parr, MD, at Essex Water, had spent nearly 25 years in the private sector but he had little or no experience of takeovers, mergers, acquisitions, or other joint ventures. However, in the development of the partnership with Lyonnaise the informal discussions between Parr and his opposite number were particularly important. Negotiations were well-developed informally before more formal discussions involving the participation of third parties such as merchant banks took place. The merger resulted in a partnership between Essex Water PLC and Lyonnaise des Eaux – Essex has not become a subsidiary company of the French organization.

Consolidation of Lyonnaise des Eaux's position in the UK

Since 1988 Lyonnaise des Eaux has established a sound base in the UK. It has interests in four water supply companies: Essex, Suffolk, Newcastle, and Sunderland. In addition, it has a minority holding in both the Bristol and Anglia Water Authorities. These holdings are purely in the water sector of the business, but Lyonnaise has interests in activities such as: waste disposal, water treatment and purification services. In 1990 Lyonnaise acquired the Duvaise Company, a major international construction organization. Thus, in two-and-a-half years the French company has consolidated comprehensive business interests in the UK.

During the 1980s Lyonnaise developed trading interests in other parts of the world, most notably Eastern Europe, especially the former East Germany, and the Middle and Far East.

The need to diversify

Even with privatization it was generally felt that the water industry in the UK was static; it hinged on one product, the supply of water. The business culture was product-based, whereas in a successful commercial operation the strategic focus normally depends upon adapting and responding to the market place. Few water companies in the UK were taking full advantage of privatization, for example, few took the opportunity to develop additional products, such as water testing services.

'. . . most have just been concerned with reducing the harmful effects of privatization as they see it, in cultural terms little seems to have changed as a

result of privatization. Most appear to be developing a defensive strategy.'
A spokesman at Essex Water

The current structure of Essex Water PLC

Essex Water has a relatively small board of six members, this includes two French directors. Since 1988 David Parr has held the position of Chief Executive of Lyonnaise des Eaux in the UK. In addition to his responsibilities within Essex Water, he is also Chief Executive of the Suffolk Water Company. See Fig. 2.8.1 for the organization structure of Essex Water.

Product development and strategic planning

Prior to becoming involved with Lyonnaise, Essex's primary business was in water supply. During 1990 it was developing the idea of becoming a PLC and senior management felt that to attract shareholders it would have to diversify away from its core business.

The French water industry has been in private hands for over a hundred years and the private sector expertise that Lyonnaise had developed has been of great value to Essex Water. Lyonnaise has provided Essex Water with ideas, opportunities and substantial resources. After the merger Essex Water had the confidence to take risks, this had not been the case previously.

'The French company brought a fresh approach to Essex Water, bringing new ideas without being a "prescriptive or authoritarian parent".'
David Parr

A strategic decision was taken that diversification should be achieved wherever possible by utilizing and developing in-house expertise rather than bringing in outsiders. To this end, with the assistance of an external consultant, an audit was carried out to identify existing skills and those required for the future. Senior management at Essex were keen to ensure that all their employees were fully involved in this process and committed to it.

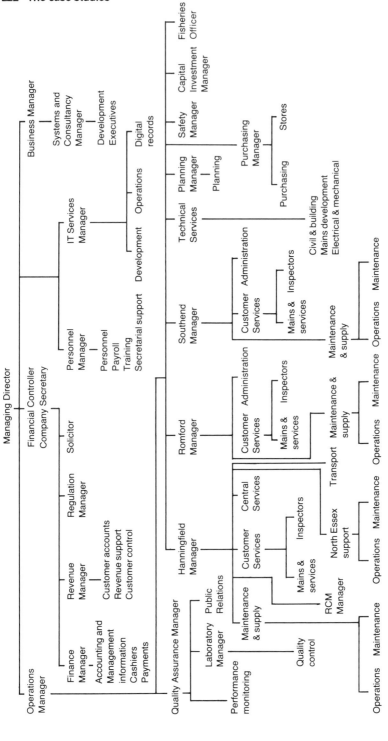

Fig. 2.8.1   Essex Water Company PLC organization and structure

The development of the product portfolio

Out of the management audit, Essex Water identified certain key strengths and areas that the business could diversify into. Three new business areas were developed as a result of this process and they were established as separate subsidiaries of Lyonnaise UK PLC. This structure enables shareholders, managers and others to distinguish these subsidiary businesses from the core activity, monitor their viability and ensure that Essex Water rate payers' funds are not diverted. The business areas are:

- Essex Water Projects;
- Water Analytical;
- AQUIT 2000 and Eurecart.

Essex Water Projects (EWP)

The aim of EWP is to provide a high-quality emergency, general plumbing and underground pipework service to all domestic and commercial customers in Essex and ultimately further afield. A 24-hour control room has been set up, manned by staff who can advise callers and schedule calls. To provide management expertise in this area an existing plumbing company was acquired. The company argues that the strength of the business is the reputation and security of Essex combined with widespread promotion and careful quality monitoring. This is a niche market as the specific area of underground work was not well served by existing operators.

Essex Analytical

Essex Water have developed extensive skills in the area of specialist water analysis, for example, the analysis of trace levels of pesticides. These services are now offered to other organizations including water companies. In the rapidly changing context of environmental awareness, the strategy is to adopt a low-key commercial stance but to be ready for opportunities as they arise.

AQUIT 2000 and Eurecart

These two business areas are based on Essex's experience of installing IT systems to run a large utility network. In the area of information technology, Essex Water has developed an integrated database, drawing together 20 or 30 software systems – some of which are management-control systems, others geographic systems, geographic information, and network-modelling systems. For example, in the water industry there are requirements for sophisticated communications systems because service engineers are widespread, mobile, and on call 24 hours a day. In addition, comprehensive statistical information is required for the UK water regulatory authorities.

With a customer base of half a million, the company needs fairly substantial mainframe and other support computers. All of this interactive customer-orientated information is accumulated into a ten-year plan, then a five-year plan, and then 50 action plans. Twenty or 30 of these are combined into a database called 'AQUIT 2000 – Water Information 2000'.

IT skills, both in computer technology developments and in the operational needs of the company, are being offered to the water industry both in the UK and abroad through Lyonnaise. In addition, two software packages are being marketed. One is a Customer Service Management system enabling staff to accept calls and give immediate feedback on incidents (for example, burst main pipes), or to distribute calls to the appropriate areas for logging and tracking new incidents through to completion of any work needed. Equally, the system can handle billing enquiries, routine information and complaints. All these items are recorded for management action.

The second system is a geographic information one which goes beyond the storing of 'maps on computers' to the use of data from other related sources for operational and planning applications, for example, asset performance and customer records.

Lyonnaise des Eaux's contribution to development

With the establishment of the additional business sectors, Essex Water now has a global portfolio of products. Each of these business areas are semi-autonomous units within Essex Water and Lyonnaise has contributed substantial financial resources to each.

The French company provided a ready-made network to disseminate some of these key activities overseas, avoiding the expensive exercise of setting up sales networks for overseas business development. Thus, the association with Lyonnaise has enabled Essex Water to project itself straight on to the world scene. For example, in partnership with Lyonnaise it is participating in a project with research organizations in Japan and the USA to develop a best-practice book on water supply. In addition, a team from Essex and Lyonnaise carried out a study and costing project for water distribution in Jordan, in part this project was financed by the World Bank. On its own, Essex Water could not have envisaged accumulating the necessary resources to consider bidding for such a prestigious contract.

'Projects such as these hold the key to international market development for a small UK company such as Essex Water, and they greatly increase the morale of the work force.'
David Parr

By 1991 Essex Water had developed three separate, but integral parts of the company's portfolio in addition to its core business of providing water. The three areas are small in comparison to the core business and in a number of respects they are at the embryonic stage. These areas are viewed as 'tomorrow's growth areas'.

Training and corporate success

Essex Water recognizes that people's skills are absolutely essential to the growth and development of the company. Training in the company is more concerned with overall staff development than training in the conventional sense. In terms of staff development the company has established two key principles:

- the planning process;
- the people process.

The planning process

David Parr feels that it is important that the business looks forward, has a vision of the future, develops a corporate plan, and distils this into action plans. In this process the Chief Executive aims to fully involve his staff at all levels. For example, about twice a year selected staff are taken away from operations to participate in the planning process. Good communications is regarded as essential to the development of the company.

The people process

For David Parr the people process is about developing people's skills, 'identifying talents, moving people forward, stretching them' and thus complementing the planning process. A central part of the process is identifying promising people and developing their skills. These skills can be interpersonal, managerial, professional, and/or technical.

In David Parr's view some people revel in this dynamic environment, and much of the work that is done is through mixed functional and mixed level groups and is thus outside the formal hierarchical structure.

> 'Management style at Essex Water focuses on team building, staff development and good internal communications but all of this focuses on the customer.'
> David Parr

Prior to the partnership with Lyonnaise, not only was Essex Water product-orientated rather than customer-orientated, but the technical staff such as the chemists and engineers were viewed as the elite within the organization. In David Parr's view it is not the technical staff 'who now drive the business but the customer'. He recognizes that the company has a number of different types of customer.

> '. . .sometimes people come to Essex as an individual, sometimes as a member of an influence group, for example, Friends of the Earth, sometimes as a Customer Service Committee, and sometimes as the Director-General of the whole UK water industry.'
> David Parr

Price and service quality and value

Over the last few years there has been a change in the public's perception of water as a resource. For example, the general public had little understanding of the costs involved in providing good quality water and the industry as a whole had a low profile. It is now more concerned with its public image. A major objective of the industry was to keep prices low. To change the public's perception of the industry, Essex Water has organized a number of events, for example, open days, and presentations in schools and other organizations.

Essex Water – David Parr's vision for the future

Under the privatization rules the water industry has become a series of commercial businesses. In this new culture Parr believes that Essex Water needs to set itself targets that year on year can be improved. This not only implies technological, but also organizational improvement.

Questions/discussion topics

1. To what extent might the UK water privatization policy have provided the initial spur to European expansion by Essex Water?

2. Using the Ansoff model for strategic market development, what could the future service expansion options be for Essex Water?

3. How important is management style and corporate culture to product and market development?

4. Where does management development training fit into market performance in this case study?

Case 9
Airbus Industrie – a study in European collaboration*

Ron Allison and Ian Barnes

Advice to readers

This case study illustrates the process of collaboration between companies in different states of the European Community, using civil aviation as an example. The Airbus project itself predates the Single European Market initiative by a number of years, but it illustrates one of its most important themes: the need for European industry to develop an appropriate response to a global market characterized by a necessity for large-scale production.

The model which Airbus adopted is important, for it is the most significant example of European collaboration in action to date. It is a model which has been widely used by the Community for a range of its R&D programmes such as ESPRIT and BRITE. The case shows that there are strong political, as well as financial, elements in the process of collaboration. In the example of civil aircraft the existence of appropriate political will is essential to overcome the nationalism which has been a feature of the sector in the past. The start-up costs of such projects are high; political support is important in helping to unlock the required funding.

Background

There have been dramatic changes in the pattern of competition in the commercial aircraft industry since the late 1960s. At that time, three US airframe producers – Boeing, Lockheed, and McDonnell Douglas – dominated the global market, but in 1967 a consortium of European producers

* The authors would like to thank Dr Rosina Jones and Derrick Chadburn of Humberside Business School for their contributions to the early development of this case study.

was created and this now offers a significant and increasing challenge to the former US dominance.

On 26 September 1967, the British, French, and German Governments signed an agreement for the production of the first of the Airbus aircraft – the A300 – as long as three national carriers placed orders for a total of 75 aircraft. Airbus Industrie was initially composed of Aerospatiale (France), British Aerospace (Britain), Construcciones Aeronauticas (Spain), and Messerschmitt-Boelkow-Blohm (Germany). By 1991, the European collaborative project had six models under production, or development, and had increased its share of the world market from 5 per cent in the mid-1970s to over 30 per cent. It had delivered 650 aircraft, and had a backlog of orders for another 1,038, worth $71 billion.

This success, along with other competitive factors, led to Lockheed withdrawing from the civil aviation market, and severe pressures being placed upon the remaining US rivals. The two remaining US producers attribute the growth of Airbus to the high levels of State help that the partners in the enterprise receive, whilst Airbus defenders point rather to the success of the collaborative process.

Economic issues in aircraft production

Modern aerospace projects are reliant on high technology and this means that there is often a long lead time between a programme's conception and its delivery. This adds greatly to the degree of risk involved and the projects frequently overrun in terms of cost. Advances in technology can give a competitive advantage, but there are times when the leaders in this respect are overtaken by those who follow, and then there is an advantage in not being first in the field.

Where States support projects, they frequently do so on the basis of national prestige, hence the Anglo-French Concorde carried on being built long after it was clearly not economically viable. On the other hand, without State support it is difficult to keep a civil aerospace industry going in Europe.

Because of the huge development costs associated with modern aircraft design and production, there is a need for high volumes of production, so that these fixed costs can be spread over a larger number of aircraft. The economist's concept of a minimum efficient scale (MES) is of considerable importance in aircraft production. MES is the scale of production where average costs are at, or close to, their minimum level. This is the plant size associated with the bottom of the long-run average cost (LAC) curve, or where the LAC curve enters a very gradual decline. Even in 1969, when aircraft production was nowhere as 'high tech' as it later became, Pratten (1971) estimated that, for one type of aircraft alone, MES as a percentage of the UK market was greater than 100; i.e. there was room only for a maximum of one UK aircraft manufacturer if costs were to be kept at a competitive level. He further pointed out that the cost penalties of being at half the MES were significant at around 20 per cent. The crucial importance of high-volume production is a major explanation for the formation of Airbus Industrie.

In addition, with high volumes it is possible to move down the learning curve, and so produce at lower cost with higher quality based upon experience. In economist's jargon, a learning curve 'defines the marginal productivity of inputs as a function of the cumulative level of output'. Normally, the learning curve is expressed in terms of the number of labour hours required to produce an additional unit of output. As cumulative output increases so both shop-floor workers and managers become more experienced and the existing technology is used more effectively. Studies have shown that learning benefits are largest where new and advanced technology is being used and where production is highly capital-intensive. Not surprisingly, in view of this, the aircraft industry has attracted much empirical research into learning benefits and several studies have shown a learning curve in the 80 per cent region, i.e. each successive unit of output requires only 80 per cent of the previous input quantity.

The high costs of development mean that there are advantages in producing a family of aircraft. It follows that components can be shared, and in many cases, if there is a range of aircraft, it is possible to meet all the needs of a customer. Hence, customer loyalty can be fostered, and they can be encouraged to deal with just the one supplier of not only aircraft, but also the important market for the supply of spare parts.

In the past, European manufacturers seemed unable to compete effectively, they were selling into relatively small home markets, often with narrow specifications. The costs of development were duplicated as each country sought to promote its own champion. In many cases the only serious purchasers were the national flag-carrying airlines, who had little choice but to make the purchase, or those countries who were encouraged to buy the products as part of an aid package. There were frequent doubts about the technical quality of the projects, and generally, they sold badly.

This, therefore, left the US producers in a dominant market position, and in the case of the so called 'jumbo jet', Boeing was the only producer in the world. Effectively, this meant that Boeing could demand the highest price that the market could stand for these large aircraft.

The civil aerospace industry competes on a global basis and it is an industry which requires a huge amount of investment. For example, the development cost of the projected Airbus model A350 is estimated to be $3 billion. The risks are high, the consequence of a model which does not sell well is that the heavy R&D costs will not be recovered.

Unlike many industries of its size and importance, even in the recent past, civil aircraft building was normally conducted by a variety of companies operating within nation states, although frequently linked internationally by licensing, subcontracting, and collaboration agreements. It is an industry where, as already indicated, the major companies are tied very closely to the national political system. This is because of the strategic importance of the industry, especially as the civil aerospace companies are also producers of military equipment. Additionally, it can be a high value-added export industry, as is the case with the Boeing company in the USA.

Government funding in the aerospace industry

The civil aerospace industry in Europe has benefited from much government financial support. This has been accomplished by financing research projects, or underwriting losses on projects. Governments have also helped indirectly by feeding money into the companies via military programmes. Where military research is being conducted by a company, it is often the case that there is an overspill of technology into civil aircraft technology in terms of materials, fuels, electronics and engines.

Civil airliners can, of course, be used for military purposes, for example, as troop transporters or carriers of equipment. For the national governments there is an added bonus, in that support for high-technology areas like this tends to lead to increased investment as guaranteed government support gives firms the confidence to invest more than they would have done otherwise. Estimates place the investment multiplier for aerospace as high as 2.2. In this way the industry helps to promote economic growth. Governments have given indirect help to their aerospace industries by subsidizing export financing or by persuading national flag-carrying airliners to buy the product.

In return for the assistance the industry receives, governments expect to be able to influence the decision-making process, in order to further their international relations policy. Heads of State have frequently seen the industry as being a diplomatic tool, to be used to cement relations with other countries. There is frequently a linkage with military projects, and the size of the contracts involved is seen as sufficient to warrant very top-level involvement in negotiations over sales, or the nature of collaboration.

The move towards European collaboration

By the late 1960s the potential benefits of collaboration in civil aircraft production in Europe were seen to be considerable. Failure of the 'go-it-alone' national efforts indicated that a co-operative solution had to be found. In the field of military aircraft a degree of collaboration made sense, so it also seemed a rational move to adopt the concept for civil aircraft projects.

Collaboration across national borders meant that the costs of development would be shared and there would be limited duplication of research efforts. It also meant that access would be open to existing technological expertise in different states. There would be a wider access to venture capital, and risks would be shared among partners. When the huge costs of developing new aircraft were considered, it was clear that new projects were likely to be beyond the means of individual companies and even national governments. Problems of gaining acceptability of technical standards across Europe would be reduced, as all partners would see it in their interest to ensure that the product was totally acceptable in all markets. Finally, national airlines could be persuaded to purchase the aircraft, so increasing the prospect of sufficient sales to gain the economies of scale required to move down the LAC curve and to become competitive in third markets, i.e. those outside the home country and the EC.

All of these benefits pre-supposed that a project could be started and financed up to the point where it became viable. The costs of gaining a presence in the world airline market were always likely to be huge, given that Airbus was in effect a new entrant.

Instead of a number of national champions all struggling to compete within the narrow confines of the Western European market, collaboration offered the prospect of enhanced market power. Instead of the aircraft manufacturers being relatively insignificant national concerns, the right kind of network of collaboration offered the prospect of creating a global power. With the backing of a number of national governments to ensure that access to third markets was made easier, and a production and research capacity to match the larger global players, it would be possible to offer a meaningful challenge. In addition, the presence of a major European producer offered an additional benefit – the impact of competition on prices. For example, the Boeing monopoly of the jumbo jet market has meant that they have been able to dictate their terms to airlines who had no alternative supplier. Finally, if collaboration offered the prospect of enhancing European integration, then it could expect support from the European Community.

Issues in international collaboration

Collaborating with other companies across national boundaries is not easy, indeed many firms have not even resolved the communication difficulties of operating within one plant. There needs to be a clear definition of the objectives, and an accurate assessment of the financial, technical, and commercial parameters involved. Areas of responsibility have to be made clear, and all those involved in the project must feel a sense of ownership for it. There has to be confidence between partners, and an equitable method of sharing the profits or losses. In order to maximize confidence it is best if collaboration takes place over a long period of time, involving a number of projects. At the same time there has to be an awareness and acceptance of differing industrial cultures.

The choice of the collaborative model, as a competitive response to the US domination of the world civil aircraft market, was driven essentially by the high entry costs in the aircraft manufacturing industry. In addition, there has been a need to establish credibility with the airlines who purchase the products of the industry. Also, collaboration offers an opportunity to gain from a much wider research and manufacturing experience. New technology is difficult to fully develop nationally, and in isolation. Even the most inventive of societies produces only a fraction of the total of new patents and processes required.

Scale economies

Because of the crucial importance of scale economies, in an ideal world the degree of specialization in the EC would develop to such an extent that there would be only one manufacturer of aircraft. Failing this, national producers may benefit from a sharing of information, and a greater degree of specialization on aspects of technology which they feel most comfortable with. Each successive stage in developing new technology becomes more expensive, and individual Member States may not have the resources to compete adequately. The arguments for greater collaboration include:

- cost reductions, for example, economies of scale and experience-based savings;
- the ability to share technology, so that there is not a need to duplicate expensive R&D costs;
- sharing risks, especially with large-scale projects, where there may be a risk of failure;
- reduced problems with technical standards, in that where new standards emerge, they do so in more than one Member State;
- market power, that is the ability to ensure that whatever emerges is not lost because the company lacks size or a presence in other markets. In the case of aircraft manufacture, the fact that many of the airlines are State-owned, means that they can be 'persuaded' to buy specific aircraft. This in turn ensures that volumes are sufficient to reduce costs, and make the manufacture more viable.

It would be wrong to assume that collaboration was a universal panacea. The increasing use of collaboration as a method of operating within the European market has revealed a number of significant problems. These include:

(a) A lack of control over vital parts of the project. There is often a lack of understanding of foreign business cultures and working methods, which leads to very different outcomes from those expected.

(b) No sense of ownership, because the costs and risks are being shared, means that in some cases projects do not receive the same priority as those generated domestically within the organization.

(c) Costs can increase very substantially at the early stages of programmes. This is often because of the need for executives to travel and develop adequate communications. Also compromises have frequently to be made about alternative methods of working.

(d) Setting up and running collaborative projects takes up too much time, especially for senior managers.

(e) State, or EC funding is required to make projects viable, and even then the levels of funding do not always compensate for the extra costs involved. This is especially the case where funding is only available on a competitive basis.

(f)   There is a danger that collaboration is regarded as being nothing short of protectionism by other global producers, especially where large-scale subsidies are involved as part of the launch costs of a project. This may in turn encourage damaging trade disputes.

The decision to collaborate therefore depends on the extent to which the positive aspects of collaboration can be said to outweigh the negative aspects.

The market for aircraft

Within the European context, air travel is growing rapidly. In the past, growth of traffic rates was only between 2 and 4 per cent, however, between the start of 1987 and mid-1989, there was a growth rate of 20 per cent, and it is estimated that traffic will further increase by 1992 and double by the year 2000. This offers a huge potential market for the aerospace industry. It is estimated that the world aerospace market will grow by 20 per cent by the year 2000. The turnover of the European aerospace industry in 1988 was around ECU 35 billion per annum, with it employing nearly half a million workers.

Despite some early successes with the British Comet and Viscount aircraft, the Americans, and particularly the Boeing company, dominated the European producers in the post-war period. In the early 1970s Europe had only 5 per cent of the world's military and civil aerospace orders. This rose to 25 per cent by the mid-1980s with approximately 30 per cent of its revenue coming from external markets. Competition in the world's markets is, however, very intense, especially from the Americans. In the market for civil aircraft, the quality of technology is particularly important and is becoming increasingly more expensive to obtain. The European manufacturers currently spend about a third of the amount on research compared to their American rivals.

Demand

The pattern of demand for the industry's products tends to be cyclical, depending in part on the pattern of passenger growth. Because the airlines are trying to guess the market in advance, there are times when they over-estimate the demand, and this can result in a surplus of aircraft. Also, new technology can stimulate demand by making older aircraft less profitable for the airlines to use.

The choice of one particular kind of aircraft as against another depends upon a variety of factors, such as what the airline requires in terms of the aircraft's range, its payload and its suitability to operate out of particular airports. Increasingly, environmental considerations are of importance, particularly with regard to the noise levels at take-off. The general technical merit of the aircraft is, of course, a major issue, as are factors such as fleet standardization, the availability of spare parts and the training needs of the pilot and crew. Finally, the kind of financial package available to the purchaser is of vital importance.

Until recently, Europe's record in the global civil aerospace market has been poor. This is in part because the US producers have been able to take advantage of a large domestic market and so gain production economies. This has meant that the higher wages paid in the USA can be offset by higher levels of productivity. Added to this, Boeing, in particular, has shown itself very good in the past at producing a high-quality product, and has sold it with skilful marketing, good consumer liaison and imaginative financial packages. Success in the home market has meant that it is easier to sell competitively into third markets.

The Airbus Industrie

Europe's response to the challenge of creating a viable alternative to the dominance of the American producers was the creation of Airbus Industrie. The initial agreement was signed in September 1967, which was more than five years before the UK obtained membership of the EC. Thus, the model which was adopted, can be seen as a recognition of the need to integrate the operations of Europe's industry. This reflects the aspirations to achieve the longer-term goals of the Treaty of Rome, which were restated as part of the Single Market campaign of the 1980s.

Airbus partners

British Aerospace (BAe)

British Aerospace's 20 per cent share was finally taken up in 1979, some twelve years after the initial launch of the A300 project. This fact, together with the relatively low percentage share, does perhaps reflect the British company's ambivalence about participation and its scepticism about the consortium achieving anything remotely resembling real commercial success when it eventually becomes a public listed company sometime in the 1990s.

BAe produces the wings for Airbus and leans heavily on its history, experience and expertise as a military aircraft producer, and its strategic position in the UK economy for both protection and support from the UK Government in its dealings with its consortium partners.

Aerospatiale

Aerospatiale enjoys a 37.9 per cent share in Airbus and is very much the national champion of France in this sector. It is fiercely proud of its share in the project and of the strategic importance of the assembly line of the final aircraft in Toulouse. France views the Airbus project as representing the epitome of French specialist knowledge. In Jean Pierson, the Airbus Manufacturing Director, the French have a powerful influence over policy. He is a pioneer of the Concorde project and clearly does not subscribe to the mainly British lobby now pressing for more accountability, tighter management and increased financial controls.

Deutsche Aerospace (DA)

Deutsche Aerospace (formerly Messerschmitt-Boelkow-Blohm now owned by Daimler Benz) also enjoys a 37.9 per cent share in the Airbus project, but due to a manifestly different political and cultural heritage appear not have exercised as dominant an influence to date as their French counterparts. However, with growing expertise – they started from a base of zero experience in civil aircraft production – they have rapidly descended the learning curve and are now beginning to flex their bargaining muscle.

Grave dissatisfaction and resentment at having to bear the costs of the destructive industrial disputes at BAe in 1989/90 in terms of reduced Airbus output (from 12 per month to 1.2) have led DA to demand both financial recompense and the setting-up of a second assembly line in Hamburg to rival Toulouse. In addition, DA has demanded a secondary system of sourcing of most, if not all components, to avoid high-risk dependency on any major component supplier, for example, the BAe wings.

The Germans have succeeded in getting the second assembly line, but secondary sourcing is still to be achieved; however, the indications are that the Germans will take a much more prominent role in the project in the future.

CASA

CASA, the Spanish partner, with a meagre 4.2 per cent share, pales into insignificance compared with the major partners in terms of share and political clout. For them, participation has clearly been sufficient and the spin-offs for an economy desperately seeking to establish itself quickly in the EC as a credible and effective partner appear to date to have been adequate reward.

When pressure comes for expansion to include other companies and/or countries, as surely it will given the full order book and insufficient production capacity amongst the existing partners, and as development costs mount and governments tighten their belts in the face of global recession, it will be interesting to observe whether CASA seeks to limit participation of any new partners by itself bidding for an increased share in the project.

Objectives achieved

In 1990, the European partners achieved their objective of carving out a 30 per cent share of the civil market for large airliners, but are yet to achieve leadership in terms of sales for wide-bodied aircraft. It remains to be seen if their arrival on the global scene will succeed in maintaining the tilt in balance in the world aviation market they have brought about, or if the inherent cultural and political differences between them will prove insurmountable in the attempt to create a genuine, and profitable, alternative to Boeing and McDonnell Douglas.

Structure

Airbus consists of 1,500 administrative and sales staff who have their headquarters near the Aerospatiale operation in Toulouse. The operation of assembling the aircraft is currently carried out by Aerospatiale, but from 1994, a second assembly plant will be established at Finkenwerder, Hamburg. All other tasks concerned with the development of the aircraft are carried out by the partners, in roughly equal proportions to their ownership of the project.

In October 1990, the new Aerospatiale plant was opened on a 130-acre site, after £690 million had been spent on preparing for the production of the A340 four-engined long-range airliner, and the A330 twin-engined, medium-range jet. The centrepiece of the development is a £100 million high-technology assembly hall, which is partly robotized. This is designed to match the facilities which Boeing have in place in Seattle.

The Deutsche Airbus achievement in gaining the right to assemble the A321 is considered important in that there are claimed savings of £380 million by the year 2005. The first prototype of the 186-seater aircraft will not be available until 1992, with its maiden flight taking place in 1993. The key to the aircraft's early success has been the 20 firm and 20 provisional orders placed for it by Lufthansa. In May 1990, when the decision to go ahead with the German assembly line was announced, there were 109 firm orders and 74 options on the new aircraft.

The rules of Airbus mean that partners within Airbus cannot develop rival products, so that alternative consortia have to be either in smaller categories of aircraft, or be formed entirely from non-Airbus members. The precise dividing line between the class jet that Airbus wishes to make and that which might be offered by a rival consortium is uncertain. The A320 is a 150-seater aircraft, whilst BAe, with its family of 146 jets and the Fokker group's F100 and proposed F130, could well offer competition with 130-seater regional jets.

The decision-making structure of Airbus Industrie is based upon two levels. At the political level, the Heads of State of the nations involved are frequently active in lobbying each other over key decisions, and progress on some issues is linked on the basis of either a bilateral or a multilateral agreement. Thus, what would be normal commercial decisions in other organizations, such as arrangements for fitting out and customization of aircraft, have often been decided upon by governments.

At the company level, there has been a Supervisory Board, with five members, and an Executive Board with seven members, since 1989. Each of the partners has a top level representative on each, and any of the partners has the power to veto a decision.

The structure of Airbus is regarded as being very unwieldy, but the fact that the organization has been in business for over 20 years and the existence of a wide range of agreements and procedures make it difficult to reform. In the long term, it is hoped that a company structure based upon private sector lines might develop. However, radical solutions to structural problems are unlikely to be acceptable according to Jean Pierson, who prefers 'evolution rather than revolution'.

The product range and orders

As was pointed out earlier, Airbus Industrie has followed the example of Boeing and developed a family of aircraft to offer to its worldwide customers. Table 2.9.1 shows the Airbus family, although it includes one model which is no longer available (A300B2 which was superseded by the A300-600) and one which is projected – the very large A350. The A350 is not seen as a competitor against the current jumbo jet (the Boeing 747) but as a new aircraft for the 747 replacement market early in the next century.

Table 2.9.1   Airbus product range

Model	Seats	Range*	Boeing equivalent
A300B2	250	1,500	–
A300-600	267	4,350	737
A310	218	4,950	757
A320	150	3,000	767
A340-200	262	7,450	747
A340-300	295	6,650	747
A330	335	4,600	777
A350	650	–	–

* in nautical miles

The inaugural flight of the A340 model, an aircraft that is seen as the biggest challenge yet to Boeing's domination of the long-haul jet market, was set to occur in October 1991. By August 1991 firm orders for the aircraft and its sister, the A330, totalled 232. These figures indicate that this model is likely to enjoy considerable success.

Table 2.9.2 includes both firm orders and options. From the middle of 1989 to the middle of 1991, Airbus had captured 29 per cent of world orders for civil airliners compared with a figure of 13 per cent in the early 1980s. In 1990, Airbus achieved firm sales of 404 aircraft worth $175 billion and expects to do very well in 1991. The 1990 performance makes up 36 per cent of the jet orders won by the big three producers. Boeing got 48 per cent and McDonnell Douglas 16 per cent. This was the first time that Boeing had been pushed below 50 per cent of the total market in any one year.

Table 2.9.2   The order book at 31.10.89

Model	Orders	Customers	Deliveries
A300/A310	589	68	475
A320/A321	700	26	64
A330/A340	380	15	–

Source: Airbus Industrie

A number of significant orders have been announced for 1991. In June, the California-based firm of the International Lease Finance Corporation placed orders and options for 15 aeroplanes, worth some $960 million. In the same month an order for 15 aircraft and options for nine more were obtained from Kuwait. This order was valued at $1.9 billion. Also in June, Federal Express, the world's largest cargo and express delivery company, placed an order for up to 50 A330-600 jets worth $4 billion. In August, in a deal potentially worth a total of $3.3 billion, Singapore Airlines ordered seven A340's, and seven more subject to reconfirmation. They also placed options for a further six.

Since the mid-1980s, Airbus has secured an increasing share of the US jet market, a fact that has angered its American competitors. The Federal Express breakthrough came at a particularly critical time as all the world's aircraft manufacturers were feeling the effects of the sharp downturn in air travel due to the Gulf War and the general economic recession, and the consequent squeeze on jet orders. The Federal Express order is the third largest US order to date, and follows an order for up to 100 A320's from North West Airlines, and the order from the International Lease Finance Corporation mentioned above.

The US competition

Boeing

Boeing, with a dominant, almost two-third, share of the global market throughout the 1980s, is by far the major producer. With a thriving military aircraft division, its civil sector business is cushioned, cross-subsidized and enhanced by the company's ability to use its dominant US and global position to advantage. As the pioneer developer of the jumbo jet, Boeing led the way in the industry in trying to reduce costs and increase productivity by pursuing the development of 'families' of aircraft based on one initial research design project. It has enjoyed a virtual monopoly of long-haul aircraft sales and with the covert US Government/military support, had looked invulnerable to competitive attack until the advent of Airbus Industrie and its range of competing products.

McDonnell Douglas (MDD)

MDD, although renowned both in the USA and globally for its military and civil aircraft developments, remains clearly the second-ranked player to the giant Boeing, with a history in the 1970s of unprofitable civil projects, growing debt burdens and a flagship aeroplane with a tendency to crash, the ill-fated DC-10.

The early 1980s saw MDD abandon the production of the DC-10 and show a growing reluctance to be heavily involved in civil aircraft projects. But improving fortunes in the mid-1980s saw a restart of production of the DC-10, albeit under a new name, the MD11, once public disquiet about the former's safety had subsided sufficiently.

Pricing and finance

The actual pricing of commercial airliners is a matter of detailed negotiation between the manufacturers and the purchasing company. In most instances the sale will involve some arrangements with regard to financing of the aircraft, a factor which will be reflected in the price. In some instances deals can be made to lease aircraft, which avoids heavy borrowing, and gives greater certainty in terms of cost. Leasing is also a useful way of gaining entry into the market for smaller or newer companies.

Prices will also differ because of the size of the order, and the state of the market. In the early stages, when manufacturers are looking for orders to test for the viable launch of a new design, prices may be very cheap. Unless sufficient interest can be found, prior to the aircraft being built, the risk of development will be too high. Later, when an aircraft has actually flown, and it is shown to have achieved its design specifications, prices will rise.

Information about the finances of the Airbus project are limited. As a French Groupement d'Intérêt Economique, the consortium is not obliged to publish its accounts, or disclose levels of government subsidy. The sources of information tend to be the national governments, who release details because of the need to give information about public finances, or rivals of Airbus, who complain about subsidy levels. In an article in the

Sunday Times (9.06.91) it was stated that in 1990 Airbus Industrie made an operating profit of $100 million and that this was the first time the company had been in surplus since its inception.

Competition issues

For many years the American competitors of Airbus have complained about the level of subsidies they allege the latter has received, and is continuing to receive, from the national governments associated with the project. These subsidies, they say, violate the rules established under the General Agreement on Tariffs and Trade (GATT). Much of the recent American wrath has been directed at Daimler-Benz.

In 1988, to enable Daimler-Benz to acquire MBB (the original German firm in Airbus Industrie), the German Government introduced a limited system of exchange rate guarantees against fluctuations in the dollar/mark rates. Airline contracts tend to be dollar-denominated. It has been suggested that the cost of exchange rate guarantees for 1990 alone was $257 million, equal to a subsidy of $2.5 million per aircraft from the German Government. The EC has argued that this scheme does not constitute an export subsidy, as defined under GATT, since it is self-financing, it applies to EC as well as overseas sales, and has no impact on the sale price of Airbus aeroplanes. However, at the beginning of 1989 the American Government warned that it intended to file a claim with GATT against Airbus.

At the 1989 Paris airshow in June both Boeing and McDonnell Douglas said they would not be pressing the American Government to initiate action and that they would prefer to see an amicable solution to the dispute through negotiations currently going on between US and EC trade officials. However, the dispute resurfaced two years later, in May 1991, with fresh moves by the USA to launch a complaint against Airbus subsidies. Transport ministers of the Airbus countries wanted talks to take place under GATT's civil aircraft code which allows 'special factors' to be taken into account when assessing the degree of state support for aircraft industries. The USA wanted to deal with the matter under the GATT subsidies committee which the Europeans fear will give them a less sympathetic hearing. The matter was still unresolved by the beginning of August 1991.

The level of alleged subsidy has not been definitively established. The US Department of Commerce estimate that the project has received $13.5

billion in subsidies, and if this funding had been borrowed at commercial rates it would have cost $25.9 billion, which would have meant that the project was not commercially viable. An even higher estimate of losses came in a report by Gellman Research Associates published in September 1990. This report, made public by the US Commerce Under-Secretary for International Trade, found that by the end of 1989 Airbus had repaid only $462 million out of $8.2 billion in launch aid and other direct support received since 1971.

In addition, the European Governments have committed another $5.3 billion in subsidies over the next few years. These Governments had under-written between 60 and 92 per cent of the costs involved in developing each of Airbus's line of five aircraft types. Boeing claims that the consortium has received up to $26 billion in direct subsidies, plus billions more through indirect military subsidies and 'privileged access' to commercial research programmes.

In response to American claims of unfair competition, Airbus officials describe the subsidies they have received as 'launch aids', which they claim are being steadily repaid via a levy on each aircraft delivered. Every time an aircraft is delivered, $10 million is repaid to the national Governments. It is claimed that the successful A340 may even make a profit, as 650 had been ordered by the end of 1990, which is well above the 500 normally needed to break even in the industry. Airbus also claims that both Boeing and McDonnell Douglas receive substantial indirect subsidies from the US Government arising from their work as military contractors. The European firm puts a figure of $23 billion on such subsidies received in the last twelve years.

Jean Pierson, Airbus's Managing Director, claimed that the company made an operating profit in 1990. This is a claim that is difficult to verify, simply because of the way the company is organized. The owners of Airbus are also its main subcontractors. There are frequent debates about the price of their contribution to the project, and it has been suggested that there is an incentive to overprice, in order to limit the extent of any losses. The downturn in the world economy significantly reduced the scope for price increases to recoup these losses.

Removing subsidies

Airbus finances have been a significant part of trade talks between the EC and the USA. The USA hopes to remove totally production subsidies for Airbus, and to limit future R&D contributions to 25 per cent, to be provided through conditional loans repayable within 15 years and at a real rate of interest. The EC would like the R&D contribution to be higher at 45 per cent for future models, as long as the US Government discloses the true level of indirect support for the two American firms.

In June 1991, Airbus Industrie took a decisive step away from the hither-to complete reliance on government subsidies as it announced plans to raise up to $400 million through its first excursion into the open money markets in the group's 21-year history. The money will be used to help cover the full production costs of its latest aircraft, the 180-seat A321 (a stretched version of the 150-seat A320), which is scheduled to come into service in early 1994. The company is raising around $122 million through the issue of lira-denominated Eurobonds. A further $180 million line of credit has been arranged with the European Investment Bank and unnamed private investors. At the time the arrangements were announced, Airbus denied that the decision to seek private finance was connected to the bitter subsidy row with its US rivals.

The future

The number of passengers flown in 1991 has been affected by the economic recession and the Gulf War but both airlines and aircraft makers think that there are good long-term growth prospects for air travel. They forecast an average growth of 5 to 6 per cent per year over the next ten years.

There is an evolving long-term trend in commercial aviation towards larger capacity aircraft. Examples include the A340, the Boeing 777, and the McDonnell Douglas MD11. These types of aircraft are expected to account for about 50 per cent of the world market by the year 2000. This trend has arisen from the demands of the airlines for roomier and more efficient planes, partly in an attempt to overcome the problems arising from air traffic and airport congestion which threatens the steady long-term increase in demand. Another reason for their demands relates to passenger comfort. Business air travel surveys repeatedly show that lack of leg-room is a major complaint. This can be remedied in the new wide-bodied jets. A third factor is the growing demand for non-stop services. In the long-distance market, wide-bodied twin-engined jets with a high flying range and comfort enable airlines to operate profitably on routes such as across the USA and the transatlantic one where a jumbo jet would not be profitable. The Boeing 777 and Airbus A330 can fulfil these objectives as well as providing more seating capacity for busy short- to medium-range flights.

Another type of aircraft that the world's airlines are showing an increasing interest in is a very high capacity aircraft which could seat 600 or more passengers. Airbus is already talking about the development of such an aircraft (the A350) with potential customers. Jean Pierson suggests that a launch decision might be made in 1997 in time for the plane to enter service in 2002.

In conclusion, the Airbus product range, both existing and projected, appears to be well suited to take advantage of the likely developments in air traffic over the next ten to 15 years.

Reference

Pratten, C.F. *Economies of Scale in Manufacturing Industries*, (Cambridge, Cambridge University Press, 1971).

Questions/discussion topics

1. Does Airbus Industrie have a long-term future?

2. Subsidies usually distort trade patterns and lead to a non-optimal allocation of resources. Are there any economic arguments for continuing to provide subsidies to Airbus Industrie?

3. What are the implications for Airbus of the movement of Eastern European countries towards market economies?

Case 10
Competition and change in the British and German brewing industries*

Ron Allison, David Kinnear and Henry Schietzold

Advice to readers

This case outlines some of the developments that have been taking place in both the British and German brewing industries in recent years and provides a brief historical context. There are a number of similarities in the developments in both countries but also some important differences.

The study is also concerned with some of the issues arising from the movement from a command economy to that of a market economy, as found in the brewing industry of the former East Germany. Readers are advised to look at the questions/discussion topics before reading the case study, so that they are aware of some of the issues involved.

Introduction

In both Britain and Germany the degree of concentration of brewing operations has increased after the Second World War but the process is much further advanced in Britain. There are few brewers in Germany who would claim to operate on a national scale, whereas brewing in Britain is dominated by the six largest groups whose products are found nationwide. In both countries there has been a resurgence of the micro-brewer (brewers who brew on a small scale), although they account for a tiny part of total beer production in both cases.

The tied house/outlet system prevails in both countries as do other types of tie. Duty is considerably higher in Britain than it is in Germany. In Germany the structure of excise duty helps the small brewer, whereas in Britain no help is provided. In fact, the 'wastage allowance' is claimed to

* The authors would like to thank George Bateman, MD of Bateman's Brewery; John Smith, Marketing Manager of Ridley's Brewery; Herr Koller of Landshuter Brewery and Hans-Joachim Timme of Felsenkeller.

act against the small-scale brewer. Not only is excise duty higher in Britain, it has changed frequently and penalizes the production of higher strength beers. The permitted ingredients for beer production in Germany, destined for sale in Germany, are narrowly defined. In Britain, brewers are allowed to use many substances other than the traditional water, hops, malted barley and yeast, including a wide variety of chemicals.

Almost all of the beer sold in Germany is still brewed in Germany despite the ruling of the European Court of Justice on the *Reinheitsgebot* (see p. 270). Import penetration in Britain, although less than 10 per cent, is noticeably higher than in Germany. So far, no British brewer has taken advantage of the new markets opened up as a result of the re-unification of Germany, although West German brewers have been swift to acquire breweries in the former DDR (East Germany).

In many ways, the events in the brewing industry in the former DDR mirror what is happening to the other industries there. Although there is some middle ground, breweries are either closed or considerably modified with a substantial injection of capital and substantial reductions in the labour force. The material in the case study on the Felsenkeller brewery in Dresden and the Kindl brewery in Berlin illustrate both of these phenomenons.

In both Britain and Germany the beer market has been either stagnating or declining for the last decade or so. For many firms merger has been one strategy for survival. Other, generally smaller, firms have adopted a variety of alternative strategies and these are outlined in the Landshuter, Bateman's and Ridley's cases.

The smaller firms appear to believe that the formation of a Single European Market by 1 January 1993 will not greatly affect them, at least in the short run. But some effect has already been noticed. There have been changes in labelling requirements and standards of hygiene. Bottles in Britain are increasingly in standard metric sizes and cans are also moving this way. Thanks to a dispensation, the traditional British pint and half-pint measures for consuming draught beer will remain for some time to come. The harmonization of duties will bring some changes, but brewers seem unsure exactly how this will affect them.

A wide variety of German beers are imported into Britain and are readily available in supermarkets and off-licence chains. Apart from Guinness, there is little importation of British beers into Germany. However, many brewers in both countries are talking of increased co-operation *vis à vis* franchising, joint licensing, and other trading arrangements. So far, no

German brewer has acquired a British brewery and no British brewer has acquired a German one. It is questionable whether brewers as yet view Europe as a single market.

British brewing

Introduction

The brewing industry in Britain is highly concentrated with the six largest firms accounting for 75 per cent of beer production in 1989. In 1967 the six largest firms had 68 per cent of the market. Further information about trends in concentration is presented in Table 2.10.1.

Table 2.10.1   UK beer production by company 1967–85

Firm	1967 hl	1967 %	1972 hl	1972 %	1980 hl	1980 %	1985 hl	1985 %
Bass	3.46	18.1	4.0	18.5	4.90	20.0	4.72	20.2
Allied	2.96	15.5	3.35	15.5	3.73	16.0	2.93	12.6
Whitbread	2.11	11.1	2.50	11.6	2.87	12.0	2.63	11.3
Watney	1.80	9.4	2.28	10.6	2.81	12.0	2.08	8.9
S & N	1.53	8.0	2.22	10.3	2.44	10.0	2.14	9.2
Courage	1.09	5.7	1.70	7.9	2.20	9.0	2.02	8.7
Guinness	0.93	4.9	1.13	5.2	1.16	5.0	0.73	3.2

Notes
1. Figures in first column are annual output in millions of hectolitres.
2. Figures in second column are market shares of each company.
3. Some of these firms have undergone name changes over the years.

Source: Adapted from figures published by Anthony Cockerill, Manchester Business School.

The number of long-established brewing firms has steadily declined throughout the twentieth century as has the number of breweries, although a feature of the 1970s and 1980s was the appearance of new (small-scale) breweries and home-brew public houses. Not all these new ventures have been successful and their numbers fluctuate considerably. Table 2.10.2 provides an indication of how the number of firms and breweries have declined since 1900.

The huge decrease in both the number of brewing companies and the number of breweries between 1950 and 1960, and 1960 and 1970 may be readily observed. The number of brewing firms fell by 32 per cent and 61 per cent respectively in these two decades, and the corresponding fall in the number of breweries was 37 and 51 per cent. The decline has continued since 1970, although the rate of decline has slowed. In the 40 years since 1950, the number of old established brewing firms fell by 82 per cent and the number of old established breweries by 81 per cent.

Table 2.10.2   Number of brewing companies and breweries in the UK

Year	Companies	Old breweries	New breweries	Total
1900	1,466	6,477	–	6,477
1920	941	2,914	–	2,914
1930	559	1,418	–	1,418
1940	428	840	–	840
1950	362	567	–	567
1960	247	358	–	358
1967	117	243	–	243
1970	96	177	–	177
1975	82	147	–	147
1981	80	138	49	187
1985	73	121	96	217
1986	68	117	94	211
1987	67	113	75	188
1988	65	107	67	174
1989	64	105	–	–

Source: Adapted from The Brewers' Society Statistical Handbook, 1990.

Beer consumption

Other significant changes have been occurring in the post-1945 UK beer market. Table 2.10.3 provides an indication of beer consumption since 1960. From the table it may be seen that beer consumption peaked in 1979 and declined between 1980 and 1987. In 1988 and 1989 there was a slight increase in consumption but UK production is currently less than it was in the late 1970s. Imports are still relatively small. In volume terms they have doubled over the last 30 years and their share of the total market has grown from 5.4 per cent in 1960 to 7.2 per cent in 1989. Similarly, exports have almost doubled in volume over the period, but in percentage terms they have only increased from 1.6 per cent of total production to 2.2 per cent.

Table 2.10.3   UK beer consumption 1960–89

Year	Production	Exports	Imports	Consumption
1960	43,392	714	2,441	45,833
1965	48,433	826	2,318	50,751
1970	55,148	669	2,821	57,969
1975	64,566	880	2,957	67,523
1979	67,416	783	2,747	70,163
1980	64,830	750	2,578	67,408
1985	59,655	984	3,688	63,343
1986	59,439	1,011	3,858	63,297
1987	59,897	1,140	4,093	63,990
1988	60,155	1,232	4,350	64,505
1989	60,015	1,336	4,533	64,548

Note: The figures are in thousands of hectolitres. Also one UK barrel of 36 gallons equals 1.637 hectolitres. Thus one hectolitre equals 22 gallons.

Source: Adapted from The Brewers' Society Statistical Handbook, 1990.

The type of beer being produced and consumed has also changed considerably as has its packaging. This is shown in Table 2.10.4.

Table 2.10.4   UK beer market by type and packaging measured in terms of percentage sales volume

Year	Ale	Lager	Draught		Bottles		Cans
			Cask	Other	Rtn	Nrtn	
1960	99.0	1.0	64		34.0	2.0	
1965	98.0	2.0	68		30.0	2.0	
1970	93.0	7.0	73		24.0	3.0	
1975	80.3	19.7	75.8	16.7	0.6	6.9	
1980	69.3	30.7	78.9	10.3	0.5	10.3	
1985	59.1	40.9	16.6	60.6	6.6	2.4	13.8
1986	56.6	43.4	15.7	60.1	6.3	2.7	15.2
1987	53.4	46.6	15.1	59.3	6.4	2.9	16.4
1988	51.4	48.6	14.5	58.9	6.7	2.8	17.2
1989	49.6	50.4	14.0	58.1	6.4	2.9	18.5

Notes:
1. Non returnable bottles (Nrtn) includes Polyethylene Terephthalate (PET).
2. Cask conditioned and other draught beers aggregated until 1984.
3. Non-returnable bottles and cans aggregated until 1974.

Source: Adapted from The Brewers' Society Handbook, 1990.

The changes shown in Tables 2.10.3 and 2.10.4, together with advances in technology almost certainly explain some of the enthusiasm shown over the last 40 years for what has been described as the 'merger mania' in the brewing industry.

Changes in the industry

The trend towards mergers has already been mentioned. A significant event in the post-1945 merger movement occurred in 1959 although no merger actually took place. In 1959 Sears Holdings, a conglomerate based in the footware industry, made a bid for Watney Mann. A major reason for the bid was the fact that Watney's licensed properties appeared in the balance sheet at their 1929 valuation – an extreme example perhaps of asset valuation at historic cost. This unsuccessful bid, and the threat from Taylor's Canadian Breweries, forced many of the leading brewers to think seriously about the management of their assets and the generally low rates of return on their capital. By the end of the 1960s, the six largest firms in the industry had emerged through a number of mergers.

Other developmental changes have also taken place. The first was the diversification carried out by all the larger companies and many of the smaller ones. Often this expansion was into brewing-related activities such as other alcoholic products, travel and leisure, hotels, and food. The diversification was two-way. Some brewers acquired other companies. For example, Allied Breweries merged with the food group J. Lyons. In other cases brewers were taken over by non-brewers. For example, Imperial Tobacco bought Courage and Grand Metropolitan (Hotels) bought up Watney Mann after earlier acquiring Trumans.

The next stage was the UK brewers involvement in the globalization of the industry. Once again there was a two-way process. Some UK brewers were acquired by foreign-based multinational enterprises – for instance Courage breweries were bought by the Australian based Elders IXL concern. In other cases, UK companies set up operations overseas. For example, Allied Breweries own the Dutch firm of Oranjeboom. This globalization is likely to continue. In July 1991 it was reported in *The Guardian* that Grolsch, the Dutch brewer, which had doubled in size after acquiring a German beer group earlier in the year, was looking to acquire a British regional brewer. The intention is to acquire a quality regional ale brand to be built up into a national brand and marketed alongside Grolsch in the UK.

The latest developments are the changes 'forced' upon the industry by the recommendations of the recent Monopolies and Mergers Commission (MMC) investigation into the supply of beer (see p. 257).

Industry structure

The MMC identified over 200 breweries in the UK and categorized them as:

- six national brewers (Allied, Bass, Courage, Grand Metropolitan, Scottish & Newcastle, and Whitbread). These brewers account for 75 per cent of UK beer production, 74 per cent of the brewer-owned retail estate, and 86 per cent of loan ties;
- eleven regional brewers (Boddington, Cameron, Devenish, Greenall Whitley, Greene King, Mansfield, Marston, Robinson, Thwaites, Vaux, and Wolverhampton & Dudley). These brewers account for 11 per cent of beer production, 15 per cent of the brewer-owned retail estate, and 8 per cent of loan ties;
- 41 local brewers that account for 6 per cent of beer production, 10 per cent of the tied estate, and 4 per cent of loan ties;
- three brewers without tied estate (Carlsberg, Guinness, and Northern Clubs Federation). These account for about 8 per cent of beer production and around 1 per cent of loan ties. They have no tied estate;
- 160 other brewers all of whom operate on a very small scale. They account for less than 1 per cent of UK beer production.

The report defined the categories of brewers as follows:

- **national brewers**: 'the very large brewers whose business extends over much of the UK, even if their tied estate is in some cases concentrated in particular regions';
- **regional brewers**: 'have a business which is mainly, but not necessarily wholly, concentrated in a single region of the UK';
- **local brewers**: 'have their main business in a particular locality but may have business in some other areas of the UK';
- **brewers without tied estate (BWTEs)**: 'are brewers whose main business is the brewing of beer for sale to other brewers or to wholesalers for distribution to the retail trade';
- **others** are: 'brewers which do not belong to The Brewers' Society and are in the main, but not wholly, very small brewers supplying limited

amounts of beer directly to the public through a single or small number of owned outlets and to a limited extent by wholesale trade'.

Products

Table 2.10.4 distinguishes ale from lager, cask draught beer from other draught beer, and bottles, both returnable and non-returnable, from cans. Ale includes mild, stout and bitter. All three types of beer have been brewed in the UK for centuries. The sales of mild beer have been steadily declining for many years. In 1982 draught mild beer accounted for 8 per cent of sales by volume, in 1985 this had fallen to 6.4 per cent and by 1989 sales were only 4.4 per cent of total production. Draught bitter production has also fallen. This, together with stout, accounted for 47 per cent of sales volume in 1982 but only 34.8 per cent in 1989. The apparently remorseless growth in the sales of lager is very noticeable.

Cask beer is beer that is conditioned in the cellar of the public house in which it is sold and is often known as 'real ale'. Other draught beers are conditioned at the brewery – a process which usually involves filtering and pasteurization.

Table 2.10.4 also shows the steady increase in the amount of beer and lager that is sold in cans, which may have profound implications for the smaller brewer.

The British beer market

The British beer market differs from that in the other EC countries in several respects. These are summarized in Table 2.10.5.

Table 2.10.5   Some comparative aspects of the EC beer market in 1988

Country	Consumption (litres per head)	Beer sales (% on draught)	Average Strength (% alcohol vol)
Belgium	119	45	4.7
Denmark	127	40	5.0
France	39	25	4.6
Eire	94	86	4.0
Holland	83	30	5.0
Germany	143	28	4.7
UK	111	73	3.7

Source: Adapted from *The Brewers' Society Statistical Handbook*, 1990.

With the exception of Eire, more beer is sold in draught form in Britain than in any of the other EC countries. In fact, this is true on a worldwide basis. Only in Czechoslovakia, New Zealand, Belgium and Spain it is 40 per cent or more. The main reason is probably a social one connected with the unique role that the public house plays in the social life of the British. The second point of interest is the relatively low strength of beer sold in the UK. This would appear to be directly related to the way in which excise duty on beer is levied and the scale of these duties.

Excise duty on beer

Between 1950 and October 1988 there was a flat rate of duty for beers with an original gravity between 1,016 and 1,030 degrees together with an additional duty for every degree above 1,030. From October 1988, every degree above 1,000 degrees was levied at £0.90 per hectolitre. This was raised to £0.97 in March 1990. Consequently a hectolitre of average strength beer (1,037 original gravity) attracts £35.89 in duty which is equivalent to just over 20 pence per pint. As a simplification, the strength of beer (% alcohol by volume) may be said to vary directly with its original gravity. Thus, the stronger the beer the higher the amount of duty its price will incorporate. This is compounded as VAT is additionally levied on beer.

Two facts emerge from this. The first is that the rate of excise duty is high compared with the rate levied by our EC partners. The second is that the structure of excise duty penalizes the production of higher gravity beers. This is not the case in the other major beer-producing EC countries.

It has been argued that the UK system of excise duty penalizes the smaller brewer. In the UK all brewers pay the same rate of duty per hectolitre regardless of the size of the brewery. In Belgium, Germany and Holland duty is levied on a sliding scale of production rather than original gravity. Thus, the smaller brewer pays less duty per hectolitre than the larger brewer. In the UK the smaller brewer is also at a disadvantage over the allowances provided to brewers for production losses. It is assumed by Customs and Excise that 6 per cent of beer is lost during the brewing process and thus duty is not levied on this amount. During evidence given to the MMC enquiry, the Small Independent Brewers' Association (SIBA) suggested that for technical reasons associated with the small size of their plant, small brewers lose about 10 per cent of their production. Whereas larger brewers use more sophisticated equipment and losses are typically 2 to 4 per cent of production.

Branding

In the 1960s and 1970s large brewers attempted to market bitter (for example, Allied's Double Diamond and Watney's Red Barrel) on a national basis, but ultimately these attempts were unsuccessful. The pressure group The Campaign for Real Ale (CAMRA) came to prominence in the 1970s and there was a revival of interest in 'real ale' which had almost disappeared from many areas of Britain. National branding of draught bitter is now less and marketing tends to stress the local nature of the beers (even though they may be brewed in a huge brewery many miles from the local market).

Lager

The increase in the importance of lager has been accompanied by national branding with correspondingly large advertising budgets. Some lagers (Heineken and Carlsberg, for instance) are promoted as being a world brand.

Different strategies have been followed by regional and local brewers and the appeal to local tastes and traditions often features in their promotional activities. Some of the smaller brewers brew and market their own lagers, others brew it under licence. Some have reciprocal trading agreements from which they obtain lager from national firms.

Advertising and marketing

All brewers attempt to differentiate their products by branding, and marketing in general and advertising in particular, are important weapons. The MMC investigation studied the expenditure in 1985 by brewers on marketing and advertising. It is not always possible to make a precise distinction between advertising and marketing but the former generally includes radio, press, posters and television, whilst the latter includes consumer/trade activity, point of sales materials, and promotions. The results are summarized in Table 2.10.6.

Table 2.10.6   Advertising and marketing expenditure by brewers in the UK in 1985 (£m)

	National	BWTE	Regional	Local	Total
Advertising	72.1	13.4	4.7	1.7	91.9
Marketing	72.3	10.1	3.6	2.0	88.0
Total	**144.4**	**23.5**	**8.3**	**3.7**	**179.9**

Source: Adapted from The Supply of Beer, HMSO Cm 651 1989

From the table it may be seen that there is a rough equivalence between the amounts spent on advertising and marketing, although both the BWTEs and regional brewers spend more on advertising than on marketing. The national brewers spend just over two-and-a-half times as much as the smaller brewers on advertising and marketing and the BWTEs three times as much.

The Monopolies and Mergers Commission (MMC) report on British brewing

On 4 August 1986 the Office of Fair Trading asked the MMC to investigate various aspects relating to the supply of beer in the UK. The report was presented to Parliament by the Secretary of State for Trade and Industry in March 1989. The main recommendations embodied in the report were as follows:

(a) **The property tie** – a ceiling of 2,000 on the number of on-licensed premises which any brewing company or group may own. This ceiling will require the divestment of some 22,000 premises by UK national brewers. (No regional or local brewer had reached 2,000 premises at the time the report was published.) No product-tying covenant should be attached to any sale.
(b) **The loan tie** – the elimination of all loan ties but those in force at the date of publication should be allowed to run their course.
(c) **The product tie** – tenant should be allowed to purchase a minimum of one brand of draught beer from a supplier other than the landlord. There should be no tie for non/low-alcohol beers, nor for wines, spirits, ciders, soft drinks or mineral waters.

(d) **Terms and conditions of tenants** – that tenancies of all on-licensed premises should be bought within the provisions of the Landlord and Tenant Act 1954, Part II.

(e) **Wholesale price lists** – that brewers should publish wholesale price lists for the on-licensed trade which set out the discounts that are generally available.

The Brewers' Society called the report a 'charter for chaos' and launched a substantial campaign against its findings. In part it succeeded and some of the recommendations were watered down. By the end of March 1991 Grand Metropolitan and Courage had done their pub for breweries swap. Grand Metropolitan announced it was to stop making beer. Courage will continue to brew and run fewer pubs. Scottish and Newcastle (S&N) had sold 150 outlets to bring itself below the Government's 2,000 outlet level – the level at which a brewer is defined as big. As a consequence, S&N does not have to allow guest beers in any of its outlets. Bass says it will sell, or otherwise free from its control, more than 2,600 pubs. Whitbread has asked for more time in which to sell 2,100 of its 6,200 outlets as it claims the autumn 1992 deadline is too near. Allied-Lyons has yet to make up its mind what to do.

Evidence about the number of tenants who have decided to stock a guest beer is not clear cut. Allied says that about 250 of its 3,600 tenanted outlets were serving a guest beer before the regulations came into force. Another 300 have now done so. Whitbread says that about 6 per cent of its tenants do so. Less than 10 per cent of Bass tenants are said to stock a guest beer. There have been accusations about intimidation by brewery representatives over the issue. A survey suggested that 60 per cent of tenants felt there was no pressure not to stock guest beers, whilst 27 per cent thought that there was pressure. The Office of Fair Trading is pursuing a number of complaints but the matter had not been resolved by the beginning of June 1991.

Towards the end of March 1991 a 'secret plan' to create a huge new brewery group was revealed in the press. The scheme would bring together the brewing operations of Whitbread and Allied-Lyons, and the new group would have about 27 per cent of the UK beer market. It is thought that if the plan goes ahead it would be investigated by the MMC.

A number of the issues outlined above are illustrated by looking more closely at two British breweries, Bateman's Brewery and Ridley's.

Bateman's brewery

Introduction

George Bateman and Son Limited is an independent local brewer situated at Wainfleet, near Skegness, in Lincolnshire. The private limited company was founded in 1874 and the present brewery was built in 1880. Although none of the original equipment survives some of the plant is between 40 and 60 years old.

The plant

The carriage cask system of fermentation was employed until 1953. With this system, the wort was placed in wooden casks set above long open troughs. During the early and vigorous fermentation, yeast and wort overflowed into the troughs. This was returned by hand to the casks every three hours or so. Carriage cask production was expensive, both in terms of the labour intensity and loss of wort (up to 8 per cent). Modern stainless steel fermenting tanks are now used at this stage of production. The newest piece of equipment is a bottling line which was installed early in 1990. Although it fits in well with the marketing strategy of the firm, it represented a large outlay for a comparatively small brewer and the investment decision caused much heart searching by the management team.

Bateman's reputation and success

In one sense the brewery is a local firm with an associated reputation and following. Almost all of the tied estate of 80 houses, that take around 50 per cent of the output, lies within 50 miles of the brewery. However, for its size there is an extensive free trade, numbering around 400 customers, and this is widespread. Draught beer is taken to a number of London outlets and one lorry-load a week is taken to Kent. Additionally, a new strand of the corporate strategy is the establishment of 'flagship' pubs in cities that include Derby, Hull, Newark, and Nottingham. Preliminary indications are that these ventures are successful. The development of these houses and the free trade has undoubtedly been helped by the firm's success, and the resulting favourable publicity, in recent CAMRA Great British Beer Festival competitions. Its higher-strength premium bitter (XXXB) was the supreme champion in 1986, champion special beer in 1987 and 1988. The mild beer was judged Britain's third best mild at the 1989 festival and at the same festival the Victory Ale came second in the Strong Ale Class.

A commemorative bottled beer – Battle of Britain Ale – was brewed in 1989 and 1990. This high-strength beer (6 per cent alcohol by volume) is supplied in distinctive 50cl bottles. It is available in local supermarkets and some specialist outlets. Other special bottled beers are under active consideration. Two sales directors were engaged in 1989 to develop these niche marketing products. A strategy of selling beer in two-litre PET containers was considered and rejected. One reason was the problem of Bateman's being a small-scale producer and trying to compete in a low-margin market with high-volume producers. Another reason relates to impending EC legislation that will require 70 per cent of beer containers to be recyclable. The plastic used in PET containers cannot be recycled and given Bateman's product mix this would cause difficulties in reaching this target. They are, however, enjoying great success with a unique nine-and-half-litre PET beersphere for parties and weddings.

Production costs

The size of the brewery means that it is well below the level of minimum economic scale in terms of brewing costs. But with regard to the overall cost of production, Bateman's is able to compete with larger rivals as the other main components of total cost – distribution and promotion – are fewer. However, its total cost could be even less if it did not handle its own distribution. Bateman's distributes its beer to all its tied estate and its free trade in the East Midlands. Free trade outlets outside this area are served by wholesalers that have, in turn, been supplied by Bateman's. A fleet of seven red high-sided lorries, bearing the distinctive windmill logo, and a number of similarly painted smaller vans are used for these tasks. The reason why contractors are not used for distribution is that the firm believes it has a 'duty' regarding employment in an area where unemployment is high and opportunities are sparse. The firm employs 121 people. Eight are employed in Boston and Grantham, 25 in the County Hotel in Skegness, and 88 at the brewery or administered from it.

Diversification

There has been a limited amount of (related) diversification. The firm owns three hotels in Skegness. One of these, which is considered to be one of the best appointed hotels on the east coast, has 45 bedrooms and employs 25 staff. The other venture outside brewing is the acquisition of a small wine merchants. This firm, J.E. Ridlington & Son, has one outlet in Boston and one in Grantham. These outlets also act as distribution depots. But the present Chairman of the Board of Directors and Managing Director, George Bateman, views the firm as still being primarily a brewer of beer. As he remarked in November 1990, 'There is not much point in carrying on otherwise and I and my family are dedicated to the brewing of our own beer'.

The product mix

The product range consists of five draught beers: mild, an ordinary bitter (XB), a strong bitter (XXXB), Victory Ale, and a seasonal strong beer (Winter Warmer). There are also five bottled beers. Victory Ale accounts for 50 per cent of bottled-beer sales. Following the company's niche marketing strategy, the range of bottled beers is likely to expand. Currently, there is no barley wine. The production of this ceased 20 years ago when a national bottled beer of this type was introduced to the tied estate. Draught beer constitutes 80 per cent of the brewery's total production.

Bateman's market

The reputation of Bateman's as brewers of high quality beer rests firmly on their real ale, and the national move back to this type of draught beer has been of considerable benefit to the firm. In most of its trading areas there is a good demand for real ale. A major reason why Bateman's did not join the keg beer bandwagon of the 1950s was the capital expense in equipping its public houses for the dispensation system necessary for its sale. Although the firm is very much a 'real ale' brewer, two keg beers for some of its free trade customers are currently produced.

The firm believes that demand for its beer is sensitive with respect to price, especially in the free trade. The pricing policy of the firm is to be competitive and where possible to price a little below its larger rivals.

Export opportunities

There has been some success in export markets. Following a visit to the Milan Trade Fair in 1984 by George Bateman, an order was secured to supply 23,000 bottles of strong pale ale every three weeks to an agent in Italy. This increased the output of the brewery by a significant amount (8 per cent). However, problems later occurred in this market and the agreement has now lapsed. Beer, both in bottles and larger plastic beer-spheres, is being shipped to Canada and Houston, Texas. Possibilities for sales in both Germany and Japan are being actively pursued.

The impact of the Single European Market

It is thought that the formation of the Single European Market will have some significance to small brewers such as Bateman's. Changes to labelling, such as declaring the alcohol content by volume, rather than stating the original gravity (OG) have already been required. Competition policy may lead to revised tenancy agreements. The move towards harmonization of duties may aid the firm. It is the custom in many of the other EC countries for excise duty on beer to be levied on a sliding scale (for an example, see the section on the German brewing industry). Adoption of this practice within the whole Community would help brewers the size of Bateman's to compete with larger firms. Excise duty on beer in Britain is levied when the beer is brewed. It is likely that soon duty in all EC countries will be levied when it leaves the factory gate. This will aid the cash flow of firms, particularly with respect to beers which are matured for longer periods of time. On the other hand, there is the possibility that there will be regulations that will result in additional expense.

The Department of Trade and Industry has provided opportunities for support in the lead up to the completion of the Single European Market, although Bateman's found that the advice given was not very helpful as it was 'far too general'.

The effects of the MMC report

One of the competitive strategies of the firm is to make selective additions to the tied estate. Following the Monopolies Commission report into the supply of beer, a number of public houses within the Bateman's area have already come on to the market. Many of these are regarded as being unsuitable for acquisition as they have a low turnover, are too expensive, run-down, or are adjacent to existing outlets. The requirement that publicans have the right to stock a guest beer from a small brewer has so far been of very limited benefit. However, some of the former tied estate of large brewers is now free trade and this has provided opportunities for increased sales.

Future trends

It is the firm's view that the growth of lager sales will probably continue, but slowly and level off at somewhere around 60 per cent of the total market. It anticipates that the growth of beer consumption at home will also continue and this is one of the factors behind the decision to produce specialized bottled beers. Niche marketing of this nature can provide an important sales opportunity for firms of Bateman's size.

Publicity

The corporate image is based around concepts of tradition, responsibility to the local community, value for money, and quality. The main slogan of the firm, widely used in publicity material, 'Good Honest Ales' dates back to 1925. Only small sums of money are spent on direct publicity but the company is very publicity-conscious. For example, the winner of the 1990 UK Ladies Snooker Championship was sponsored by Bateman's. The free publicity gained as a result of its success in a number of Great British Beer Festivals has also been very helpful. Valuable word of mouth publicity is gained through evening brewery tours. Almost every weeknight of the year sees a tour of the brewery by one or more coach loads of beer enthusiasts. The firm only breaks even on these events but often the visitors stay in local Bateman's pubs and further sample its products.

Conclusions

The company believes it has a promising future as an independent brewer in what is almost certain to become an increasingly concentrated and competitive market place. Its strategic thrust is aimed at strengthening its position in this environment.

Ridley's Brewery

Introduction

The brewery of T.D. Ridley & Sons is located at Hartford End, a few miles from Chelmsford, Essex, and was built in 1842, so by coincidence it will be celebrating its 150th anniversary in 1992. Although there have been alterations and additions over the years, the brewery proper still looks much as it did when first built. The firm itself dates back even earlier in the nineteenth century. The business began with the marriage of William Ridley to the daughter of a Hartford End mill owner. Their son, Thomas Ridley, expanded the business from milling and malting to incorporate brewing. Today the company mainly brews beer, although there has been some recent diversification into food and property development.

The plant

Most of the equipment is relatively modern but a link with the past is the original oak fermenting tanks, although these were lined with copper in the early 1900s. The latest addition to the site is an administration block which was occupied at the end of October 1990.

Ridley's reputation

Ridley's is primarily a 'local' brewer serving a local market. The tied house estate of 65 public houses is located within a 25-mile radius of the brewery and the relatively extensive free trade of around 350 outlets is concentrated in south, mid-, and north Essex. The firm has worked hard to build up a local following by acquiring a reputation for good service and reliability and emphasizing its importance as a local employer. In total there are 100 employees.

The product mix

The product range comprises five bottled beers, three draught bitters and a draught mild. About 75 per cent of the brewery output is produced as draught beer with the remaining 25 per cent being bottled or canned. There is a bottling line which is also used for contract bottling. Customers include Guinness, Watneys, and Whitbread. The contract bottling helps to lower unit costs by keeping the throughput of the plant high. Canned beer was introduced to the product range in October 1990. The only beer which is presently being canned is the premium beer 'Old Bob'. Negotiations are currently under way with a national supermarket chain that is considering adding this beer to its existing, and extensive, range of premium beers.

British supermarkets are only interested in stocking cans, non-returnable bottles or the larger PET containers. For a variety of reasons, Ridley's have decided not to compete in the latter market. Currently, all draught and bottled and canned beer is distributed by the brewery.

Production costs

The brewery recognizes that its costs of brewing beer are higher than the large brewers, but because of its localized markets its distribution costs are relatively low. Additionally, it spends, by large brewery terms, small amounts of money on publicity and advertising. Overall, the higher production costs are balanced by the lower distribution and promotion costs allowing the firm to compete effectively with larger rivals.

Ridley's employs 100 people in the production and distribution of beer and has an annual turnover of around £6.5 million.

Ridley's market

The national trends regarding beer consumption and production apply to Ridley's. Mild sales have declined and lager sales have increased, although there appears to be a slow move back to traditional draught bitter. Currently, sales of draught IPA are buoyant. No lager is produced by the firm but four (Carlsberg, Foster's, Heineken, and Holsten) are sold in their tied house estate. Ridley's is well known for its production of 'real ale' and all of its tied houses sell it, but two keg bitters are produced for the free trade. There is an important local market, the Grays area, for this type of beer.

The brewery believes that because of the competitive local market in which it performs, sales of beer are sensitive with respect to price and it is for this reason that changes have been made in their pricing policy. Until recently public houses owned by the company paid comparatively low rents but there was a surcharge on beers. Prices are now charged at the same rate as the free trade sector of the industry. The Ridley's owned outlets have had their rents proportionately increased to compensate for the loss of income to the company. As a result of this change in policy, it is envisaged that overall sales will increase for there is now no monetary advantage in the temptation for licensees to purchase products from a source other than the brewery.

Diversification

Although the firm still regards itself as primarily a brewer of beer, there has been some recent diversification away from brewing. In 1988 Ridley Country Chandlers was established. The beautifully produced 1990 catalogue ('*A Catalogue of Country Eatables*') shows an extensive range of premium products listed under the following headings: Country Lane Preserves and Jellies, Victorian Garden Preserves and Jellies, Fruit and

Wine Preserves and Jellies, Ridley's Country Delights, Appletree Hill Fruit Chutneys, Ridley's Country Condiments, Traditional Spiced Fruits, Ridley's Fine Teas, Chocolates, Seasonal Accompaniments, and Ridley's Gift Collections.

The Ridley family own extensive holdings of land and following changes in the senior management team in 1990, a property company has been established to develop these holdings. It is not possible to say yet how this further example of diversification will develop.

Export opportunities

In the recent past, bottled beer was exported to both Italy and the USA. However, difficulties involving the reliability of the import agencies in these two countries were experienced and these experiments have been discontinued for the time being.

The effects of the Single European Market

The firm believes that in some respects the completion of the Single European Market by 1 January 1993 will make the task of exporting easier. A prime example is the simplification of the necessary paperwork. Ridley's only produce 'traditional' English beer and this is regarded as being a distinct submarket of the general beer market, particularly with respect to draught beer. Thus, competition from European brewers, who do not produce this type of beer, is regarded as minimal. It is felt that for this reason, the Single European Market will not result in increased competition. It may help in the sourcing of imported beer for sale in Ridley public houses. For instance, at present Holsten beer may only be purchased from one particular source – an agency that has exclusive rights to this beer.

The firm is actively engaged in a search for a European brewery to franchise products with or to enter into reciprocal trade with. Negotiations are being carried out for market research to be undertaken to see what opportunities are open to them.

The effects of the MMC report

The number of tied outlets has not changed significantly in recent years. Following the recommendations of the Monopolies and Mergers Commission investigation and report on the supply of beer, public houses currently owned by National Brewers are being offered for sale. If the right locations at the right price become available, then Ridley's will endeavour to add some of these to their existing estate. An important factor will be the location of such properties. The firm is not interested in buying properties in areas where sales from existing pubs would be affected by sales from acquisitions. Rather, property that will be complementary to the existing business will be sought out.

Although the number of tied houses has remained almost unchanged in recent years, there has been a programme of refurbishment and improvement. This work is expensive and places a strain on the resources of the smaller brewer. Unlike many larger brewers, Ridley's have not spent money on developing theme pubs. Around two-thirds of the brewery production is sold to the free-house trade.

One of the recommendations (12.136.a) of the MMC's supply of beer report was that 'Tenants should be allowed to purchase a minimum of one brand of draught beer from a supplier other than their landlord or the landlord-nominated supplier.' In theory this should provide a good opportunity for the smaller independent brewers to increase the number of their outlets. However, press reports have indicated that some large brewers are putting pressure on their tenants not to buy from other brewers. Ridley's view is that in general the National Brewers have not pressurized their tenants but that some regional managers of national firms have caused difficulties. By the beginning of 1991, sales of Ridley's draught beer to these possible new outlets have not been extensive.

Future trends

The trend towards increasing lager sales and falling mild and bitter sales was mentioned earlier. From Ridley's perspective, there are indications that this trend may be coming to an end. The firm has experienced something of a real ale revival. For example, sales of IPA increased by 50 per cent in 1990. The firm believes this is not a temporary phenomenon and that sales of IPA will remain buoyant. Another trend is the increase in containerized beer consumption in the home at the expense of draught beer sales in the public house. This trend, and the likelihood that it will continue, was an important factor in the decision to begin canning some of their range.

Information about the formation of the Single European Market, its requirements and likely consequences was obtained mainly from the Department of Trade and Industry. However, much of the material and information on offer is thought not to be particularly relevant or suitable to the needs of the smaller independent brewer. It was recognized early on, though, that the firm had to adapt to all the Single European Market requirements that were relevant. One example where changes have already occurred is the labelling requirements. Formerly, an indication of the strength of beer was provided by information of the original gravity (OG) of the wort. It is already a European requirement that the labels or lettering of containerized beer provide the percentage of alcohol by volume.

Publicity

Part of the corporate strategy of the firm, broadly speaking, is to concentrate on producing quality beers which are widely acceptable. Words and phrases which appear in the printed publicity material include 'traditional', 'heritage', and 'small is beautiful'. The approach though is generally subtle. As is the case with many small firms, TV advertising is considered to be unacceptably expensive. Advertising on the sides of local buses for the launch of IPA and Old Bob was thought to have been very effective. Local radio is to be experimented with. The high reputation of the brewery's products, given the limited amounts spent on promotional activities, has come mainly from word of mouth, although the Campaign for Real Ale (CAMRA) has been a consistent advocate over the years, and there is a very favourable mention in the book *Local Brew: Traditional Breweries and Their Ales*. As John Smith, the firm's Sales Director, said in an interview which provided material for this case study, 'quality talks in the end'.

Conclusions

The management believes that there is an assured future for the firm, notwithstanding the trend in the British brewing industry towards fewer and larger firms. In line with this belief there are plans for expansion of both output and owned outlets.

Brewing in Germany

Introduction

The beer market in the former West Germany is highly fragmented. At the beginning of 1990 there were approximately 1,170 breweries producing around 5,000 different brands of beer. The five largest companies account for only 28 per cent of the market and this represents a relatively low level of concentration. To an extent, though, this is misleading as there are some large groupings of breweries. In 1973 the four largest firms accounted for 20 per cent of the market but the four largest financial groupings had about 40 per cent of it.

A large grouping links Dortmunder Union Brauerei (DUB) with Schultheiss of Berlin, and several other breweries. Dortmunder Actien is linked with Binding of Frankfurt and with Kindl of Berlin. The group is owned by the food company Oetker and is an example of a German brewing conglomerate. Another large conglomerate used to be under the control of the Reemstma cigarette company. One of the members, Hannen in Rhineland-Westphalia, was sold to Carlsberg of Denmark, while Henninger of Frankfurt and Tucher of Nuremberg have joined another group. In Bavaria, two of Munich's breweries, Paulaner and Hacker-Pschorr, are part of property groups.

Beer consumption

Beer consumption in Germany is the highest in the world at a per capita figure of 144 litres per annum. This is down from a peak of 151 litres in 1976 and 147 litres in 1987. Excise duty has remained unchanged since 1952 and the German excise duty legislation incorporates four strength bands. Over 98 per cent of all beer sold is in the third category which has an average strength of around 5 per cent by volume. In each of the bands there are ranges which benefit the smaller brewer. Although there are still a very large number of breweries, both absolutely and relatively compared with Britain, the number of brewers has decreased by over 50 per cent in the last 30 years.

Sales outlets

It is estimated that there are about 18,000 beer wholesalers in the former Federal Republic of Germany. About 30 per cent are directly or indirectly owned by brewers. Brewers also own around 22 per cent of all on-licensed outlets accounting for 28 per cent of all beer sold in this sector. Some of the larger regional brewers have substantial chains of outlets. Additionally, there are very strong ties between brewers and another 25 per cent of the remaining outlets. These take various forms, including development finance, promotional investment, and discounts in return for the exclusivity on beer and non-alcoholic drink supplies.

Problems

There are a number of problems facing German brewers. The market has been stagnating for a number of years, there is substantial overcapacity and about half of the breweries are operating at a loss. Further, output per brewery is low, being 80,000 hectolitres on average. Despite the problems, and in the face of fierce competition, a number of breweries have achieved a considerable degree of success. Some are mentioned in a later section.

The *Reinheitsgebot* (Beer Purity Laws)

The Beer Purity Law originated in Bavaria in 1516. The rules governing the manufacture of beer are set out in Article 9 of the *Biersteurgesetz*. Article 9(1) provides that bottom fermented beer (comprising 84 per cent of production) may be manufactured only from malted barley, hops, yeast, and water. Article 9(2) relates to top fermented beer and additionally permits the use of other malts, technically pure cane sugar, beet sugar or invert sugar and glucose and colourants derived from those sugars. Article 9(3) states that malt means any cereal artificially germinated. Rice, maize, and sorghum, though, are excluded from the cereals allowed under the definition of malt.

Most, if not all British, American, and other European top fermented beers use sugar and banned cereals, and many of the bottom fermented beers contain rice. These beers also use chemicals to act as head retainers, stabilizers, to extend shelf life, etc. and thus could not be sold in Germany.

Contravention of the Treaty of Rome

In 1984 the Commission of the European Community took the Federal Republic of Germany to court alleging a failure of a Member State to fulfil its obligations. Action was taken under Article 169 of the Treaty of Rome. This Article states that if the Commission considers that a Member State has failed to fulfil an obligation under the Treaty, it shall deliver a reasoned opinion on the matter. If the State does not comply with the opinion, the Commission may bring the matter before the Court of Justice.

During the proceedings of the Court of Justice of the European Community several brewers in Bavaria were caught brewing in breach of the law and in the resulting scandal there was a suicide. It also emerged that several brewers in the north of Germany were using brewing sugars and additives in beer destined for export.

Paragraph 54 of the March 1987 judgment stated '. . . it must be held that by prohibiting the marketing of beers lawfully manufactured and marketed by another Member State if they do not comply with Articles 9 and 10 of the *Biersteurgesetz*, the Federal Republic of Germany has failed to fulfil its obligations under Article 30 of the EEC Treaty'. Article 30 prohibits quantitative restrictions on imports between Member States.

So far imported beers have taken only a very small part of the total market. In 1986, before the Court of Justice ruling, the market share of imported beers was 1.2 per cent. In 1990 it was still under 2 per cent.

Trends in beer consumption and production

There have been some marked trends in beer consumption and production in the last two decades. Draught beer has been in steady decline since 1960 when it accounted for 40 per cent of total production. In 1970 it was about 32 per cent of total output, and by 1989 had declined to 28 per cent. Output of the beer types *Premiumbiere, Pils, Specialitäten* (i.e. wheat beer), and *Alkoholfreie Biere* are increasing, *Alt* and *Kölsch* are in steady state, and *Konsumbiere* and *Export* are in decline. In the 1950s and 1960s beer was seen as *flüssigen Brot* (liquid bread) – a thirst-quenching, mass-consumption drink. The image of beer is now changing to a more quality-oriented and sophisticated beverage.

Müller and Schwalbach, in an article in the *Journal of Industrial Economics* in June 1980, distinguished three categories of beer produced in Germany. The first is *Billig Bier* (cheap beer). The name is derived from its widespread use as a loss leader by large supermarket chains. There are two types of *Billig Bier*, the first being that produced by large breweries with excess capacity. This is of the same quality as a premium beer and is sold at short-run marginal costs under a non-brand name. The second type is produced by several medium-sized breweries which specialize in selling non-advertised, non-promoted *Billig Bier* directly through retailers and distributors.

Konsumbiere is sold at a 'popular price' and refers to the regular brands of regional breweries, including those operating on a small scale. Normally, they are not well advertised and are sold in pubs and other outlets close to the brewery. Some of the larger brewers from other regions do compete in these local markets, though, and they use extensive advertising as a weapon of penetration into the market.

Premium beers are heavily advertised as being of superior quality and have extensive regional, and sometimes national, distribution. Prices tend to be higher, partly on account of the distribution costs and partly because production costs are higher – best quality hops, longer maturation, etc.

Interestingly, some small- and medium-sized breweries in the range of 0.3 to 2.0 million hectolitres have been successful in this market. They have traded on their traditional brand name and quality image. Conversely, some of the large breweries have been less successful because of strong product loyalty by consumers to traditional brands.

Survival and growth strategies

Despite the stagnation of the German beer market as a whole in the 1980s, a number of breweries have been successful.

Warsteiner

Warsteiner has adopted the strategy of producing a single product – a premium *Pils* – and distributing it over a wide geographical area. It is available in both draught and bottle form. Output increased by 320,000 hectolitres between 1983 and 1989. From 1988 to 1989 production went up 320,000 hectolitres, an increase in percentage terms of 12.2. In the same period turnover increased by 14.5 per cent from 393 to 450 million DM. Transport costs are high, as is advertising, but profits have increased because of scale economies and the higher price associated with a premium product.

Diebels

Diebels is a *Privatbrauerei* (i.e. not a member of a large group) that doubled its output between 1979 and 1989. It also decided on the strategy of producing a single product. In this instance it was *Altbier*. This is a dark top fermented beer that is closer to British beer in character than other German beers. *Altbier* accounts for only 5 to 6 per cent of the total German beer market. Diebels marketed its *Altbier* as a premium product and took sales away from the former market leader Hannen which incurred considerable losses. Diebels now has a market share of 35 per cent in North Rhine-Westphalia.

Binding

The brewing firm of Binding started the development of an alcohol-free beer in 1973. The name chosen was Clausthaler. The chances of success seemed remote as this type of beer was then regarded by consumers as being *kastriertes* (castrated) or *bleifreies* (leadfree) and Birell, an earlier attempt by another brewery, had failed. Clausthaler was launched in 1979 with an interesting marketing strategy. The beer was sold by a well-trained sales staff and the price was pitched and maintained at a relatively high level. Initially the beer was sold to the catering trade and then to the staff canteens of large businesses. It was then offered to sports clubs as their patrons are more receptive to non-alcoholic drinks than the general public at large. Normal large retail outlets were deliberately neglected to avoid the cut-throat competition that a new brand normally faces. Sales have risen from 33,000 hectolitres in 1980 to 850,000 hectolitres in 1989. Over 11 million DM was spent on advertising in 1989. The beer now accounts for over 30 per cent of Binding's turnover. Around 250,000 hectolitres is exported to 35 different countries, including Britain. Competition in Germany is now stronger but the firm expects that a good marketing strategy and the 'innovation bonus' will enable them to remain the market leader.

Maisel and Erdinger

Wheat beer (*Weissbier*) has increased in popularity in Germany in recent years. Two breweries have endeavoured to specialize on a national scale in the production of this type of beer. Geb. Maisel of Bayreuth started at the beginning of the 1970s to distribute *Weissbier* nationally and a market re-launch in 1984 successfully positioned their beer as the premium brand in the market. Production in 1989 was around 850,000 hectolitres and an output of one million hectolitres is the next target. (Another *Weissbier* specialist is Erdinger Weissbräu.)

In 1966 output of this beer was only 50,000 hectolitres but by 1989 it had risen to 700,000 hectolitres. Although this ranked it thirty-third in terms of output in Germany, this is still relatively small-scale production and it is profitable only because it sells at premium beer prices.

Recent developments in German brewing

During 1990 breweries in the former East Germany (DDR) lost one-third of their turnover to breweries in the former West Germany (FDR). Production was down from 24.8 million hectolitres in 1989 to 15.9 million hectolitres in 1990. Brewing industry analysts believe that many of the DDR breweries have a chance to survive if they can produce the range of beers that the market requires, although the 150 breweries that existed at the time of re-unification are expected to fall to around 50 in 1991. Not surprisingly, in view of the above market developments, 1990 was a record year for FDR brewers. Total output was up by 11 per cent on 1989 at 103 million hectolitres. Most of this growth was at the expense of DDR breweries.

Bitburger is an illustration of a brewer that has benefited from the opportunities provided by the new market in the east of the country. It is one of the few German brewers that sells its beer nationally. It has a similar strategy to Warsteiner in that it produces one type of beer and markets it throughout Germany. In 1990 it had its best year ever in 175 years of brewing, selling over 3 million hectolitres. Turnover increased by 14 per cent to 420 million DM. Much of this improvement in performance was due to the market opportunities arising from re-unification. Already 2 per cent of its turnover is in the former DDR and this is increasing. Future strategy includes the buying of former DDR breweries and further opportunities are seen in Poland and Hungary. Trading partners already exist in these countries and the work force has increased as a result.

Grolsch is the second largest Dutch brewer (after Heineken) and its annual output of around two million hectolitres is distributed in 35 different countries. In 1990 it acquired the Wicküler group based in Wuppertal. As a result, turnover has nearly doubled from 360 to 700 million DM. The price paid for the group was around 100 million DM. Until now there has been very little foreign investment in German breweries but the stimulus of 1992 may lead to similar acquisitions.

Another 'new' development is the brewing of a foreign beer under licence by a German brewer for sale in Germany. In 1991 the Holsten brewery in Hamburg began brewing the Australian Foster's lager, in accordance with the *Reinheitsgebot*.

Landshuter Brauerei

Introduction

The Landshuter Brauerei (Koller-Fleischmann) is one of the two breweries still operating in Landshut, a small town of some 60,000 people that is 60 kilometres from Munich. Landshut has seen considerable concentration in brewing in the twentieth century. In 1911 there were still 17 breweries in the town. The third remaining post-1945 independent was bought up by Paulaner from Munich in 1987.

The Landshuter company dates back to 1493, although the present owners (the Koller family) did not enter the industry until 1848. Uninterrupted brewing took place on the Altstadt site from 1493 to 1958.

This site now serves as the head office and restaurant. There was a move to the present site in 1958, where a new brewery was built in 1968. Rock cellars of considerable antiquity on this site are still used for the storage of beer. In 1923 there was a merger of the Koller and Landshuter brewing firms with the Koller family retaining control. Herr Koller, the present Chief Executive, represents the sixth generation of the family involved. His daughter is the company architect and has been responsible for some important refurbishment of brewery-owned property.

The brewery employs 55 workers to produce an annual output of 70,000 hectolitres. There are still around 760 breweries in Bavaria (out of a world total of 2,700). In a highly fragmented industry, the brewery, in Bavarian terms, is regarded as being of medium size. Some 40 restaurants are owned by the firm as well as cafes and houses. A noticeable feature of the Bavarian brewing industry is the ownership of private houses by brewers. (The Munich brewers, Löwenbräu, are said to be the largest owners of houses in Munich.) The outlets owned by the firm are tied to the brewery for their supplies of beer. There are some independent outlets in Landshut and its surrounding area that can buy beer from a source of their own choice, but these are small in number.

Landshuter's markets

The firm has about 800 customers and included in its market are restaurants, cafes, *Abhol Markt* (discount beer shops) and individuals. The firm still delivers crates of beer to private customers and the drivers have the keys to some houses. Seventy-five per cent of the output is sold within 80 kilometres of Landshut. This localization of sales is known as *'rund um den Kamin'* (around the chimney). The remaining 25 per cent of production is sold further away or exported. Beer is delivered by the firm to the Austrian market. Beer destined for Italy is collected. Following re-unification, there is an expanding market in the former DDR. No beer is currently exported to Britain.

The product mix

In Germany as a whole about 80 per cent of beer is bottled or canned and 20 per cent is sold in draught form. For the Landshuter Brauerei, the breakdown is 72 per cent bottled and 28 per cent draught. This proportion has remained constant over the last ten years. The split in sales depends to a large extent on the nature of the retail outlets. Restaurants and hotels sell mainly draught beer, whilst private customers, shops, and export markets take, almost exclusively, beer in bottles or cans.

Price differentiation

A feature of the German beer market is the relatively large price differential between beer consumed in bars, hotels, etc. and beer purchased in containers for consumption at home. The comparison is not straightforward. For instance, the price of beer in bars varies according to the type of beer, the size of town, its location within Germany and the location of the bar within the town. Beer in bottles and cans varies in price according to the brewer, type of beer and type of retail outlet. For instance, in November 1990, a 0.2 litre glass of beer in a bar on the Kufürstendamm in Berlin cost 2.80 DM, whereas a half-litre glass of local beer could be bought in a restaurant in Landshut for the same price. In the famous Hofbräuhaus in Munich a litre stein costs 7.80 DM. For comparative purposes, a price of around 10 DM per litre could be regarded as typical. A 50cl can of Warsteiner, one of the few brands of beer that is easily obtainable throughout most of Germany, costs 1.49 DM in a small Berlin supermarket. Similar-sized bottles of Löwenbräu, Löwenbräu Premium, and Spaten, cost respectively 1.15, 1.38, and 1.25 DM in a small Munich supermarket. In an *Abhol Markt* in Landshut a crate of twenty 50cl bottles cost 15 DM. At a typical price of 2.50 DM per litre for beer for consumption at home, the ratio of on-premises to off-premises beer prices is of the order of 4 to 1.

Such price differentiation is much less in Britain. A pint of bitter in a public house varies according to its location in a town and whether it is in the south or north of the country, but a price of £1.30 is not untypical. Beer in bottles and cans varies according to type and variety of retail outlet but somewhere around £2.80 for a 2-litre plastic bottle of normal strength bitter from a supermarket is typical. This gives a price ratio of 1.20 to 0.80 or 1.5 to 1.

Herr Koller attributed the large differential in Germany primarily to the intense competition in the take-home trade. *Abhol Markt* proprietors are very keen to keep the price of beer as low as possible and work on the small profit margin, high sales volume principle. For example, on a 15 DM crate of beer, the profit is only 1 DM.

Capital investment

Although by Bavarian standards the Landshuter brewery is medium sized, it is not large enough to reap scale economies. It, like many similar-sized breweries, has a bottling plant. Although this is a significant piece of investment, a long-term view is taken: in the long run this, and other examples of capital expenditure, save on staff and thus justify the expenditure.

Publicity

Offsetting the higher production costs is the fact that comparatively little is spent on publicity and distribution. Large brewers spend large amounts on marketing and distribution. However, there is strong customer loyalty for Landshuter's products and this obviates the need for much promotion. The beer market in Bavaria is regarded as being a local market. The 'national' brewers such as Warsteiner and Bitburger are not seen as a threat. In the words of Herr Koller, 'They are too far from Landshut, and decision making takes too long for their customers' needs'. Local brewers pride themselves on the quickness and flexibility of their response to their customers' requests. Even the major brewers in Munich (only 60 km away) such as Hacker-Pschorr, Löwenbräu, Paulaner, and Spaten are seen as being distant. Paulaner is said to have lost business in Landshut from some of the outlets it acquired following its takeover of a local brewery, for this very reason.

The impact of the Single European Market

The firm believes that the Single European Market will have little impact on it and other brewers in Bavaria, mainly because of the geographical location of Bavaria – it is too far from possible new competitors. An additional factor is the localization of the beer market and customer loyalty. The *Reinheitsgebot* has been declared illegal in regard to imported beer, but imported beer still has only 1 per cent of the German market, and one firm, Tuborg, has 60 per cent of that. Many German brewers believe that the publicity arising from the overturning of the *Reinheitsgebot* actually strengthened the position of German beer as German consumers believe in products with high-quality ingredients.

Concern was evinced by Herr Koller regarding one aspect of the Single European Market – the harmonization of duties on beer. At the beginning of 1991, a crate of twenty 50cl bottles attracted a duty of 1.40 DM in

Germany. Equivalent figures for Ireland and Denmark are 21.72 and 10.98 DM respectively. It has not yet been decided what the common rate will be but 3.55 DM is a possibility. A rate such as this will aid the competitive position of brewers in countries such as Britain where the existing duty is already high.

A related point concerns the tax on wine. It is low in countries such as France and Italy, and there are no moves to increase it. Thus, wine producers in these countries and in Germany will gain a comparative advantage. As a result, consumers might buy less beer and more wine. However, beer prices are still fairly low, so there is some room for manoeuvre.

Future trends

Beer consumption in Germany has been in slight decline in recent years, but there is evidence that this has levelled off. Per capita consumption in Germany as a whole is 143 litres and in Bavaria 230 litres. Landshuter does not think that trends in beer consumption are a problem.

However, there has been a change in consumers' tastes and preferences and the brewery has responded to this. More light (2.6 per cent of alcohol by volume) beer and alcohol-free beer is being produced. *Weisse* (wheat) beer is now very popular. The brewery started producing this type of beer in 1984 and it now accounts for 25 per cent of total production. Twenty years ago there was only a very small demand for this specialist beer. Eighty per cent of the beer sold in local discotheques is *Weisse* beer. Part of the popularity of this type of beer might be explained by two common misconceptions – that it doesn't have the intoxicating powers of other beers, and that it is not as fattening as other beers. Both perceptions are false.

As the consumption of *Weisse* beer has increased, the sales of *Helles* (light in colour) beer have decreased. The sale of *Dunkles* (dark) beer are small but steady at about 5 per cent of total production. There is a small, but committed, clientele for this product. At one time dark beer used to be very popular and one of the reasons may have been because of the chemical properties of the water supply. The local water is high in calcium and this is suited to the brewing of dark beer. With modern chemical treatments, however, calcium is easily removed and the resulting softer water particularly suits the production of light-coloured beers. One type of *Helles* beer, *Pils*, accounts for 10 per cent of Landshuter's production.

Although the number of breweries continue to decrease both in Germany as a whole and Bavaria itself, Herr Koller believes that for reasons outlined above, and especially consumer loyalty, tradition, and flexibility in responding to the market place, his brewery has an assured future.

Berliner Kindl brewery

Introduction

The Kindl brewery is situated on Indira Ghandi Strasse in the eastern sector of Berlin. The brewery was founded in the nineteenth century but most of the current buildings were constructed in 1926. Following the end of World War II, and until re-unification in 1990, it lay in the DDR. It was one of six breweries in the eastern sector and with the others formed the Berlin Getränkekombinat. The other brewing members of the combination were the Schultheiss specialist *Weisse* brewery in Schönhauser Allee, the Schultheiss brewery in Leninallee, the Bärenquell brewery in Schöneweide, the Berliner Bürgerbräu, and the Engelhardt Brauerei. The final member was the Spreequell plant. This did not brew beer, but produced mineral water and carbonated drinks. For a number of years, the Bürgerbräu plant exported beer, and its bottled Berliner Pils was obtainable from Tesco until early 1990.

Because of the events leading up to and following re-unification, the Getränkekombinat ceased to exist in July 1990. The two Schultheiss breweries were closed in 1990. For a time the Bärenquell had a reciprocal trading agreement with the Henninger brewery of Frankfurt and in the early part of 1991 became part of the Henninger group. The Bürgerbräu brewery obtained assistance from the West Berlin Kindl brewery for several months, but later decided to try and make its own way as an independent firm. The East Berlin Kindl and Engelhardt breweries were grouped to form the Brau und Erfrischungsgetränke AG (BEAG) and in October 1990 this became part of the large group that owns Dortmunder Union Brauerei (DUB), West Berlin Schultheiss, Schloßer of Düsseldorf, and Valentines of Heidelberg. Collectively this large group is called Brau und Brunnen. The Engelhardt brewery was closed in March 1991.

Until the end of 1990, and unusual, in terms of current German practice, a maltings formed part of the plant. The maltings was greatly expanded between 1972 and 1974 and output of malted barley has risen from 7,000 to 33,000 tonnes per year. In the past, there have been problems associated with the quality of the barley supplied and used. From 1 January 1991 the maltings has been an independent firm operating within the BEAG. With its new status has come choice of suppliers and this together with better agricultural methods and improved disease-resistant strains of barley, should mean these problems will be overcome.

In the first eight months following the formation of the BEAG, significant changes have occurred to the plant, production methods, the product mix, marketing and distribution. Further changes will undoubtedly follow.

The plant

The present brewhouse dates from 1974 and was built by Sieman, a West German firm. Its capacity is three times that of the old one. In November 1990 there was one operative bottling line and bottle washing machine. Both were rather antiquated physically and technically. A hot caustic soda solution (the norm in brewing) was used for bottle cleaning and there had been problems with imperfectly rinsed bottles finding their way into the hands of consumers. A new electronic caustic soda detector, to replace the previous, and not wholly effective, machine was installed and was working well. A new bottle labelling machine was installed in July 1990. A new, very fast bottling line (fully automated and computer-controlled) and washer came on stream in mid-December 1990. On the new line, 55,000 bottles per hour are cleaned, filled, capped, labelled and placed in crates. The labour force in this department has been reduced by one-third and breakages are much less frequent than before. Work has begun on the installation of the second new bottling line and washer and this was expected to be ready by May 1991. Thus, washing and bottling facilities are being upgraded and capacity increased in line with the production strategy detailed below.

In the dispatch department, a new palleting machine became operative in October 1990. This is fully automated and computer-controlled and is very much 'state of the art'. It was built by a well-known firm of machinery makers, SEN. Following its introduction, a number of dispatch department workers lost their jobs and productivity rose accordingly.

The new investment involves significant sums of money. For instance, each of the new bottling lines has cost around 13.5 million DM. Up to December 1990, over 30 million DM of new investment had been made, in contrast to the years of starvation in pre-unification days. Another 11 million DM has been earmarked for spending in 1991. This will be spent on renewing technical equipment, advertising in general, and in particular promoting the BEAG trademark *Berliner Pilsener*.

Production methods

Until the organizational changes of 1990, some raw barley had been added to the mash when Pilsener was produced. Former East German brewers are now required to brew beer according to the *Reinheitsgebot*, and they have until the end of 1992 to change their practices. As far as is known, all former DDR brewers had complied with the purity laws by the end of 1990. Thus, there has been a gradual phasing out of raw barley, in order to avoid sudden changes in taste. This transition to permitted ingredients was completed by the end of 1990. A further change, to improve the shelf life of bottled beers, is the use of some saccharified and low-protein malt. East German hops do not have the reputation of those grown in West Germany, and the beer is now brewed with *Hallertauer* and northern brewer hops from West Germany and *Saaz* hops from Czechoslovakia.

Beer is produced in batches of 1,000 hectolitres and until late in 1990, seven batches were produced every 24 hours on a round the clock basis. Subsequently, around five brews a day have been produced. After the mashing period, the hops (in both extract and pelleted form) are added to the wort and there is a boiling period of 90 minutes. The wort is then cooled to six degrees Celsius and the hops removed by centrifugal force. Liquid yeast is then added and there is a primary fermentation of five to six days at 12 degrees Celsius followed by a lagering period of 12 to 14 days in large vessels called reactors. Unusually, both the fermentation and lagering take place in the same vessel. This lagering period is short by traditional standards (three to six weeks).

Following the incorporation into the BEAG, the brewery has become much less labour-intensive and labour productivity has increased. In February 1990, 2,625 workers were employed in the six members of the Kombinat. This fell to 1,972 by the end of August and a figure of 1,765 was planned for February 1991. Further reductions are in store. In the Kindl brewery there were 1,500 workers on its books at the beginning of 1990 and annual production was around 1.3 million hectolitres. By the end of 1990, combined employment in the Kindl and Engelhardt breweries had fallen to less than 900. Job losses have been at a high rate in the Kindl brewery, echoing the situation in the former DDR as a whole. By the beginning of 1991, most of the 'surplus' labour had been shed and productivity was expected to be near typical West German brewing standards by July 1991.

The product mix

The Kindl brewery produces both draught and bottled beer but it is many years since the brewery possessed a casking line. The draught beer used to be transported by road tankers to large pubs and restaurants that were equipped with bulk storage tanks. After re-unification, draught beer is taken by tanker to the West Berlin Schultheiss brewery in the West Krüzberg area some 15 km away for kegging. It is then transported back to the eastern sector of Berlin for sale. Schultheiss beer, using Schultheiss yeast, malt and technology (but obviously not their water) has been brewed at the Kindl brewery since December 1990. It is bottled there in half-litre bottles bearing the Schultheiss label. Around 550,000 hectolitres of this beer is to be brewed in the Kindl brewery in 1991. Around 500,000 hectolitres of Berliner Pilsener, destined for sale in East Berlin will also be brewed. In addition to the two beers discussed above, several other beers are brewed and bottled. These include a *Premium Pils* and a *Bockbier*.

Marketing and distribution

Before the changes in 1990, there was comparatively little effort put into marketing as the term is understood in the EC. Bottled and draught beer was supplied to secure outlets, there was no effective competition from other members of the Getränkekombinat, and no competition from imported beers. Custom and practice largely determined the choice of outlets. High quality hotels tended to take the bulk of the higher quality beers. Generally, outlets selling beer were not free to change their source of supply. In summary, each brewery, including Kindl, had a captive market and hence no need, or point, to market the product, as the term is understood in market-oriented economies.

Suddenly, though, the Kindl brewery found itself operating in a harsh and competitive environment and this has resulted in considerable attention being paid to marketing the products. In the former DDR consumers could not easily tell which of the Kombinat breweries the beer they were drinking came from. Beer mats, if provided, were plain, there were no labels on the draught dispensers, glasses were not marked, etc. The labels on the bottles, which generally were not eye-catching anyway, were the only visual clue as to the origins of the beer. Following the organizational changes already discussed, new attractive labels for the bottles, to tempt the consumer, have been devised. The beer glasses have also been revamped, both in style and finish. Advertising, which was formerly completely unknown, has been introduced. As well as the brewery's name appearing on glasses and beer mats, eye-catching posters have appeared, there are newspaper insertions and a regular TV spot. The adherence to the *Reinheitsgebot* is featured.

Because there was no need, the Kindl brewery did not employ a marketing manager. The nearest equivalent post was an *Absatz Direktor* who was responsible for distribution, lorry routes, etc. His was one of the first senior management posts to be abolished. Now all distribution and marketing is handled centrally from the Schultheiss brewery in the Krüzberg district of Berlin.

Despite these changes, there are problems in selling the beer. For the first time ever, there is strong competition in eastern German supermarkets from western German beers. Additionally, it is proving difficult to get on to the supermarket buyers' lists. There is only space on the shelves for so many products and beer from eastern Germany does not have a high priority. Currently, beer is viewed in the same way by consumers in the former DDR as many other products originating from this area – rightly or wrongly it is seen as being inferior.

There is another problem with outlets. The Handelsorganisation and Konsum combines, that ran most of the bars and shops in the eastern sector of Berlin, have been very busy negotiating contracts with brewers from western Germany and these contracts have been largely at the expense of brewers from the eastern part of the country. Many of the bars have been sold off and in the process they have been loan-tied to western brewers. As a consequence, towards the end of 1990, the Kindl brewery came to regard these two organizations as an enemy. To combat their policies one of the tactics Kindl has employed is to sell beer direct to the public from the back of lorries parked in front of supermarkets.

As a measure of the difficulties being faced in a 'competitive' (in fact there is a large degree of monopoly power because of the control of outlets) German market, compared to the former non-competitive State market, the output of the Kindl brewery had fallen by one half within a year of its acquisition by the western German brewer.

Production under a command economy

Within a very short time span, almost overnight, the brewery has seen enormous changes to the environment in which production occurs and selling and distribution is effected. Until recently, managers had very little freedom. Output targets were determined by the central planners and materials allocated in accordance with these targets. Central Government planners gave broad targets to the Wirtschaftsrat der Bezirkes (WdB). In essence these were local planning councils responsible for every industry in a district. They had very wide powers over planning in general and investment decisions. The WdB interpreted these targets and implemented them by giving detailed instructions to the firms under its control. Included in its powers were decisions about funding. Thus, there was very little scope for the exercise of initiative by plant managers. For instance, although it was possible for rewards to be made for achieving production targets, there was no incentive to keep down the level of costs in order to achieve an *Überschuss* (surplus). Any 'profit' resulting from increased efficiency would be 'taken' by the WdB, and the Government itself, and used as they thought appropriate. Firms were strictly monitored, for instance, they had to provide output details on a daily basis.

Problems

Various problems were experienced with the materials, and managers had no control over their sourcing. Barley for malting varied in quality and suitability. It was Government policy to concentrate the production of many articles in one factory. Thus, if there was a breakdown in the crown stopper, bottle label factory, etc. there were then knock-on effects at the brewery which managers were powerless to remedy.

Managers had to deal with another centralized decision-making body – the Wissenschaftlich Ökonomisches Zentrum (WTÖZ). This organization, which was located in Berlin, had a responsibility for scientific, technical and economic aspects of the brewing and malting industries in the DDR. It allocated raw materials such as malt and hops to the various brewing Getränkekombinat. It also decided on the distribution of items such as bottles and plastic crates. The latter were often in short supply and decisions about them tended to have important consequences. Once these broad allocations had been determined, the Getränkekombinat allocated the materials to individual breweries. The WTÖZ and other planning organizations, including Government ministries and the WdB, worked together to try and co-ordinate their policy decisions.

The labour force

The level of the labour force was largely determined centrally as well, although there was some limited discretion allowed in practice over extra labour being hired to cope with periods of peak demand. There were two such peak periods. A reserve of 150,000 crates (each containing 25 half-litre bottles) was required to cope with summer and Christmas seasonal demand. It was practically impossible for managers to make permanent workers redundant. Labour was similar to the other inputs – its quantity, and price, were centrally determined.

Pricing and wages

The prices of the inputs used and the end products were in effect shadow prices, laid down centrally, and bearing little relation to costs. Wages, by EC standards, were low. At the end of 1990 workers at the Kindl brewery were being paid 45 per cent below their West German counterparts. Limited bonuses, of around 150 to 500 Östmarks, could on occasion be earned by some workers. Investment decisions were not taken by the Kindl management. Once again these were at the remit of the central planners. It has already been mentioned that one of the other breweries in the Getränkekombinat – the Berliner Bürgerbrau – exported beer and thus earned valuable hard currency. Sometimes, part of these earnings could be used to buy western equipment or spare parts for existing equipment. However, as the economy of the DDR worsened, more and more of these earnings were diverted elsewhere. The consequence was that as machinery broke down production suffered because of the delay in repairing it.

Strengths and weaknesses of the system

In many respects, the Kindl brewery represented, in microcosm, an illustration of the strengths and weaknesses of central planning and control of an economy. On the positive side, there was security of employment for workers in the brewery and elsewhere in the production chain, although ultimately the price paid was to be high.

On the negative side, there was little or no incentive for managers to be efficient, and a consequence was the general low productivity of the labour force. Equipment was generally old and unproductive. Modern production techniques were often not employed. At the time of re-unification the output per worker in brewing was around 1,000 hectolitres in the DDR. In West German breweries it is typically 2,000–5,000 hectolitres.

The Felsenkeller Brauerei

Introduction

The Felsenkeller brewery, founded in 1857, consists of an attractive range of stone buildings nestling under a cliff on the outskirts of Dresden. The stone for the buildings was obtained by quarrying into the hillside. The resulting large caves have been used ever since for storing the beer produced by the brewery. They have given the name of the brewery, as *Felsen* and *Keller* in German mean rock and cellar respectively.

Output

The output of beer in 1857 was 3,000 hectolitres. Production increased steadily over the years, reaching 380,000 hectolitres by 1928. Output was only 92,000 hectolitres in 1949, presumably because of material shortages in the aftermath of the Second World War. By 1960 the output had risen to 396,000 hectolitres. This upward trend continued until a peak of 606,000 hectolitres was attained in 1981. This fell to 576,000 hectolitres in 1988 and 540,000 hectolitres in 1989. The re-unification events of 1990 caused output to slump to 300,000 hectolitres. This was less than 50 per cent of capacity. As a rationalization measure, production of beer has been concentrated in other breweries in Dresden and brewing ceased in mid-October.

Two main and interrelated reasons for this greatly reduced demand were provided by Herr Hans-Joachim Timme, the *Felsenkeller Betriebsdirektor*. Firstly, the Dresden consumers, faced for the first time in nearly 50 years with the chance to buy beer brewed in West Germany, made an initial decision that it was better beer *per se*. Secondly, there was the 'newness factor': 'The West German beer was new to the people and the people say new is better' (Herr Timme).

The future

Although brewing has ceased, beer from other breweries in Dresden will be casked – 200,000 hectolitres a year at the Felsenkeller site. It will also be used as a distribution depot for bottled beer from Munich (Spaten) and Hamburg (Holsten). Pepsi-Cola will also be distributed. The effect on employment has been severe. By the middle of November 1990, the work force had fallen from 250 to 100. All levels have been affected. For example, the *Betriebsdirektor* (plant manager), after 30 years at the brewery and at the age of 57, was made redundant in March 1991. The Head Brewer was retrained in November 1990 as a fork-lift truck driver!

Physically, the plant had been well maintained, and was varied in terms of age and technology. The brew house equipment was quite modern as was the casking plant. One of the two furnaces and boilers though, dated back to 1924 and was supplied by the Scottish firm of Babcock and

Wilcox. Although it was still in use in late 1990, the brewery's continued existence seems doubtful in view of its inefficiency and also the fact that it is fired with environmentally unfriendly brown coal briquettes.

Reference

The Brewers' Society: Statistical Handbook (London, Brewing Publications Ltd, 1990).

Cockerill, T.A.J., 'Economies of scale, industrial structure efficiency: the brewing industry in nine nations' *The economics of industrial structure* (Culembory, Netherlands, Nijhoff, 1977)

Downham, P., and Johnson, G., 'The UK brewing industry' in *Exploring Corporate Strategy*, by G. Johnson and K. Scholes (Hemel Hempstead, Prentice Hall International, 1989).

Dunn, M. *Local Brew: Traditional Breweries and their Ales*, (London, Robert Hale, 1986).

The Monopolies and Mergers Commission, *The supply of beer* (London, HMSO Cm 651, 1989).

Muller, J., and Schwalbach, J., 'Structural change in West Germany's brewing industry: some efficiency considerations, *The Journal of industrial economics*, June, 1980.

Questions/discussion topics

1. Account for the merger trends in the post-1945 British brewing industry.

2. What are the main sources of scale economies in the brewing industry?

3. What factors might act as entry barriers in the British brewing industry?

4. How does the brewing industry accord with Michael Porter's concepts of strategic groups and mobility barriers?

5. Why has the German brewing industry remained relatively fragmented? Is this likely to continue?

6. Critically discuss the competitive strategies of the British and German companies outlined in the case studies.

7. Carry out a SWOT analysis of the small breweries in both Germany and Britain outlined in the case.

Index

accounting 46, 55
acquisitions 4, 40
Advanced Communication Technology in
  Europe Programme (RACE) 53
agriculture 20, 24, 32, 37
aircraft production 8, 32, 42, 52
Ansoff, H Igor 5, 9
auditing 6

banking 7, 15, 19, 37, 46–7
  European Central Bank 26, 28, 29
barriers to trade 23–4, 30, 40, 52
  fiscal 26
  physical 24–5
  technical 25–6, 43
brewing 8–9, 34, 42
British Standards Organization (BSI) 43
Bundesbank 29
business advice 6

cars 32–3, 51 *see also* motoring assistance
  services
case studies
  aims and themes 1–2
  description 4–5
  issues to address 2–4
  organizations subject of 6–9
  skills required by students 5
Cassis de Dijon case (1979) 25
CEN (standards organization) 43
CENELEC (standards organization) 43
Central and Eastern Europe 6, 8, 13, 34–9, 40,
  56
Channel Tunnel 51
Charter of Fundamental Social Rights 30, 45
Clerc, Wily de 32
COMETT Programme 54
Commission, role of 14, 15–16, 17, 18, 19, 20,
  21, 22
Committee of Permanent Representatives
  (COREPER) 17, 20
competition 1, 4, 55
  banking 47
  legislation, impact of 40–3
  training, effect on 54
  transport 50
  White Paper programme 24
Completing the Internal Market see White
  Paper, Commission

Council for Mutual Economic Assistance
  (CMEA) 35
Council of Ministers, role of 14, 16–18,
  19–20, 21, 22
custom posts *see* frontier controls

defence 29, 44
Delors, Jacques 27–8, 29, 33
Department of Trade and Industry (DTI) 17,
  22, 56
Directorates-General (DGs) 15–16
distribution of goods 3–4, 43

Economic and Monetary Union (EMU) 26–9,
  40
Economic and Social Committee (ESC)
  14–15, 19
education *see* training, vocational
employment 6, 24, 30, 45, 46, 55
environment
  PHARE Programme 37
  policy, EC 31, 40, 50
  standards 43, 54
  White Paper programme 24, 25
EURATOM *see* European Atomic Energy
  Community (EAEC)
European Atomic Energy Community (EAEC)
  13
European Bank for Reconstruction and
  Development (EBRD) 37
European Central Bank 26, 28, 29
European Coal and Steel Community (ECSC)
  13
European Collaboration Linkage of Agriculture
  and Industry through research (ECLAIR) 53
European Community (EC)
  aims 13–15
  historical background 13
  institutions and bodies 15–19
  law, type of 22
  policy-making 19–21
European Council 17
European Court of Auditors 15, 19
European Court of Justice (ECJ) 14, 18–19,
  20, 25, 50
European Currency Unit (ECU) 27, 28, 29
European Economic Community (EEC) 13
European Free Trade Association (EFTA) 6,
  33, 40, 43, 56

European Investment Bank (EIB) 15, 19, 37
European Monetary System (EMS) 20, 27
European Parliament (EP), role of 13, 14, 16, 18, 19, 20–1
European Research and Technology Community 30
European Strategic Programme for Research and Development in Information Technology (ESPRIT) 53
Exchange Rate Mechanism (ERM) 27

financial services 25, 26, 46
FORCE Programme 54
frontier controls 23, 24, 26, 29, 46

G24 group 37
General Agreement on Tariffs and Trade (GATT) 32

health and safety 25, 30, 43, 45, 50
hydraulics 7

immigration controls see frontier controls
industrial relations 30
insurance 7, 26, 46, 48–9
interest rates 27, 29

joint ventures 38–9, 40

legislation, EC 16, 22, 29
   employment 6, 30, 45, 46, 55
LINGUA Programme 54

management consultancy 6
mark, CE 43
marketing 2–3, 4, 43, 55
mergers 4, 42
Ministry of Agriculture, Fisheries and Food (MAFF) 17
motoring assistance services 8, see also cars

PETRA Programme 54
PHARE Programme 37
pharmaceuticals 7, 25
policy-making, EC 19–21
political union 29–30
Porter, M E 5, 9
pricing 4, 7, 40, 42, 55
production of goods 3, 25, 43, 55

public procurement 1, 6, 33, 44

qualifications, people with 25, 54
quality 7, 40, 53, 55

reciprocity 32
recognition, mutual 25, 35, 43
Representatives, UK Permanent (UKREP) 17–18
research and development 4, 18, 20, 30, 42, 52–3

safety, health and 25, 30, 43, 45, 50
Schuman, Robert 13
services sector 4, 25–6, 38
Single Administrative Document (SAD) 24, 33
Single European Act (SEA) 13, 18, 24, 30, 31, 50, 52
standards
   banking 47
   education 7
   environment 43, 54
   health and safety 25, 43
   research and development 52, 53
   technical 6, 33, 43, 44

taxation 6, 26
tenders 44, 45
Total Quality Management (TQM) 7
training, vocational 7–8, 18, 20, 30, 37, 53–5
Training and Enterprise Councils (TECs) 7
transport 3, 24, 25, 26, 45, 49–52
Treaty of Paris (1951) 13, 16, 20, 22, 27
Treaty of Rome (1957) 13, 16, 17, 20, 22, 23, 29, 31
   competition rules 41, 42
   EMU Stage One 27–8
   SEA amendment 24
   transport policy 49

voting-power of EC members 17

water 8, 45
Werner Report 27
White Paper, Commission (1985) 23, 24, 33
   external implications 31, 32
   fiscal barriers 26
   recognition, mutual 25
   transport measures 50